Masons, Tricksters and Cartographers

Masons, Tricksters and Cartographers

Comparative Studies in the Sociology of Scientific and Indigenous Knowledge

David Turnbull

Routledge
Taylor & Francis Group

LONDON AND NEW YORK

Reprinted 2003
by Routledge
2 Park Square, Milton Park, Abingdon, Oxon, OX14 4RN

Transferred to Digital Printing 2005

Routledge is an imprint of the Taylor & Francis Group

British Library Cataloguing in Publication Data

A catalogue record for this book is available from the British Library.

ISBN: 90-5823-001-5 (soft cover)

Printed and bound by Antony Rowe Ltd, Eastbourne

Cover: 'Fools Cap Map' anon c. 1590. the main title translates as 'Know thyself', the subtitle as 'Tis folly to be wise'. The cartouche suggests it was drawn by Epicthonius Cosmopolites, translated as 'Everyman indigenous to himself'. By permission of the Bodleian Library, University of Oxford, Douce Portfolio 142 no 92.

Contents

Figures

Acknowledgements

Over the years I have benefited from the work of others and from conversations with many people in a wide range of places and disciplines. It is not possible to list them all, but I would like to thank all those who made a specific contribution either to my thinking or more personally by way of encouragement and support. I would particularly like to thank Judy Armstrong, Maggie Brady, Michael Bravo, Damien Broderick, Ian Burn, Barry Butcher, Wade Chambers, Catherine Delano-Smith, Henry Krips, Bruno Latour, John Law, Kingsley Palmer, Lex Smits, Leigh Star, Helen Verran, David Woodward, Brian Wynne and John Ziman. I also want to thank the Center for Cultural Studies for their generous support in preparing the illustrations.

I owe a special debt of thanks to Sandy and Alexander who have seen me through many a dark night of the soul and this book is dedicated to them.

Some of the material in this book I have published elsewhere in other forms.

The introduction draws on *Technoscience Worlds* (Geelong: Deakin University Press, 1991); 'Reframing Science and Other Local Knowledge Traditions', *Futures*, Vol. 29, 6 (1997), pp. 551–62; 'Rationality, Objectivity, and Method', reproduced with permission of Elsevier Science, pp. 16–21 in Helaine Selin, ed., *Encyclopedia of the History of Science, Technology and Medicine in Non-western Cultures* (Dordrecht: Kluwer Academic Publishers, 1997).

Chapter 1 is a modified version of 'Local Knowledge and Comparative Scientific Traditions', *Knowledge and Policy*, Vol. 6, 3/4 (1993), pp. 29–54 with material from 'Reframing Science and Other Local Knowledge Traditions', *Futures*, Vol. 29, 6 (1997), pp. 551–62; 'Maps and Mapmaking of the Australian Aboriginal People', pp. 37–39 in Helaine Selin, ed., *Encyclopedia of the History of Science, Technology and Medicine in Non-western Cultures* (Dordrecht: Kluwer Academic Publishers, 1997).

Chapter 2 is an updated version of 'The Ad Hoc Collective Work of Building Gothic Cathedrals with Templates, String, and Geometry', *Science Technology and Human Values*, Vol. 18 (1993), pp. 315–40. This material is used with permission of Sage Publications.

Chapter 3 takes material from two articles; 'Cartography and Science in Early Modern Europe: Mapping the Construction of Knowledge Spaces', *Imago Mundi*, Vol. 48 (1996), pp. 5–24; 'Constructing Knowledge Spaces and Locating Sites of Resistance in the Early Modern Cartographic Transformation', in R. Paulston, ed., *Social Cartography: Mapping Ways of Seeing Social and Educational Change* (New York: Garland Publishing Inc., 1996), pp. 53–79 and 'Cook and Tupaia, a Tale of Cartographic Méconnaissance?', in M. Lincoln, ed., *Science and Exploration: European Voyages to the Southern Oceans in the Eighteenth Century* (London: Boydell and Brewer, 1999, pp. 117–132).

Chapter 4 uses material from *Mapping the World in the Mind: An Investigation of the Unwritten Knowledge of the Micronesian Navigators* (Geelong: Deakin University Press, 1991) and 'Comparing Knowledge Systems: Pacific Navigation and Western Science', in J. Morrison, P. Geraghty and L. Crowl, eds., *Science of the Pacific Island Peoples: Vol. 1, Ocean and Coastal Studies* (Suva: Institute of Pacific Studies, 1994), pp. 129–44. This is reproduced with permission of the Institute of Pacific Studies.

Chapter 5 is a revision of 'The Push for a Malarial Vaccine', *Social Studies of Science*, Vol. 19 (1989), pp. 283–300.

Chapter 6 is a revision of 'Rendering Turbulence Orderly', *Social Studies of Science*, Vol. 25 (1995), pp. 9–33.

The conclusion includes some revised material from 'Relativism, Reflexivity and the Sociology of Scientific Knowledge', *Metascience: Annual Review of the Australasian Association for the History, Philosophy and Social Studies of Science*, Vol. 1/2 (1984), pp. 47–61.

INTRODUCTION
FROM RATIONALITY TO MESSINESS: RETHINKING TECHNOSCIENTIFIC KNOWLEDGE

Modernity and its Problems

This book began as a series of essays on the way knowledge is constructed by different groups of people: masons, Polynesian navigators, malariologists, turbulence engineers and cartographers. Now the book is finished it seems to be a reflection on modernity and the problems we have in understanding it. This slightly odd effect of an unplanned outcome may be the common authorial sensation of the book having a voice of its own. But I suspect it illustrates the illusory nature of one of the core tenets of modernity—that the technoscientific knowledge, upon which the concept of modernity is based, epitomises planning, rationality and order.[1] This book is in large part a reexamination of the supposed planned and rational character of technoscientific knowledge. Rather than being governed by logic and method, modernity's drive for order conceals its messy, contingent, unplanned and arational character. If we wish to rethink the way we produce knowledge and the forms of knowledge we value, we need to recognise, even celebrate, its unplanned and messy nature.

The book assumes that there is not just one universal form of knowledge (Western science), but a variety of knowledges.[2] Moreover, a cross-cultural, comparative form of analysis is required to understand our own knowledge traditions. For this reason I consider examples from a variety of periods and cultures in order to explore the ways in which we are constituted as knowng subjects through the very processes of knowing that we construct. At the same time I think it is incumbent on me to examine the nature of the sociological stance that provides for such an analysis. In that reflexive sense my position could be characterised as postmodern, but I aim to break with the limitations of both the postmodern and the modern and argue for the transmodern—a way station at which some kind of synthesis of the two can be achieved, without the excesses of either.

Behind the theorising there are a number of intersecting, fundamental and seemingly intractable questions concerning the knowledge produced by science and technology which reflect the conditions of modernity in the late twentieth century. Can we ensure that the world will continue to exist, that we will not bring about its destruction either catastrophically by blowing it up or more insidiously by destroying the atmosphere or the environment? Can we ensure that the world's habitability is sustained, that the environment and its resources are not subject to degradation and depletion so that the quality of existence is not continuously impaired? Can we ensure that people from all cultures have lives that are valuable and fulfilling, that everyone has access to the necessities of life so that the minority does not live at the expense of the majority with the attendant repressive economic, social and military regimes? Can we maintain biological and cultural diversity in the face of global processes of homogenisation? Finally, can we at the same time give salience to the fundamental and perennial questions of the meaning and purpose of human existence?

These questions are intimately connected to science and technology, to our ways of inquiring about the world and our ways of transforming it. Science and technology seem responsible for the greatest paradoxes yet faced by humankind. At the very point in history where we appear to be able to explain the formation of the universe itself, when we have the ability to utilise energies as great as those of the sun, the majority of the world's population still live in poverty, the resources that made 'modern civilisation' possible are fast being depleted, and the byproducts of that civilisation threaten to transform the climate of the whole world.

We face a doubly confounding paradox, for not only are our scientific and technological inquiries manifestly both very productive and very destructive but we must inevitably depend upon them to resolve the very contradictions they have produced. What compounds this even further is that we know little about the nature of inquiry; we hardly know what science and technology are, let alone what makes them tick or how to control them. We know little about them since, as Langdon Winner points out, the intimate connections between knowledge and power have lead to the promulgation of myths and misunderstandings about the nature of science and technology. We are, as he says, in a state of 'technological somnambulism ... the interesting puzzle in our times is that we so willingly sleepwalk through the process of reconstituting the conditions of human existence.'[3]

Decentring Science and Curing Somnambulism

My aim is to unravel some of the myths and misunderstandings about science and technology by proposing a different set of narratives. The perspective adopted is that of the sociology of scientific knowledge (often referred to as SSK) and as such is both constructivist and inter-actionist. As Joseph Margolis puts it, '[we are] constituted and recon-stituted *by* such cultural forces in the same instant in which the "world" is constituted and reconstituted by our changing inquiries and interventions ... *the human self is itself technologically and praxically constituted.*'[4]

In the view of Elting Morison, an historian of American technology, our task is to:

> design and control things so that the artificial surroundings we create for ourselves will serve our interests better than the supplanted natural environment did ... how to organise a technological world we can live in ... The criteria for such design and control cannot be established by a search for the maximum potential in each particular machine or system—how to better cool a room; how to blow up more easily some part of the world we do not at the moment want. The criteria derive from some general scheme that all the parts and pieces can fit into and serve. Such a scheme cannot be based only on our knowledge of what machines can be built to do, which is almost anything. It must be grounded in the sense of ourselves as the governing point. The controlling factor in the design problem is what we take the human condition to be.[5]

Analytically, the task is to reveal both the processes that bring scientific and technological knowledge about and the ways in which they in turn order our lives. But we also need to ask how we can bring these insights to bear on the problems of modernity. How can we have technoscience that does not dominate nature but is compatible with it, that does not exploit and demean people but enhances their lives? How can we develop new criteria to achieve these ends and how can we ensure that these criteria are implemented? Many of these subsidiary questions can be expressed in a way which brings them within the ambit of this book. How can we ensure that we do not impose a universal monoculture either biologically or socially? How can we reframe science and technology in such a way that we encourage biological and cultural diversity? Our survival is dependent on both.

While I propose ways of thinking about these issues it is not possible to produce any definitive solutions. The modern world, as we are all too well aware, is complex and constantly changing; any suggested answers must be similarly complex and diverse. I offer an approach which makes science and technology questionable and criticisable. In other words I hope to create ways of framing problems that make them potentially resolvable, rather than intractable paradoxes or ineffable mysteries.

There are both programmatic and methodological reasons for taking this kind of position. John Law, for example, argues that the sociology of scientific knowledge has had a developmental trajectory. It had its beginnings in a problem of epistemology, questioning the nature and authority of scientific knowledge, expanding its focus and growing to encompass the problem of heterogeneity or how to explain social order. In his view the sociology of scientific knowledge has only recently matured to the point where it can deal with the problem of distribution, that is the inequities of class, race and gender.[6] Methodologically, the sociology of scientific knowledge is also inherently relativistic and reflexive. One way to handle the problems this makes for the grounding of the claims of the analyst is to acknowledge the political nature of the enterprise. To put the problem of distribution on the agenda from the start provides an answer to the reflexive problems that raise so many apparently intractable difficulties for some people within the sociology of scientific knowledge.[7] It makes clear the analyst's own position and criteria. At the same time it also forestalls the simple anti-relativist arguments based on self-contradiction or 'anything goes'. I shall develop these points more fully in the conclusion.

The general claim of this book is that much can be learned about the production of scientific and technological knowledge from a consideration of the differing ways in which its heterogeneous components are assembled. Knowledge is in effect a 'motley'.[8] The process of knowledge assemblage is a dialectical one in which forms of social space are coproduced. The interactive, contingent assemblage of space and knowledge, sustained and created by social labour, results in what I call a 'knowledge space'.

This messy, spatialised perspective stands in marked contrast with the 'received view' of the nature and relationship of scientific and technological knowledge as having their own separate and logical dynamics. Science is autonomous, rational, objective and universal. Technology is applied science guided by instrumental and economic rationality. The sociology of scientific knowledge has, of course, spent the last forty years or so deconstructing these claims by setting scientific and technological knowledge in a sociohistorical context and

examining their complex interactions. Such deconstructions and exam-
inations, whilst prolific and insightful, have had limited success in
changing the broader community understanding. Not surprising, given
that the nature of science and technology and their relationship is contested territory, with high stakes invested in their authority and credibility. Science as rational, autonomous, and objective not only
represents the establishment position, but in recent years its more
vociferous proponents have moved onto the offensive in the 'science
wars' salient of the wider 'culture wars'.[9] Nonetheless there is currently
a kind of 'Kuhnian orthodoxy' in the sociology of science in which
scientific knowledge is held to have a less than fully determinate relationship to reality. There are significant differences and disputes within
the sociology of science about the constraints of 'reality' on knowledge.
But, by and large, it is the received view, at least within the discipline,
that scientific knowledge is not immune to sociological analysis.[10]

There are now few sociologists who would defend a view like
Werner Stark's: 'social developments do not determine the content of
scientific developments simply because they do not determine natural
facts.'[11] Equally there are few historians of science who would
treat science as a purely autonomous intellectual enterprise in the way
that Alexander Koyré did when he described science as 'essentially
theoria, a search for the truth … an inherent and autonomous development', or Charles Gillispie who claimed that 'science which is about
nature cannot be determined in its content by the social relations of
scientists'.[12]

Indeed, in recent years it has become apparent that across the broad
mainstream, orthodox analysts of science, including historians and
philosophers, are starting to change their minds about the origins,
nature and status of science. They are, in a sense, coming of age. They
are undergoing what Cunningham and Williams have neatly identified
as a process of 'decentring'—recognising that there are other ways of
knowing the world in addition to the Eurocentric and egocentric as
exemplified in the term 'Western science'.[13] This maturation has followed in the wake of the more radical critiques of science brought to
the sociology of scientific knowledge by feminists, post-colonialists,
and left-wing theorists.[14] It is now widely recognised that there was
always a concealed tension in the easy elision between science, a supposedly 'universal' body of objective knowledge, and 'Western' science,
a body of knowledge having specific and unique origins in 'the scientific revolution' of seventeenth-century north-western Europe.
Historians and sociologists alike are now more ready to acknowledge

that a specific form of knowledge production, best thought of as 'modern science', is a relatively recent, local activity that was co-produced with industrial capitalism. Science, in the general sense of systematic knowledge, was never uniquely Western, having exemplifications in a wide variety of cultures both ancient and modern, including Islam, India and China, the Americas, Africa and the Pacific.

However, there is a great diversity of knowledge traditions around the world and despite the decentring in the more historically informed disciplines, the epistemological and political stakes are still very high in the struggle over what counts as knowledge, and whether modern science should be seen as setting the epistemological standard. The position I have adopted here will do little to appease opponents of the sociology of scientific knowledge, but I argue that my approach meets some of their criticisms while also allowing for a performative, historically contingent and cross-culturally comparative account which is committed to the idea that technoscience can be and should be other than it is. This book will suggest ways in which all knowledge traditions, including Western technoscience, can be compared as forms of local knowledge so that their differential power effects can be explained but without privileging any of them epistemologically.

Of Pawpaws and Cabbages, Roses and Nettles

In order to get to the position from which it is plausible to see scientific knowledge as the contingent assemblage of local knowledge, I want to look briefly at some of the classical underpinnings of Western science, and to review some of the arguments that make a sociological approach to understanding knowledge possible at all. It is this very possibility that its opponents, like Stark, have sought to deny, arguing that if something is to count as real knowledge it must be true, both throughout time and from one culture to another. If knowledge is historically and culturally invariable, how then can there be anything to be analysed sociologically? After all, sociology is concerned with social variation and thus would seem to have little to contribute to an analysis of knowledge that is rational, objective and produced according to the canons of scientific method, and which is consequently universal. In other words, from this perspective, sociology can be informative about social and institutional factors affecting the rate and direction of scientific change but cannot deal with the content of scientific knowledge.[15]

Technoscience has become the authoritative form of knowledge in the world today. According to the myth, the key to this unparalleled success lies in science's embodiment of the highest form of rationality and objectivity in the scientific method. This mythical underpinning of science also provides the rationale for the celebration of modernism and the current domination of the West, a view unselfconsciously exemplified by the philosopher Ernest Gellner, who claims 'If a doctrine conflicts with the acceptance of the superiority of scientific-industrial societies over others, then it really is out.'[16]

Therein lies the first set of intrinsic problems and contradictions which this myth conceals. Modernism is supposedly synonymous with development and social improvement, but science and technology can no longer be treated as unalloyed agents of progress. The other equally difficult emergent problem for the mythological account of science is that it has been seen as quintessentially Western; absent in the developing countries or an undeveloped possibility in the Islamic, Chinese and Indian cultures. This can no longer be accepted as a simple fact but has now to be seen as an ideological marker in the creation of the 'other'. We have then a typically complex and contradictory 'modern' problem. It is becoming apparent that the grand project of modernism—a universal scientific culture—has started to show significant pathologies and stands in need of radical rebuilding in order to encourage cultural diversity. Just as biological diversity has become recognised as an ecological necessity, so too has our cultural survival come to be seen as dependent on a diversity of knowledge. However, such ecological insights are in part drawn from Western science. Consequently, we are faced with the necessity of trying to reach the 'transmodern' where knowledges from differing traditions, non-Western and Western, can be enabled to work together. From the perspective of a political historian 'the central problem of social and political theory today is to decide the nature of communicatory reason between irreducibly different cultures'.[17] If that bridge between knowledge traditions is to be built, we need to ask ourselves in what ways can science be reconstituted.

The strongest and most persuasive arguments for the possibility of universal, objective knowledge are based on two assumptions. Firstly, that there is one uniquely correct ordering of the natural phenomena of the world and secondly, that there is a set of procedures sufficiently powerful to determine what that ordering is. However what philosophers from Duhem to Rorty have shown is that our scientific and technological ways of knowing about the world, far from being epistemologically secure or privileged, are riddled with *indeterminacies*.[18]

All our ordering is partial and incomplete. Now we are told, for example, that we should recognise that the pawpaw is closely related to the cabbage and the rose to the nettle according to Kew Garden's new botanical system of classification by genetic history rather than by morphology. ·

Science as Practice

It was Thomas Kuhn, in his seminal text *The Structure of Scientific Revolutions,* who set the opening agenda for SSK by portraying its communal character and reliance on established tradition, and drew attention to the salience of practice in science. He famously invoked the notion of a paradigm to explain scientific change, but used it in two major and distinct senses; *disciplinary matrix,* and *exemplar.* Kuhn's first usage of the term paradigm is something akin to a global theory such as Newtonian physics and is subject to revolutionary change—the main topic of his book. His second usage of paradigm as exemplar is much closer to the standard meaning of paradigm—a sample problem solution which can be extrapolated to other problems. Within a *disciplinary matrix*, which Kuhn takes to be a constellation of communal commitments, he discerns a variety of elements, including symbolic generalisations, metaphysical presuppositions, and values. Conjointly, these elements enable the scientists in a particular field to reach communal agreement on what count as significant questions and puzzles, what modes of analysis are appropriate and what kind of solutions are acceptable. *Exemplars* by contrast, are shared examples of puzzle solutions and are based essentially on agreements about which kinds of problems are sufficiently similar as to be treated in the same way. These 'learned similarity relations' provide the ability to perceive otherwise disparate problem situations as alike and thence to apply known techniques and solutions. Importantly they are not verbally defined, but are the product of tacit knowledge which is 'learned by doing science rather than by acquiring rules for doing it.'[19]

Critics and commentators have paid most attention to Kuhn's first usage of the term paradigm as a global theory that defines the possible questions and acceptable answers. While this focus raises important problems about how paradigms structure scientists' experience and the difficulties of translating and moving between paradigms, it misses the crucial practical sense of paradigm as exemplar. Kuhn himself saw this as central in understanding how scientists learn to make sense of the world through finding ways of bridging indeterminacies and making judgements in conditions of uncertainty.

In his book *Knowledge and Power* Joseph Rouse points out that there are alternative readings of Kuhn, depending on which sense of paradigm is taken as paramount. The traditional philosophical perspective tends to favour the question of how scientific theories change. They focus on Kuhn's cycle of 'normal science' within a paradigm, crisis resulting from the paradigm reaching the limits of its capacity, revolution, and finally, acceptance of a new but incommensurable paradigm. On this representationalist model a scientific paradigm is essentially a theoretical entity constituting a world view. However, a more performative approach suggests that:

> Paradigms are not primarily agreed-upon theoretical commitments but exemplary ways of conceptualising and intervening in particular empirical contexts. Acquiring a paradigm is more like acquiring and applying a skill than like understanding and believing a statement.[20]

Traditional philosophy of science has always had difficulties getting abstract universal propositions to apply to particular, local, practical situations. Cartwright argues that 'the fundamental laws do not govern reality. What they govern has only the appearance of reality and the appearance is far tidier than reality itself'. She concludes that:

> We construct both the theories and the objects to which they apply, then match them piecemeal onto real situations, deriving—sometimes with great precision—a bit of what happens, but generally not getting all the facts straight at once.[21]

For Cartwright, and also for Ian Hacking, models are 'the intellectual tools that help us understand phenomena and build bits and pieces of experimental technology. They enable us to intervene in processes and to create new and hitherto unimagined phenomena.'[22] But models are by their nature artificial, finite, constructs. Nonetheless they can be inconsistent and yet still prove useful even in the light of theory change. So even on this philosophical understanding of models, what enables us to find out about and operate in the world, is a site specific practice—getting a model to work. It is not the application of a universal law. Nor could it be, since in order for laws to be applied they must be so constrained by the input of specific data that they are no longer laws but at best empirical generalisations.

Rouse brings together these insights from Kuhn and Cartwright and offers the following description of scientific practice:

> In scientific research, we obtain a practical mastery of locally situated phenomena. The problem is how to standardise and generalise that achievement so that it is replicable in different local contexts. We must try to understand how scientists get from one local knowledge to another rather than from universal knowledge to its local instantiation ...[23]

The major locus of contemporary scientific research is the laboratory which, as the name implies, is where work is done. In other words it is where nature is physically transformed. But, as Rouse points out, the actual materials worked on in the laboratory are seldom 'natural'; they are themselves artificial, being the product of prior processing. Consider for example the mice used as experimental subjects all the over the world.[24] These mice have been specially bred and are reared in isolation from the natural environment. Without such specially created materials, the kinds of fine distinctions made in scientific experiments are simply not possible. The laboratory itself also has to be organised in a very tightly controlled way to prevent unwanted effects. Once the artificial materials are assembled in the specially contrived environment of the laboratory they are subjected to experimentation using highly sophisticated instruments and techniques. Experiments, precisely because they are highly contrived, are usually hard to do. Much of the scientists' time, energy and skills are devoted to 'tinkering', to getting the experiment to work.[25] Thus the process of scientific research is in large part a technical processing of artifacts in highly constrained circumstances and the essential problem is no longer that which is central to much philosophy of science, i.e. theory change, but one of knowledge transmission: how to get a local exemplar, a particular solution worked out in one laboratory, to work in another laboratory, and then how to get it to work outside the laboratory. These vital secondary and tertiary stages usually require that the knowledge is adapted to local needs or that the environment is adapted to the knowledge. Once this local, site-specific character of scientific knowledge production is recognised, then, as Rouse argues, science can be conceived as an interrelated field of practices rather than as a network of statements. The difference between these two positions is highly significant.

Emphasising the local in this way necessitates a re-evaluation of the role of theory, which is typically held by philosophers and physicists to provide the main dynamic and rationale of science as well as being the source of its universality. A pervasive example of the primacy given to theory in current philosophy of science is the explanation of scientific development in terms of theory change.[26] Rather more grandiloquently, Karl Popper claims that all science is cosmology while Gerald Holton sees physics as a 'quest for the Holy Grail', which is no less than the 'mastery of the whole world of experience, by subsuming it under one unified theoretical structure'. It is this claim to be able to produce mimetic totalising theory that Western culture has used simultaneously to promote and reinforce its own stability and dominance and to justify the dispossession of other peoples.[27] It constitutes part of the ideological justification of scientific objectivity, the 'god-trick' as Harraway calls it: the illusion that there can be a positionless vision of everything.[28] The allegiance to mimesis has been severely undermined by analysts like Rorty, but theory has also been found to have a less substantive role at the level of practice. Analytical studies and empirical examples like those of cathedrals and malaria in Chapters Two and Five show it cannot provide the sole guide to experimental research and on occasion has little or no role at all.[29] The conception of grand unified theories guiding research is also incompatible with one of the findings in the sociology of science: 'consensus is not necessary for cooperation nor for the successful conduct of work'.[30] This slightly confounding but key sociological perspective is succinctly captured in Star's description:

> Scientific theory building is deeply heterogeneous: different viewpoints are constantly being adduced and reconciled ... Each actor, site, or node of a scientific community has a viewpoint, a partial truth consisting of local beliefs, local practices, local constants, and resources, none of which are fully verifiable across all sites. The aggregation of all viewpoints is the source of the robustness of science.[31]

Theories then have the characteristics of what Star calls 'boundary objects', that is, they are 'objects which are both plastic enough to adapt to local needs and constraints of the several parties employing them, yet robust enough to maintain a common identity across sites.'[32] Thus theorising is itself an assemblage of heterogeneous, local practices. The problem with the theory-dominant attitude, as Rouse points out, is that:

> the local site of investigation, the experimental construction, the technical facilities involved in that construction, the particular networks of social

relations within which the investigators are situated, and the practical difficulties of getting on with research are incidental to scientific knowledge.[33]

If we allow theory the less dominant role of 'the pattern that connects',[34] an increased emphasis falls on human activity in the production of scientific knowledge. It is in large part because of its philosophical origins in the epistemological critiques of foundationalism that SSK was initially heavily concerned with the problems of representation. Recent work has shown a shift towards the performative nature of knowledge production.[35]

This realignment of emphasis has several effects. Firstly, it provides a more materialist account that serves to restrict the infinite regress of interpretation and hence allows for the possibility of a minimal form of objectivity in the limitations of the material world.[36] Secondly, a renewed focus on the performative links the work, the engagement with the material world that is so central to technoscience, with the Wittgensteinian point that meaning is a matter of usage, of embodied performance.

Just as they are constitutive of our life world, our ways of understanding and of controlling the material world are transforming both that world and ourselves, and in so doing form a kind of knowledge space. The kinds of spaces that we construct in the process of assembling, standardising, transmitting and utilising knowledge govern our lives today. Not only do we have to build extensions of the laboratory into society for the knowledge produced there to be effective, but certain kinds of relationships and behaviours are required of us. Knowledge spaces are as much moral as they are epistemological, political or technical. Hence, the spatialisation of knowledge also leads to the necessity for putting the problem of distribution on the agenda.

Many distribution problems are dependent on the notion of a great divide. One of the greatest divides is that between Western and so-called primitive knowledge systems, which has turned crucially on the question of the rationality of science. If, as the arguments above suggest, science has forms of rationality of its own, but none that are especially privileged, how do we both account for, and deal with, similarity and difference between cultures? How is it, that the peoples of the world are sufficiently alike to have universally developed complex languages, and yet those languages and their accompanying knowledge systems have produced profoundly different cultures? And how are we to ensure communication between them whilst simultaneously preserving cultural diversity?

I have argued that the sociology of scientific knowledge with a more performative emphasis leads us to see that technology and science are essentially social activities concerned with the production and application of local knowledge. The questions that then have to be answered are: how does that local knowledge move beyond the site of its production, how do all the heterogenous components, people, practices and places become linked, what sort of space does this assemblage create and how do modes of moving and assembling knowledge differ between cultures and periods? In the rest of the book I try to provide answers to these questions.

The Structure of the Book

Chapter One examines the process of knowledge assemblage and develops the concept of knowledge spaces. I argue that the common element in all knowledge systems is their localness, and that their differences lie in the way that local knowledge is assembled through social strategies and technical devices for establishing equivalences and connections between otherwise heterogeneous and incompatible components. Science too is dependent on the assemblage of heterogeneous inputs, but that assemblage is not achieved by the application of logical and rational rules or conformity to a method or plan. Indeed, it is not even dependent on a clearly articulated consensus. Rather the assemblage results from work, the work of negotiation and judgement that each of the participants has to put in to create the equivalences and connections that produce order and meaning. Perhaps it has to be acknowledged that there is a minimal rationality assumption, that links between rationalities can be created by common human endeavour. So, given the lack of universal criteria of rationality, the problem of working disparate knowledge systems together is one of creating a shared knowledge space in which equivalences and connections between differing rationalities can be constructed. Communication, understanding, equality and diversity will not be achieved by others adopting Western information, knowledge, science and rationality. It will only come from finding ways to work together in joint rationalities and in knowledge spaces constituted through these joint rationalities.

An effective way of rethinking how knowledge is assembled and of undoing some of our preconceptions about 'science' and 'technology' is to examine an example of premodern construction in Western Europe. In Chapter Two I look at how complex innovative structures like

Chartres cathedral were built without architects, plans, structural mechanics or a common measure. Chartres is a motley, an ad hoc mess, put together with talk, tradition and templates. Through the adoption of a variety of such social strategies and technical devices, a knowledge space was created where the work of many men could be assembled.

The classic modern exemplar of scientific assemblage is the map. In Chapter Three I show the ways in which maps, science and the state coproduce one another in a cartographic knowledge space. But a knowledge space, like all such spaces, is a contingent assemblage and contains within it paradoxes and contradictions. So, despite their apparent hegemony, modern scientific maps offer sites of resistance and the possibility of other ways of knowing the world.

From within the knowledge space of Western science the only alternatives that seem possible are restricted to variations in perspective and technology. The contingency of our knowledge assemblage is most fully revealed in exploring a completely different way of assembling knowledge of the world that utilises none of the Western prerequisites—paper, calculation, and instruments. In Chapter Four I examine the ways the Pacific Islanders organised knowledge spatially and were able to systematically colonise the world's largest ocean.

In the next two chapters I examine the kinds of messy contingent assembly that occur in contemporary Western science and the kinds of problems involved to trying to get the world to fit a particular kind of solution. Chapter Five looks at the difficulties enountered in extending the knowledge space created in trying to produce a malaria vaccine. Much money and effort has been devoted to developing such a vaccine, yet malaria is itself a motley, constantly reassembling and escaping the confines of the knowledge space. Malaria is irredeemably messy and local, yet we continue to try for monocultural, global solutions at the expense of local knowledge and local people.

In Chapter Six I look at another example of laboratory-based Western science—turbulence research in a school of engineering. In the process of considering the ways the scientists involved attempt to impose order on the turbulence of their field both inside the wind tunnel and outside in their social world, I am forced once again to examine my own imposed ordering. Indeed this book is itself a motley, a contingent assemblage.

Finally I return to the themes of rationality and modernity and the possibilities for the joint preservation of the liberatory elements of the enlightenment project and a wide diversity of other knowledge traditions. One way to fully embrace the relativism and reflexivity of the sociology of scientific knowledge and not shirk the kind of political responsibility inherent in it, is to work towards the transmodern through the recognition of the contingently assembled nature of all knowledge. It is the considerable social labour involved in the accomplishment of contingent assemblage that is denied in universalisation of knowledge. Yet it is precisely this social labour which must be celebrated if we are to find ways of changing the world and maintaining diversity.

Notes

1 J. Law, *Organizing Modernity*, (Oxford: Blackwell, 1994).

2 P. Worsley, *Knowledges: Culture, Counterculture, Subculture*, (New York: New Press, 1997).

3 Langdon Winner, *The Whale and the Reactor* (Chicago: University of Chicago Press, 1986), p. 10. See also Barry Jones, *Sleepers Wake! Technology and the Future of Work*, (Melbourne: Oxford University Press, 1982).

4 Joseph Margolis, 'The Technological Self', in E. F. Byrne and J. C. Pitt, eds., *Technological Transformation: Contextual and Conceptual Implications*, (Dordrecht: Kluwer Academic Publications, 1989), pp. 1–16, p. 4.

5 E. E. Morison, *From Know-How to Nowhere: The Development of American Technology*, (Oxford: Blackwell, 1974), pp. 3–4.

6 John Law, ed., *A Sociology of Monsters: Essays on Power, Technology and Domination*, Sociological Review Monograph 38, (London: Routledge, 1991), pp. 1–25.

7 For example Steve Woolgar, ed., *Knowledge and Reflexivity: New Frontiers in the Sociology of Knowledge*, (London: Sage, 1988), Steve Woolgar, *Science: The Very Idea*, (London: Tavistock, 1988).

8 The evocative term 'motley' is used by Ian Hacking, 'The Self-Vindication of the Laboratory Sciences', in A. Pickering, ed., *Science as Practice and Culture*, (Chicago: University of Chicago Press, 1992), pp. 29–64.

9 See vol 46/7 of *Social Text*, 1996 and my concluding chapter. For examples of the critics of SSK see Paul Gross and Norman Levitt, *Higher Superstition: The Academic Left and its Quarrels with Science*, (Baltimore: Johns Hopkins University Press, 1994) and Keith Windschuttle, *The Killing of History: How a Discipline is Being Murdered by Literary Critics and Social Theorists*, (Sydney: Macleay Press, 1994).

10 For recent work see Collins, H. and T. Pinch 1998, *The Golem at Large: What You Should Know About Technology*, Cambridge University Press, Cambridge; Collins, H. and T. Pinch 1998, *The Golem: What You Should Know About Science*, Cambridge University Press, Cambridge.

11 Werner Stark, *The Sociology of Knowledge*, (London: Routledge and Kegan Paul, 1958), p. 171.

12 Roy Porter, 'The History of Science and the History of Society', in R. C. Olby, G. N. Cantor, J. R. R. Christie and M. J. S. Hodge, eds., *Companion to the History of Modern Science*, (London: Routledge, 1990), pp. 32–46, p. 36.

13 Andrew Cunningham and Perry Williams, 'De-centring the "Big Picture": *The Origins of Modern Science* and the Modern Origins of Science', *British Journal for the History of Science (BJHS)*, Vol. 26, 4, (1993), pp. 407–432, p. 429.

14 See for example John Law, ed., *Power, Action and Belief: A New Sociology of Knowledge?*, (London: Routledge & Kegan Paul, 1986); J. Law, *A Sociology of Monsters*, (London: Routledge, 1991); Sandra Harding, ed., *The 'Racial' Economy of Science: Toward a Democratic Future*, (Bloomington: Indiana University Press, 1993); Zia Sardar, ed., *The Revenge of Athena: Science, Exploitation and the Third World*, (London: Mansell, 1988); Les Levidow and Bob Young, *Science, Technology and the Labour Process*, (London: Free Association Books, 1985).

15 For example, Joseph Ben-David, *The Scientist's Role in Society: A Comparative Study*, (Englewood Cliffs: Prentice Hall, 1971).

16 Gellner cited in Anne Salmond, 'Maori Epistemologies', in J. Overing, ed., *Reason and Morality*, (London: Tavistock Pbls., 1985), pp. 240–63, p. 259.

17 Alastair Davidson, 'Arbitrage', *Thesis Eleven*, Vol. 38, (1994), pp. 158–62.

18 Pierre Duhem, *The Aim and Structure of Physical Theory*, (Princeton: Princeton University Press, 1954); W. V. O. Quine, *Word and Object*, (Cambridge, Mass: MIT Press, 1960); Ludwig Wittgenstein, *Philosophical Investigations*, (Oxford: Blackwell, 1958); R. Rorty, *Philosophy and the Mirror of Nature*, (Princeton: Princeton University Press, 1979).

19 T. Kuhn, *The Structure of Scientific Revolutions*, (Chicago: University of Chicago Press, 1970), p. 191.

20 Joseph Rouse, *Knowledge and Power: Towards a Political Philosophy of Science*, (Ithaca: Cornell University Press, 1987), p. 30.

21 Nancy Cartwright, *How The Laws of Physics Lie*, (Oxford: Clarendon Press, 1983), p. 162.

22 Ian Hacking, *Representing and Intervening: Introductory Topics in the Philosophy of Natural Science*, (Cambridge: Cambridge University Press, 1983), p. 37.

23 Rouse, *Knowledge and Power*, pp. 21–23.

24 Max Charlesworth, Lyndsay Farrall, Terry Stokes and David Turnbull, *Life Among The Scientists: An Anthropological Study of an Australian Scientific Community*, (Melbourne: Oxford University Press, 1989).

25 Karen Knorr-Cetina, 'Tinkering Toward Success: Prelude to a Theory of Scientific Practice', *Theory and Society*, Vol. 8, (1979), pp. 347–76.

[26] Arthur Donovan, Larry Laudan, et al., eds., *Scrutinizing Science: Empirical Studies of Scientific Change*, (Baltimore: Johns Hopkins University Press, 1992).

[27] Graham Huggan, 'Decolonising the Map: Post-colonialism, Post-structuralism and the Cartographic Connection', in I. Adam and H. Tiffin, ed., *Past The Last Post: Theorising Post-Colonialism and Post-Modernism*, (New York: Harvester Wheatsheaf, 1991), pp. 125–138, p. 126.

[28] Donna Haraway, *Simians, Cyborgs and Women: The Reinvention of Nature*, (London: Free Association Books, 1991), p. 189.

[29] N. Cartwright, *How The Laws of Physics Lie*; Richard Rorty, *Philosophy and the Mirror of Nature*, (Princeton: Princeton University Press, 1979).

[30] Susan Leigh Star and James Griesmer, 'Institutional Ecology, "Translations" and Boundary Objects: Amateurs and Professionals in Berkeley's Museum of Vertebrate Zoology, 1907–39', *Social Studies of Science*, Vol. 19, (1989), pp. 387–420, p. 388.

[31] Susan Leigh Star, 'The Structure of Ill-Structured Solutions: Boundary Objects and Heterogeneous Distributed Problem Solving', in L. Gasser and N. Huhns, eds., *Distributed Artificial Intelligence*, (New York: Morgan Kauffman Publications, 1989), pp. 37–54, p. 46.

[32] Ibid.

[33] J. Rouse, *Knowledge and Power*, p. 71.

[34] Gregory Bateson, *Mind and Nature: A Necessary Unity*, (New York: Dutton, 1979), p. 4.

[35] See for example Adele E. Clarke and Joan H. Fujimura, eds., *The Right Tools For the Job: At Work in Twentieth-Century Life Sciences*, (Princeton: Princeton University Press, 1992); Andrew Pickering, ed., *Science as Practice and Culture*, (Chicago: University of Chicago Press, 1992); A. Pickering, *The Mangle of Practice*.

[36] Randall Albury, 'The Politics of Truth: A Social Interpretation of Scientific Knowledge, with an Appplication to the Case of Sociobiology', in M. Ruse, ed., *Nature Animated*, (Dordrecht: Reidel, 1982); Andy Pickering, 'Objectivity and the Mangle of Practice', *Annals of Scholarship*, Vol. 8, (1991), pp. 409–425.

1 'ON WITH THE MOTLEY': THE CONTINGENT ASSEMBLAGE OF KNOWLEDGE SPACES

To us, science, art, ideology, law, religion, technology, mathematics, even nowadays ethics and epistemology, seem genuine enough genres of cultural expression to lead us to ask (and ask and ask) to what degree other peoples possess them and to the degree they do possess them, what form do they take, and given the form they take, what light has that to shed on our own versions of them.[1]

Comparing Knowledge Traditions

This chapter develops the argument that an explicit focus on the local-ness of knowledge production provides the possibility of a fully-fledged comparison between the ways in which understandings of the natural world have been produced by different cultures and at different times. Cross-cultural comparisons of knowledge traditions have hitherto been largely absent from SSK.[2] A necessary condition for fully equitable comparison is that Western contemporary technosciences, rather than being taken as definitional of knowledge, rationality or objectivity, should be treated as varieties of such knowledge systems. Though knowledge systems may differ in their epistemologies, methodologies, logics, cognitive structures or in their socio-economic contexts, a characteristic that they all share is their localness. However, knowledge is not simply local, it is located. It is both situated and situating. It has place and creates a space. An assemblage is made up of linked sites, people and activities; in a very important and profound sense, the creation of an assemblage is the creation of a knowledge space. The motley of scientific practice, its situated messiness, is given a spatial coherence through the social labour of creating equivalences and connections. Such knowledge spaces acquire their taken for granted air and seemingly unchallengeable naturalness through the suppression and denial of work involved in their construction. However, since they are motleys, they are polysemous and are capable of many possible modes of assemblage and of providing alternative interpretations and meanings. Hence all knowledge spaces are potential sites of resistance, as will be seen in the Chapter 3.

Knowledge spaces have a wide diversity of components: people, skills, local knowledge and equipment that are linked by social strategies and technical devices or 'heterogeneous engineering'.[3] From this spatialised perspective, universality, objectivity, rationality, efficacy and accumulation cease to be unique and special characteristics of techno-scientific knowledge, rather these traits are effects of collective work of the knowledge producers in a given knowledge space. To move knowledge from the local site and moment of its production and application to other places and times, knowledge producers deploy a variety of social strategies and technical devices for creating the equivalences and connections between otherwise heterogeneous and isolated knowledges.[4] The standardisation and homogenisation required for knowledge to be accumulated and rendered truthlike is achieved through social methods of organising the production, transmission and utilisation of knowledge. As Steven Shapin has argued, the basis of knowledge is not empirical verification, but trust: 'Trust is, quite literally, the great civility. Mundane reason is the space across which trust plays. It provides a set of presuppositions about self, others, and the world which embed trust and which permit both consensus and civil dissensus to occur.'[5] In addition to social strategies, the linking of the heterogeneous components of a knowledge tradition is achieved with technical devices which may include maps, templates, diagrams and drawings but which are typically techniques for spatial visualisation.

The work of Latour, Collins, Shapin, Star, Hacking, and Rouse among others has shown that the kind of knowledge system we call Western science depends on a variety of social, technical and literary devices and strategies—assemblages which move and engage local knowledge. I suggest that it is having the capacity for movement that enables local knowledge to constitute part of a knowledge system. This mobility requires devices and strategies that enable connectivity and equivalence, that is the linking of disparate or new knowledge and the rendering of knowledge and context sufficiently similar as to make the knowledge applicable.[6] Connectivity and equivalence are prerequisites of a knowledge system but are not characteristics of knowledge itself. They are produced by collective work and facilitated by technical devices and social strategies. Differing devices and strategies produce differing assemblages and are the source of the differences in power between knowledge systems. In order to give some flesh to the local/spatial thesis and to provide specific examples of differing social, moral and technical components in a range of cultural and historical contexts, I want to turn immediately to a brief consideration a variety of Anasazi, Inca, and Australian Aboriginal knowledge spaces. In later chapters I consider in more detail the assemblage work of the Gothic Cathedral builders (Chapter 2) and the Pacific navigators (Chapter 4).

The Anasazi

The Anasazi were a group of North American Indians who established themselves in what is now the Four Corners region (Colorado, Utah, New Mexico, Arizona) of the United States from around 200–700 A.D. They not only managed to survive in this most inhospitable region where the temperature ranges from –20°F to 100°F, and where there is only 9″ of rain often in destructive summer bursts, but they also created a complex society.[7] This society came to an abrupt end in about 1150 A.D. (possibly due to the drought between 1130 and 1180, though this is debatable). At its peak it consisted of 75 communities spread across 25,000 square miles of the San Juan Basin linked into a socioeconomic and ritual network centred on Chaco Canyon.[8]

On the floor of Chaco Canyon massive stone buildings were built up to four stories high with hundreds of rooms including vast storage areas and huge round underground Kivas or temples (see Fig. 1). Chaco was connected to many of the outlying communities by over 400 km of roads. In addition to the great buildings and the roads, the Anasazi built an enormous irrigation system with check dams, reservoirs, canals up to 50′ wide, irrigation ditches, and levelled fields with banks.[9]

The labour and materials involved were immense. It is estimated, for example, that upwards of 200,000 Piñon Pine beams up to 60′ long had to be carried into the canyon from distances of thirty miles or more. The purpose of this staggering effort, in a society that had no wheeled vehicles, seems not to have been the accommodation of large numbers of people. The archaeological record reveals a number of anomalies suggestive of a low population at each site. Despite the large number of rooms in each of these massive complexes, relatively few rooms were designed solely for habitation. One of the great buildings, Pueblo Bonito for example, may have only housed a hundred or so people. Correspondingly very few burial sites have been found. However at Pueblo Alto, on the northern rim of the canyon where the Great North road begins, there are large piles of broken pots, far more than even the most careless of populations could have accumulated. In addition, archaeologists have found large amounts of trade items

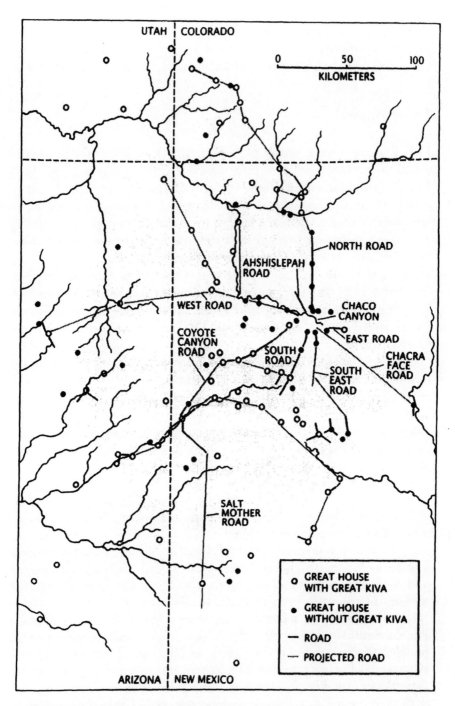

Figure 1 Kivas and roads of the Chacoan Region. Figure by Tom Prentiss. With kind permission of Nelson H. Prentiss.

imported from great distances: turquoise from 160 miles to the SE, shell from Pacific coast, copper bells and macaw feathers from Mexico, and chipped stone and pottery from Chuska 80 miles away. The road system also poses something of a mystery. The 'roads' are unusually straight and wide and without an obvious utilitarian function. All these factors suggest that 'Chaco Canyon from an archaeological perspective functioned primarily as a ceremonial centre gathering people together for the exchange of information and material goods'.[10]

It appears that the key to supporting a population estimated at up to 10,000 in such a marginal environment was the development of an agricultural and storage system which enabled them to grow and redistribute a surplus. But by itself that would not have been enough. To successfully transform an almost totally arid environment, to co-ordinate the work of large numbers of people over a vast area and to ensure the growth, storage and redistribution of food, a large amount of knowledge and information had to be developed, sustained and transmitted. This was achieved primarily with the calendar, along with ritual, myth, poetry and architecture. Clearly, however, the role of knowledge in Anasazi society, as in any other, does not have a merely functionalist role. It also reflects the desire to render the world intelligible and to celebrate existence. Why else would a culture of such complexity and sophistication develop in such an environment? Indeed one could speculate that it is the human propensity for cultural elaboration and the growth of knowledge that provides the conditions for the possibility of social development in all manner of environments. Zuidema argues that:

> Anthropologically speaking we should not look at these systems from the point of view of the prehistory of Western science and astronomy but from the standpoint of theoretically analysing the human propensity to classify the social and physical universe. Kinship and astronomy (in their broadest sense) complement each other, and provide equal opportunities, in a non-evolutionary way, of studying human variation in using limited sets of variables for the general purpose of classification.[11]

The central importance of the Anasazi knowledge system to their culture, and the power of its techniques for preservation and transmission, are revealed in the fact that it has survived largely intact from prehistoric times. It is still an active system in the Pueblo astronomy of the Hopi and Zuni Indians despite pressure from Spanish and Anglo cultures and despite the disappearance of the Anasazi.[12]

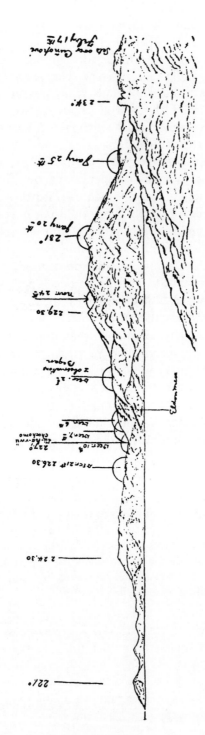

Figure 2 Hopi Horizon Calendar.

Whoever keeps the calendar, be it the town chief, *ta'wa mongwi* or *pekwin* (the sun priest), is responsible for structuring pueblo life on both a day-to-day and a yearly basis. Almost all pueblo activities, and certainly all those that are critical to village survival, both mundane and sacred, are predicted, scheduled, and executed according to the calendar, e.g., seed preparation, ditch maintenance, planting, harvesting, hunting etc., and the accompanying ceremonies.[13]

Hopi astronomical, cosmological and religious knowledge is structured by orientation. The basic axis is based on the intersection of the lines joining midsummer and midwinter rising and setting points of the sun, and is hence solstitial as opposed to our cardinal directions; in addition they place great value on up and down.[14] For the Hopi, the solstitial directions 'provide a general cosmological framework which draws apparently unrelated natural phenomena into an organic unity'.[15] This directional framework is manifested in their 'verbal art' or ritual poetry, religion, and astronomy and has its most overt expression in the calendar.[16]

The calendar is maintained by the sun priest's observation of the sun's seasonal passage past markers on the horizon and through the passage of light and shadow in buildings and rock arrangements like that on top of Fajada Butte (see Fig. 2). At the solstice the sun's rising point remains stationary on the horizon for several days making the actual solstice difficult to determine. The priest resolves this difficulty by anticipatory observation for two weeks before the solstice, which allows preparation for ceremonies.[17] It is crucial that the solstice be accurately forecast because the timing of the planting calendar is of great moment in an environment with a short growing season, and where the onset of frost must be anticipated.

There has been much debate about whether Pueblo astronomy is a science and whether it was sufficiently sophisticated to enable the prediction not just of the solar cycle but of the lunar cycle as well. The debate parallels that around Stonehenge and depends on the interpretation of very similar and problematic evidence. At the entrance to Chaco Canyon stands the massively dramatic Fajada Butte. Anna Sofaer discovered that three inclined rocks at the top of the Butte create a dagger of light that bisects a spiral petroglyph at the moment of midsummer sunrise. This extremely impressive sight demonstrates the great effectiveness with which the Anasazi understood the solar cycle and were able to utilise their physical environment to demonstrate their understanding. Sofaer went on to claim that Fajada Butte reveals intimate knowledge of relatively small long-term variations in the lunar cycle, a claim which seems somewhat overdrawn on current evidence.[18] Nonetheless, 'the site can be used at sunrise to provide a planting calender and to anticipate the summer solstice and to mark the equinoxes.'[19] Hence it is an example of a piece of representational technology that served to preserve and transmit knowledge.

McCluskey concludes of Hopi astronomy that 'considered as astronomy it shows all the concern with exact observation and the development of observational and theoretical framework that we would expect of modern astronomy.'[20] This too can be said of the Anasazi, even though their system was typically local. It strongly reflected its context of use in that it relied on specific horizon markers to record the sun's movements but was nonetheless capable of movement to different places and times, while simultaneously adapting to changing understandings and needs and providing for the growth of an extensive and complex society.[21] The potential for connectivity and equivalence is provided by the directionality that structures the calendar and social life. All events, places and people can be recognised, connected and made equatable through the system of directions represented by the calendar. For its survival and transmission this system is dependent on annual horizon observations and rituals organised by the sun priest; hence its limitations. The Anasazi knowledge system can move only as far as the priesthood can control.

The Inca

At its height the Incan empire extended over large areas of what is now Ecuador, Peru and Chile. This organisation of 5 million people in one state has been the subject of much speculation and admiration. It has been described as socialism, feudalism, despotism, a 'hydraulic society'. Its coherence has been attributed to the hierarchy, the military, the tax system, laws, bureaucracy, land rights and political jurisdiction.[22] However, an essential element was the way in which local knowledge was moved. The Inca developed a range of technical devices and social strategies that enabled all the elements of society to be assigned a spatio-temporal location, to be inscribed, accumulated and transmitted. The principal devices were the calendar, stone alignments or *ceques*, knotted string or *quipus*, and roads and runners or *chasquis*.

The Inca capital, Cuzco, was at the hub of the empire which stretched over 2,000 km from its most northern to its most southern extremities; but not only was the empire very far flung, it also incorporated a large number of pre-existing cultures and covered very variable terrain from the highest parts of the Andes to the coastal plains.[23] The key problem was how to coordinate a large population in an environment which was at best variable, and at worst marginal; and furthermore how to administer it all from one centre.

Spreading out from Cuzco were 41 radial lines marking significant rising and setting points on the horizon for the sun, moon and stars.[24] These lines were the *ceques* marked at intervals by stone cairns or shrines called *huacas* (see Fig. 3). *Ceques* not only integrated religious and astronomical knowledge, they also provided the basis for the kind of precision calendar required by a state bureaucracy that had to record and correlate information about irrigation, agriculture, trade, warfare, and all the associated taxes, manpower, labour obligations and resources, all of which operated in an intricate system of kinship, age, class and social organisation. The *ceques* were extended beyond the horizon to incorporate the whole empire and 'formed a system of coordinates by which information of very different orders was organised, as is done in our maps.'[25]

Interestingly, the Inca created very sophisticated three-dimensional maps of the landscape. The sixteenth-century Spanish historian Garcilaso de la Vega, reported that:

> ... I saw a model of Cuzco and the surrounding country, that was made of clay, small stones and little sticks. It was constructed to scale, showing both its principal and less important streets, its different districts, its suburbs and all its houses—down to the very humblest—its three brooks and the starting points of the four great highways that cross the empire; it was really a pleasure to look at it. All the neighbouring countryside was also marvelously reproduced, with its hills and mountains, its plains and valleys, its rivers and streams, including their bends; indeed, the best cosmographer in the world could not have done better.[26]

In addition to the *ceques*, the Incas developed a sophisticated system of tallying using knotted strings or *quipus* (see Figs. 4 and 5). On such knotted and looped strings it was possible, given a class of interpreters, to record a wide variety of information from instructions to details of taxes, labour obligations and agricultural supplies. The *quipus* were carried by runners or *chasquis* over the extensive road network running the entire length of the country in two parallel systems.

Quipus have been extensively analysed by the Aschers who conclude that:

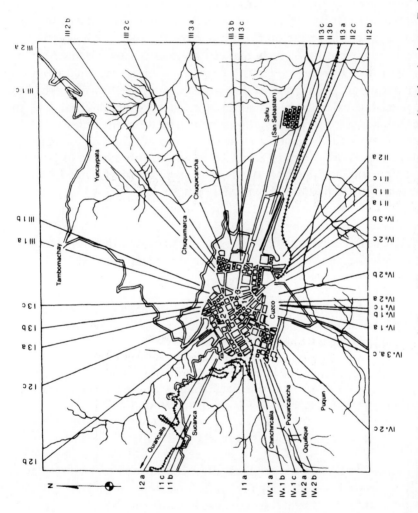

Figure 3 Inca capital Cuzco with *ceques* imposed. From *Native American Astronomy* edited by Anthony F. Aveni © 1977. By permission of the University of Texas Press.

To maintain a population that may have reached six million, knowledge of food production is indispensable. And in a land of steep mountains, knowing how to get enough food means discovering the altitudes where particular plants and animals flourish. We must postulate and indeed have

Figure 4 Incan *quipu*. In the collection of the Museo National de Anthrophología y Arquelogía, Lima, Peru. Photo by Mercia and Robert Ascher.

Figure 5 *Quipu* master. From Guaman Poma's chronicle.

evidence for, thousands of years of experimentation and the accumulation of information about plants, animals, and vertical landscapes as they relate to basic human requirements. The native Andeans dug irrigation canals, built bridges, and constructed community store houses. Clearly technical knowledge was needed to do these things, but knowing how to organise and direct large groups of people to do the work and keep the system going must also be postulated.[27]

The orderly provision of knowledge capable of being used to organise and direct large groups was one of the roles of the calendar, *quipu*, *ceques*, roads and *chasquis*. The *quipu* and the *ceques* have a very strong set of similarities and redundancies of the kind that make for a very effective communication system. Zuidema points out that:

> The *ceque* system has been compared to a giant *quipu*, laid out over the Cuzco valley and the surrounding hills that served in the local representation of the Incan cosmological system, in its spatial, hierarchical and temporal aspects...Not only can the *ceque* system be compared metaphorically to *quipu* but every local group did in fact record its *ceque* system, that is, its political, religious and calendrical organisation on a *quipu*.[28]

Elsewhere Zuidema argues that:

> As projected onto the landscape, the *ceque* system of Cuzco—with all the calendrical rituals carried out in relation to the huacas (places of worship) and ceques mentioned by it—was itself a table, like the *quipu* explaining it. The visibility of all the *ceques* from one centre meant that a person located in the Temple of the Sun had before him 'an open book'. The *ceques* organised space as a map and made reflection upon it as possible as if the person were seeing an actual map.[29]

The power of the Incan knowledge system lay in its capacity to provide connections for a diverse, messy and incommensurable set of local knowledges and to establish equivalences between disparate practices and contexts over a very large area. It was able to do this to a greater extent than, for example, the Anasazi, because the *quipus* and *ceques* were able to extend the range of their calendar beyond the horizon.

We are just beginning to recognise the power and the value of the Incan system. Not only are the old irrigation systems being rediscovered and rebuilt to supply water to regions that for centuries have provided only a subsistence existence for the locals, but the diversity of the region's grains and tubers developed using local knowledge are also offering new sustainable agricultural possibilities for the old world.[30]

The Incan example serves to illustrates the inadequacy of Jack Goody's dichotomy between oral and literate societies. Here we have a society which manifested an interest in abstract critical thought, empirical verification, lists and tables, but without writing. Just as Shapin and Schaffer found that the European scientific revolution went hand in glove with the establishment of social order, so Zuidema finds that:

> The Incan interest in exact and systematic knowledge springs not from a pragmatic interest in the measurement of volume or distance but from an interest in 'abstract and moral concepts such as "sin", "secret", "health", "obligation", and "order"'.[31]

But there is a tendency for the inexact, messy, local knowledge on which the system depends to become invisible, as van der Ploege points out in his insightful account of the ways in which Incan peasants select and maintain varieties of potatoes and their displacement by 'scientific' agricultural methods.[32] Perhaps van der Ploege's claim that 'it really seems that ignorance of the local knowledge systems, their dynamics and their scope is a crucial precondition for the diffusion of the scientific knowledge system' should be extended to include anthropological and sociological analyses of other knowledge systems.

However, it is van der Ploege's account of local knowledge or *art de la localité* which is of central importance. Local knowledge is not systematic in the nomological or law-like fashion of science, it does not lend itself to standardisation and exact planning, but neither is it atheoretical or unsystematic. Being grounded in the specificities of local conditions and practice, it is the combination of diversity, complexity, vagueness and imprecision which gives it its essentially flexible, dynamic and strategic character.

Australian Aborigines

The knowledge traditions of Australian Aborigines demonstrate similar techniques for moving and assembling local knowledge. One of the most common forms of representation in Australian Aboriginal culture is the map. Bark paintings are often maps, as are sand sculptures, body painting, and rock art. Spear throwers and log coffins may be decorated with maps (see Fig. 6). Message sticks and Toas may incorporate geographical information. Aboriginal maps in whatever form are typically landscape maps depicting known places in the

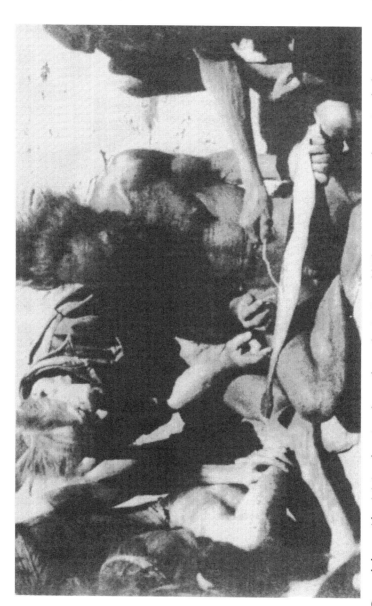

Figure 6 Central desert Aborigines showing the anthropologist Donald Thompson a map of watering holes on a spear thrower in 1957. From: *The Geographical Journal* vol 128: 3, Figure 1 Donald F. Thomson in 'The Bindibu Expedition'. With permission of the Royal Geographical Society.

geographical environment. One might ask why it is that, counter to the orthodoxy, maps are so ubiquitous in a culture that has no written language and, seemingly, has little of the social complexity held to characterise contemporary Western culture?[33] I suggest that Aboriginal culture is far from simple, having as it does one of the world's richest religious systems, and that its central values are embodied as knowledge that is spatially organised because the land and relationships to it underpin everything.

Aboriginal culture is spatialised linguistically, socially, religiously, artistically, and epistemologically. Aboriginal ontology is one of spatialised activities, of events and processes, of people and places. To talk of things is to speak of the relationships of processes at named sites. It is to consider the connections between actions of the Ancestral Beings and humans. Every moment of daily life is replete with spatial references; asking someone to move over may be phrased as 'move northwards please'. Dreams and narratives are cast in a framework of spatial coordinates.[34] Visiting groups at ceremonial gatherings distribute themselves in a spatial replication of the location of their homelands. Ceremonial and initiation grounds are spatially constructed and oriented either to other sacred sites or to the sun. The pervasiveness of spatiality in Aboriginal daily life jointly derives from the semantic structure of the language in which the subjects of sentences are not things but relations and from the centrality of the land in Aboriginal cosmology.

The land is the source of value and meaning, of rights and obligations. Everywhere is sacred since all the land was created in the Dreaming by the activities of Ancestral Beings as they moved across the landscape. These journeys left Dreaming tracks, knowledge of which is recreated in song, story, and ceremony. Everyone has a spiritual linkage to the land by virtue of birth such that they *are* the land. Knowledge of the Dreaming tracks, of the activities that created the land of one's birth, is therefore evidence of possession of the land and by the land. Continued prosperity of the land depends on the fulfilment of the ceremonials and rituals which are in effect both a celebration of ownership and a continuation of the act of creation. The landscape is the source of meaning and value and the repository of history and events and can be read as a map of itself and its own creation.

However, knowledge is the primary marker of status and item of exchange.[35] The Yolngu of Eastern Arnhemland have developed a knowledge tradition dependent on the joint articulation of two modes of patterning which makes it possible for them to know their natural environment.[36] One of those modes of patterning is genealogical—the kinship system.

> All Australian Aboriginal peoples use a formalised recursive representation of kinship as the major integrative standardised form of knowledge in much the same way the formalised recursion of tallying—number—constitutes an integrative standardised from of knowledge in Western Societies.[37]

The kinship system which the Yolgnu call *gurruṯu* provides an unlimited process of recursion that enables all things to be named and related and thus imposes an order on the social and natural world that gives it coherence and value (see Fig. 7). It provides the framework within which social obligations with regard to life, death, marriage and land can be negotiated. The other mode of patterning is provided by *djalkiri*: the stories, myths or dreamings that relate the creation of the landscape by the ancestral beings in a variety of ways including song, dance, story telling and painting. The travels and activities of the ancestors in creating the landscape form tracks or songlines that traverse the whole country. The kinship system and songlines together constitute a knowledge network that allows for everything to be connected and equivalences negotiated. Each individual is responsible for knowing, creating and sustaining the place of their birth through singing the songs and telling the stories. These performances of local knowledges in songs and stories can be linked together through ceremonies and social exchanges so that potentially everything can be known and given value and significance. The only limit to the system is the capacity to retain the land and perform the ceremonies. The kinship system provides an unlimited process of recursion that enables all things to be named and related and thus imposes an order on the social and natural world that gives it coherence and value. It provides the framework within which social obligations with regard to life, death, marriage and land can be negotiated. The other mode of patterning is provided by the stories, myths or dreamings that relate the travels and activities of the ancestors in creating the landscape in the form of tracks or songlines that traverse the whole country. The kinship system and the songlines together form a knowledge network that allows for everything to be connected. The concept of connectedness is an extremely powerful one in Aboriginal culture and is exemplified by the Yolgnu term *likan*, which in the mundane sphere means elbow—the connection of the upper and lower arm—and in the spiritual sphere connotes the connections among ancestors, persons, places and ceremonies.[38] A wide variety of Australian

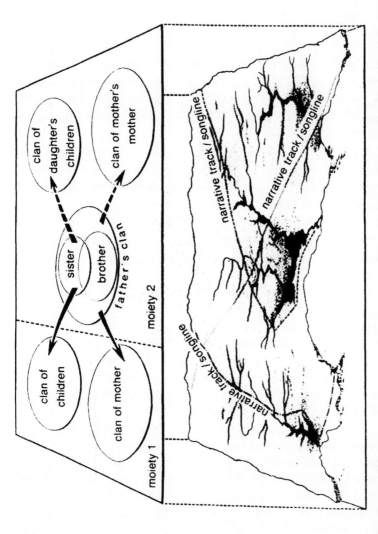

Figure 7 Aboriginal spatial knowledge as the joint articulation of genealogical and narrative patterning. From H. Watson and D. W. Chambers, *Singing The Land, Signing the Land* (Geelong, Deakin University Press, 1989). Fig. 4.3, p. 37, adapted from diagram by Richard Barwick in N. M. Williams, *The Yolngu and Their Land: A System of Land Tenure and the Fight for its Recognition* (Canberra, Australian Institute of Aboriginal Studies, 1986).

Aboriginal paintings have been interpreted as being simultaneously geographic and social; they represent both the tracks of the Ancestors and detailed maps of places. Hence bark paintings are encodings of local knowledge connections.

Sutton has analysed the modern acrylic dot paintings of the Western Desert in this way and Morphy has similarly interpreted a variety of bark paintings from Northeast Arnhemland.[39] The Kunwinjku people of Western Arnhemland paint both on bark and on their bodies at the Mardayin ceremony in the 'x-ray' style that shows internal body parts. In the Mardayin ceremony the bodies of the initiates are painted so that, in effect, their own body parts are mapped with a design that represents the body parts of the Ancestral Beings and features of the landscape. These paintings can be read as maps of the way Kunwinjku 'conceive of the spatial organisation of sites in their land in terms of an abstract model of the divided yet organically related body parts of the ancestral beings that created those lands. Such sites are described as transformations of the actual body parts of the ancestral being, and all the sites thus created are considered to be intrinsically connected'.[40]

The connective functions of paintings like these help children to learn the shape of the landscape and to have respect for it and the animals in it by integrating the activities of the ancestors, people, and places. Ownership of the land means having the right speak of it, to have the knowledge of it, and also to have responsibility for it.

While the land may have boundaries which can be known with precision, it is not good custom to display them, because they are permeable rather than fixed entities with rites of access being required and most frequently granted. Areas can be owned by more than one group and routes can be common property. Boundaries are more properly the subject of negotiation and exchange in ceremony and ritual. Moreover, Yolgnu conceptions of place do not correspond to Western legal notions of enclosure but are more typically open and extendable 'strings' of connectedness.[41]

Consequently, while Australian Aboriginal groups assemble their knowledge by constantly mapping their land, this is a very different process from that of the dominant white society. Being mapped in the white manner may have advantages, for example, in making land claims. In fact it is standard procedure for anthropologists to record Dreaming tracks on Western topographical maps as evidence that this knowledge is the property of the claimants. However this is a rather different process from that of mapping the 'precise boundaries of all Aboriginal groups in Australia', as is the aim of the recently published map *Australia's Extant and Imputed Traditional Aboriginal Territories* (1993).[42] Aboriginal conceptions of identity with the land do not equate with the notions of boundary precision, exclusion and individual property rights and the linkages to the state implicit in Western maps and knowledge spaces. Aboriginal maps, in celebrating that identity with the land, express a very different kind of knowledge space in which boundaries and their permeability are open to negotiation in ceremony and ritual.

Moving Local Knowledge

I have argued that Western science, like all knowledge in all societies, is inherently local. Further I have tried to show that other societies and cultures have developed a variety of social and technical devices for coping with that localness and enabling it to move. Some of them are technical devices of representation like the Incan *ceques* and *quipus*. Some of them are abstract cognitive constructs, like the Anasazi and Incan calendars and Aboriginal maps. All of them also require social organisation, rituals, and ceremonies and create knowledge spaces within which certain kinds of knowledge are made possible. All of them have proved capable of producing complex bodies of knowledge and in many cases have been accompanied by substantial transformations of the environment. The major differences between Western science and other knowledge systems lie in the question of power. Western science has succeeded in transforming the world and our lives in ways that no other system has. The source of the power of science on this account lies not in the nature of scientific knowledge but in its greater ability to move and apply the knowledge it produces beyond the site of its production.

If we allow that all knowledge systems, from no matter what culture or period, have spatiality and localness in common, many of the small but significant differences between knowledge traditions can be explained in terms of the differing kinds of work involved in creating 'assemblages' from the 'motley' of practices, instrumentation, theories and people. Some traditions move it and assemble it through art, ceremony and ritual, whilst science does it through forming disciplinary societies, building instruments, standardising techniques and writing articles. In both cases it is a process of knowledge assembly through making connections and negotiating equivalences between the heterogeneous components while simultaneously establishing a social order of trust and authority resulting in a knowledge space. On this basis it is possible to equitably compare and frame knowledge traditions. The social history of knowledge can be reconceived in a variety of intersecting and overlapping ways which move beyond simple contextualisation. Technoscience could, for example, be seen as a history of visualisation or as a history of measurement and rational calculation. But a particularly perspicuous perspective on the cross-cultural history of knowledge production is provided by a social history of space,[43] that is, a history of the contingent processes of making assemblages and linkages, of creating spaces in which knowledge is possible.

However, within the master narrative of modernism local knowledge is an oxymoron. Exploring this contradiction and the manifold meanings of 'local' requires a brief excursion into postmodernism as well as some of the arguments underpinning the sociology of scientific knowledge.

Though postmodernism continues to elude definition and is more likely a stage of modernism than a marked epistemological break, there is a coalescence of strands of thought in a wide variety of areas that have questioned the assumptions underlying modernism.[44] Postmodernism is most frequently equated with the collapse of the concepts of rationality and progress held to accompany the emergence of the post-industrial society and is consequently concerned with the rejection of universal explanations and totalising theories. But the strand that is most truly pervasive in the constellation of reformulated approaches to understanding the human condition is the emphasis on the local.

In physics, ecology, history, feminist theory, literary theory, anthropology, geography, economics, politics and the sociology of science the focus of attention has become the specific, the contingent, the particular, be it a text, reading, culture, population, site, region, an electron or a laboratory. Within this diversity of uses there seem to be two broad and rather different senses of local. On the one hand, there is the notion of a voice or reading. The voice may be purely individual and subjective or a collection of voices belonging to a group, class, gender, or culture. But in all cases the notion captures one of the basic characteristics of postmodernism, by way of deconstruction, that all texts or cultures are multivocal and polysemous. They have a multiplicity of meanings, readings and voices and are hence subject to 'interpretive flexibility'.[45] On the other hand, local is used both in the more explicitly geopolitical sense of place and in the experiential sense of contextual, embodied, partial, or individual. A range of disciplines from meteorology to medicine now recognise the necessity of focussing on the particular conditions at specific sites and times rather than losing that specificity in unlocalised generalisations.[46]

The sociology of scientific knowledge, in its antifoundationalism, is one of the most classically post of all modernisms. As we have already seen, it is an area in which the local is also a thematic presence, though it has only recently come into focus. Knowledge, from this constructivist perspective, can be 'local' in a range of different senses. 'It is knowledge produced and reproduced in *mutual interaction* that relies on the *presence* of other human beings on a direct, face-to-face basis.'[47] It is knowledge that is produced in contingent circumstances that are site, discipline or culture specific.[48] Local knowledge 'presupposes an active knowledgable actor, who is actually the "agent" of the unity and constant interaction of mental and manual work.[49] It is the product of open systems with heterogeneous and asynchronous inputs. 'Scientific culture is made up of all sorts of bits and pieces—material, social, conceptual—that stand in no necessary relationship to one another'.[50] In sum, scientific knowledge is 'situated knowledge'.[51]

Perhaps the most important consequence of the recognition of the localness of scientific knowledge is that it permits a parity in the comparison of the production of contemporary technoscientific knowledges with knowledge production in other cultures. Previously the possibility of a truly equitable comparison was negated by the assumption that indigenous knowledges were merely local and were to be evaluated for the extent to which they had scientific characteristics. Localness essentially subsumes many of the supposed limitations of other knowledge systems compared with Western science. So-called 'traditional' knowledge systems have frequently been portrayed as closed, pragmatic, utilitarian, value laden, indexical, context dependent, and so on; all of which was held to imply that they cannot have the same authority and credibility as science because their localness restricts them to the social and cultural circumstances of their production.[52] Science by contrast was held to be universal, non-indexical, value free, and as a consequence floating, in some mysterious way, above culture. Treating science as local simultaneously puts all knowledge systems on a par and renders vacuous any discussion of their degree of fit with transcendental criteria of scientificity, rationality, and logicality. Now the multidisciplinary approaches to understanding the technosciences which together constitute the sociology of scientific knowledge can be made more fully anthropological by the addition of a new subdiscipline—'comparative knowledge traditions'.

Knowledge Assemblage

If knowledge is local we are faced with a problem: how are the universality and connectedness that typify technoscientific knowledges achieved? Given all these discrete knowledge/practices, imbued with their concrete specificities, how can they be assembled into fields or knowledge systems? In Star's terms 'how is the robustness of findings and decision making achieved?' In Ophir and Shapin's 'How is it, if knowledge is indeed local, that certain forms of it appear global in the domain of application?'[53] The answers lie in a variety of social strategies and technical devices that provide for treating instances of knowledge/practice as similar or equivalent and for making connections, that is in enabling local knowledge/practices to move and to be assembled.

Considerable advances in understanding the movement of local knowledge have been made possible through Bruno Latour's insightful analyses. For Latour the most successful devices in the agonistic struggle are those which are mobile and also 'immutable, presentable, readable and combinable with one another'.[54] Immutable mobiles are the kinds of texts and images that the printing press and distant point perspective have made possible. These small and unexpected differences in the technology of representation are, on his account, the causes of the large and powerful effects of science. That which was previously completely indexical, having meaning only in the context of the site of production, and no means of moving beyond that site, is standardised and is made commensurable and re-presentable within the common framework provided by distant-point perspective. Hence that which has been observed, created or recorded at one site can be moved without distortion to another site. At centres of calculation such mobile representations can be accumulated, analysed and iterated in a cascade of subsequent calculations and analyses.

Latour's account has been augmented by the work of Steven Shapin and Simon Schaffer in the *Leviathan and the Air Pump*.[55] They have shown that experimental practice in science is sustained by a range of social, literary and technical devices and spaces that we take for granted, but which had to be deliberately created to overcome the fundamentally local and hence defeasible character of experimentally derived knowledge claims. In the seventeenth century, the problem for Robert Boyle, one of the earliest experimentalists, was to counter the arguments of his opponent Thomas Hobbes about the grounding of true and certain knowledge which they both agreed was essential in a country riven by dissent and conflicting opinion. Reliable knowledge of

the world, for Hobbes, was to be derived from self-evident first principles and anything that was produced experimentally was inevitably
doomed to reflect its artifactual nature and the contingencies of its production; its localness would deny it the status of fact or law. Boyle recognised the cogency of these arguments and set out to create the forms of
life within which the knowledge created at one site could be relayed to
and replicated at other sites. In order for an empirical fact to be accepted
as such it had to be witnessable by all, but the very nature of an experimental laboratory restricted the audience of witnesses. To enable knowledge to move out of the bounded private space of the laboratory into a
wider public space, Boyle sought to create what Shapin calls 'virtual witnessing'[56] for which three general sorts of devices or 'technologies' were
needed. Socially, groups of reliable witnesses had to be formed and
linked. Naturally in the seventeenth century they were gentlemen. These
gentlemen witnesses had to be able to communicate their observations to
other groups of gentlemen so that they too might witness the phenomena. This required the establishment of journals using clear and
unadorned prose that could carry the 'immutable mobiles', experimental
accounts and diagrams. In addition to these social and literary technologies the experimental apparatus had to be made technically reliable and
reproducible. But the most important consequence was the creation of an
entirely new space within which such empirical knowledge became
credible and authoritative.

Hobbes, of course, was right. Experimental knowledge is artifactual.
It is the product of human labour, of craft skill, and necessarily reflects
the contingencies of the circumstances. It is because craft skill or tacit
knowledge is such a fundamental component of knowledge production
that accounts of its generation, transmission, acceptance and application cannot be given solely in terms of texts and inscriptions. A vital
component of local knowledge is moved by people in their heads and
hands. Collins has argued that this ineradicable craft component in
science is ultimately what makes science a social practice. Because
knowledge claims about the world are based on the skilled performance of experiments their acceptance is a judgement of com-
petence not of truth. An example of the centrality of craft skill is the
TEA laser, invented in Canada by Bob Harrison in the late sixties,
which British scientists attempted to replicate in the early seventies.
'No scientist succeeded in building a laser using only information
found in published or other written sources'. Furthermore, the people
who did succeed in building one were only able to do so after extended
personal contact with somebody who had themselves built one.[57] Now

of course TEA lasers are blackboxed, their production is routine and algorithmic, but in order to become routinised Harrison's local knowledge had to be moved literally by hand.

Rouse, in considering the contemporary production process of scientific knowledge, has summarised the implications of this understanding of science.

> Science is first and foremost knowing one's way about in the laboratory (or clinic, field site, etc.). Such knowledge is of course transferable outside the laboratory site into a variety of other situations. But the transfer is not to be understood in terms of the instantiation of universally applied knowledge claims in different particular settings by applying bridge principles and plugging in particular local values for theoretical variables. It must be understood in terms of the adaptation of one local knowledge to create another. We go from one local knowledge to another rather than from universal theories to their particular instantiations.[58]

The way a scientist learns to solve problems is not by applying theory deductively but, in Kuhnian fashion, by learning to apply theory through recognising situations as similar. Hence theories are models or tools whose application results from situations being conceived as, or actually being made, equivalent. This point is implicit in the recognition that knowledge produced in a laboratory does not simply reflect nature because nature as such is seldom available in a form that can be considered directly in the lab. Specially simplified and purified artefacts are the typical subject of instrumental analysis in scientific laboratories. For the results of such an artificial process to have any efficacy in the world beyond the lab, the world itself has to be modified to conform with the rigours of science. A wide variety of institutional structures have to be put in place to achieve the equivalences needed between the microworld created inside the lab and the macroworld outside in order for the knowledge to be transmittable. The largest and most expensive example in the US is the Bureau of Standards, a massive bureaucracy costing six times the national R&D budget.[59] Without such social institutions the results of scientific research are mere artefacts. They gain their truth, efficacy and accuracy not through a passive mirroring of reality, but through an active social process that brings our understandings and reality into conformity with each other.

Though scientific culture is now being more frequently recognised as deeply heterogeneous,[60] there is, at present, no term in general usage that adequately captures the amalgam of places, bodies, voices, skills, practices, technical devices, theories, social strategies and collective work that together constitute technoscientific knowledge/practices. Foucault's epistemes, Kuhn's paradigms, Callon, Law and Latour's actor-networks, Hacking's self-vindicating constellations, Fujimura and Star's standardised packages and boundary objects and Knorr-Cetina's reconfigurations all embrace some of the range of possible components, but none seem sufficiently all encompassing.[61] Hence I adopt Deleuze and Guattari's term 'assemblage', which in their usage is like an episteme with technologies added, but which connotes the ad hoc contingency of a collage in its capacity to embrace a wide variety of incompatible components.[62] It also has the virtue of connoting active and evolving practices rather than a passive and static structure. It implies a constructed robustness without a fully interpreted and agreed upon theoretical framework, while capturing the inherently spatial nature of the practices and their relations.

Research fields or bodies of technoscientific knowledge/practice are assemblages whose otherwise disparate elements are rendered equivalent, general and cohesive through processes that John Law calls 'heterogeneous engineering'.[63] Among the many social strategies that enable the possibility of equivalence are processes of standardisation and collective work to produce agreements about what counts as an appropriate form of ordering, what counts as evidence, etc. Technical devices that provide for connections and mobility are also essential. Devices may be material or conceptual and may, as we have seen, include maps, calendars, theories, books, lists, and systems of recursion, but their common function is to enable otherwise incommensurable and isolated knowledges to move in space and time from the local site and moment of their production.

Some of these devices have been revealed relatively unproblematically through direct observation. Others are less susceptible to investigation and analysis, being embodied in our 'forms of life'. One way to catch a glimpse of these hidden presuppositions and taken for granted ways of thinking, seeing and acting, is to 'misperceive', to be jolted out of our habitual modes of understanding through allowing a process of interrogation between our knowledge system and others. Such an interrogative process of mutual inter-translation can enable us to glimpse the distortions of our 'cultural glasses' instead of looking through them as if they were simply transparent.

The Local and the Global in Interaction

This challenging of the totalising discourses of science by other knowledge systems is what Foucault had in mind when he claimed that we are 'witnessing an *insurrection of subjugated knowledges*',[64] and corresponds to an emphasis on the local that has emerged in anthropology at least since Clifford Geertz's *Interpretation of Cultures*. In his critique of global theories and his emphasis on 'thick description' Geertz pointed out that cultural meanings cannot be understood at the general level because they result from complex organisations of signs in a particular local context; that the way to reveal the structures of power attached to the global discourse is to set the local knowledge in contrast with it.[65]

Equally, there is the pervasive recognition often characterised as post-colonialism, that the West has structured the intellectual agenda and hidden its own presuppositions from view through the construction of the 'other'.[66] Nowhere is this more acute than in the assumption of 'science' as a foil against which all other knowledge should be contrasted. In the view of Marcus and Fischer we are at an 'experimental moment' where totalising styles of knowledge have been suspended 'in favour of a close consideration of such issues as contextuality, the meaning of social life to those who enact it and the explanation of exceptions and indeterminants'. In this emphasis on the local we are 'postparadigm'.[67]

However, we should not be too easily seduced by the apparently liberatory effects of celebrating the local, since it is all too easy to allow the local to become a 'new kind of globalising imperative'.[68] In order for all knowledge systems to have a voice and to allow for the possibility of inter-cultural comparison and critique, both of which are in my view essential, we have to maintain the local and the global in dialectical opposition to one another.[69] This dilemma is the most profound difficulty facing liberal democracies now that they have lost the convenient foil of communism and the world has Balkanised into special interest groups, be they genders, races, nationalities, minorities or whatever. By moving into comparative mode, there is a grave danger of the subsumption of the other into the hegemony of Western rationality. Conversely, unbridled cultural relativism can only lead to the proliferation of ghettos and dogmatic nationalisms.[70] We cannot abandon the strength of generalisations and theories, particularly their capacity for making connections and for providing the possibility of criticism. At the same time we need to recognise that theory and practice are not distinct; theorising is also a local practice. If we do not recognise this joint dialectic of theory and practice, the local and the global, we will not be able to understand and hence establish the conditions for the possibility of directing the circulation and structure of power in knowledge traditions.

The strength of the sociology of scientific knowledge is its claim to show that what we accept as science and technology could be other than it is. The great weakness of the sociology of scientific knowledge is its general failure to grasp the political nature of the enterprise and work towards change. With some exceptions, it has had a quietist tendency to adopt the neutral analyst's stance that it devotes so much time to criticising in scientists.[71] One way of capitalising on the sociology of science's strength and avoiding the reflexive dilemma is to devise ways in which alternative knowledge systems can be made to interrogate each other and work together. Recognising that all knowledge systems create their own space in which knowledge, trust and place are made, allows for just such an interrogation and working together by making visible the spatial and moral components of knowledge production.

The next chapter considers an example of assemblage work in premodern Europe. The building of Chartres cathedral created a knowledge space through talk, trust, tradition and templates; in effect, a large-scale laboratory.

Notes

1 Clifford Geertz, *Local Knowledge: Further Essays in Interpretive Anthropology*, (New York: Basic Books, 1983), p. 92.
2 Exceptions include Sandra Harding, *Is Science Multicultural? Postcolonialisms, Feminisms and Epistemologies*, (Bloomington: Indiana University Press, 1998) and David J. Hess, *Science and Technology in a Multicultural World*, (New York: Columbia University Press, 1995).
3 The term heterogeneous engineering is used by John Law, see John Law, 'On the Methods of Long Distance Control: Vessels, Navigation and the Portuguese Route to India', in J. Law, *Power, Action and Belief*, pp. 234–63.
4 John Law, 'On the Social Explanation of Technical Change: The Case of the Portuguese Maritime Expansion', *Technology and Culture*, Vol. 28, (1987), pp. 227–253.
5 Steven Shapin, *A Social History of Truth: Civility and Science in 17th Century England*, (Chicago: University of Chicago Press, 1994), p. 36.
6 Connectivity is discussed in the Chapter 3. On equivalences see Bruno Latour, *The Pasteurization of France*, (Cambridge: Harvard University Press, 1988), p. 170.
7 Stephen Lekson, Thomas C. Windes, et al., 'The Chaco Canyon Community', *Scientific American*, Vol. 259, July, (1988), pp. 100–9, p. 100.

8 W. James Judge, 'New Light on Chaco Canyon', in D. G. Noble, ed., *New Light on Chaco Canyon*, (Santa Fe: School of American Research Press, 1984), pp. 1–12. According to the archaeologist Dwight Drager the road system is linked with signal towers as part of a 'vast communication network' cited in Kendrick Frazier, *People of Chaco; A Canyon and its Culture*, (New York: W. W. Norton & Co, 1986), p. 125.

9 Patricia L. Crown and W. James Judge, eds., *Chaco and Hohokam: Prehistoric Regional Systems in the American Southwest*, (Sante Fe: School of American Research Press, 1991); K. Frazier, *People of Chaco*; Kathryn Gabriel, *Roads to Center Place: A Cultural Atlas of Chaco Canyon and the Anasazi*, (Boulder: Johnson Books, 1991); R. Gwinn Vivian, 'Conservation and Diversion: Water-control Systems in the Anasazi Southwest', in T. E. Downing and M. Gibson, eds., *Irrigation's Impact on Society*, (Tucson: University of Arizona Press, 1974), pp. 95–112.

10 W. James Judge, 'Archaeology and Astronomy; a View From the Southwest', in J. B. Carlson and W. J. Judge, eds., *Astronomy and Ceremony in the Prehistoric Southwest*, (Albuquerque: University of New Mexico, 1983), pp. 1–8, p. 6.

11 R. T. Zuidema, 'Anthropology and Archaeoastronomy', in R. A. Williamson, ed., *Archaeoastronomy in the Americas*, (Los Altos: Ballena Press, 1981), pp. 29–32, p. 31.

12 Michael Zeilik, 'Anticipation in Ceremony: The Readiness Is All', in J. B. Carlson and W. J. Judge, eds., *Astronomy and Ceremony in the Prehistoric Southwest*, (Albuquerque: University of New Mexico, 1983), pp. 25–42, p. 25.

13 Jonathon E. Reyman, 'Priests, Power and Politics: Some Implications of Socio-ceremonial Control', in J. B. Carlson and W. J. Judge, eds., *Astronomy and Ceremony in the Prehistoric Southwest*, (Albuquerque: University of New Mexico, 1983), pp. 121–42, p. 134.

14 On the six directions see Evan Hadingham, *Early Man and the Cosmos*, (New York: Walker and Co, 1984). So taken for granted is our own system of directions that we hardly notice the extent to which they constitute a framework within which we order our lives, nor do we assume them to be anything other than a natural feature of the world. Stephens, an anthropologist who lived among the Hopi, did not notice for two years that they had their own system of orientation.

15 Stephen McCluskey, 'Historical Archaeoastronomy: The Hopi Example', in A. F. Aveni, ed., *Archaeoastronomy in the New World: Proceedings of an International Conference at Oxford 1981*, (Cambridge: Cambridge University Press, 1982), pp. 31–59, pp. 33–4.

16 Jane Young, 'The Nature of the Evidence: Archaeoastronomy in the Prehistoric Southwest', in J. B. Carlson and W. J. Judge, eds., *Astronomy and Ceremony in the Prehistoric Southwest*, (Albuquerque: University of New Mexico, 1983), pp. 169–190, pp. 173ff.

[17] Zeilik, 'Anticipation in Ceremony'.

[18] John Carlson, 'Romancing The Stone, or Moonshine on the Sun Dagger', in J. B. Carlson and W. J. Judge, eds., *Astronomy and Ceremony in the Prehistoric Southwest*, (Albuquerque: University of New Mexico, 1983), pp. 71–87; Anna P. Sofaer and Rolf M. Sinclair, 'Astronomical Markings at Three Sites on Fajada Butte', in J. B. Carlson and W. J. Judge, eds., *Astronomy and Ceremony in the Prehistoric Southwest*, (Albuquerque: University Of New Mexico, 1983), pp. 43–70.

[19] Michael Zeilik, 'A Reassessment of the Fajada Butte Solar Marker', *Archaeoastronomy, Supp n9, Journal for the History of Astronomy*, Vol. 16, (1985), pp. S69–S85, p. S84.

[20] McCluskey, 'Historical Archaeoastronomy', p. 55; see also Stephen McCluskey, 'Science, Society, Objectivity, and The Southwest', in J. B. Carlson and W. J. Judge, eds., *Astronomy and Ceremony in the Prehistoric Southwest*, (Albuquerque: University of New Mexico, 1983), pp. 205–217.

[21] There is some evidence for the North American Indian recording of accurate, complex and detailed lunar and solar calendars in a mobile form as message sticks. See Alexander Marshack, 'North American Indian Calendar Sticks; The Evidence for a Widely Distributed Tradition', in A. F. Aveni, ed.,*World Archaeoastronomy: Selected Papers from the 2nd Oxford International Conference on Archaeoastronomy Held at Merida, Yucatan, Mexico, 1986*, (Cambridge: Cambridge University Press, 1989), pp. 308–324.

[22] Sally Falk Moore, *Power and Property in Inca Peru*, (Connecticut: Greenwood Press, 1985).

[23] Ronald Wright, *Cut Stones and Crossroads: Journey in Peru*, (New York: Penguin Books, 1984).

[24] R. Tom Zuidema, 'Bureaucracy and Systematic Knowledge in Andean Civilization', in G. A. Collier, R. I. Rosaldo and J. D. Wirth, eds., *The Inca and Aztec States, 1400–1800 Anthropology and History*, (New York: Academic Press, 1982), pp. 419–458.

[25] R. Tom Zuidema, 'The Sidereal Lunar Calender of the Incas', in A. Aveni, ed., *Archaeoastronomy in the New World*, (Cambridge: Cambridge University Press, 1982), pp. 59–107.

[26] Garcilaso de la Vega, *The Incas: The Royal Commentaries of the Inca*, (New York: Avon Books, 1961).

[27] M. Ascher, *Ethnomathematics: A Multicultural View of Mathematical Ideas*, (Pacific Grove: Brooks Cole, 1991); Maria Ascher and Robert Ascher, *Code of the Quipu: A Study in Media, Mathematics and Culture*, (Ann Arbor: University of Michigan Press, 1981).

[28] R. Tom Zuidema, 'The Inca Calender', in A. Aveni, ed., *Native American Astronomy*, (Austin: University of Texas Press, 1977), pp. 219–259, p. 231.

29 Zuidema, 'Bureaucracy and Systematic Knowledge in Andean Civilization', pp. 445–6.

30 Omar Sattaur, 'Native is Beautiful', *New Scientist*, Vol. June 2, (1988), pp. 54–7. 'Ancient Inca Irrigation Works Restored to Raise Record Crops', (Interpress Thirdworld News Agency, May 25 1997) on <indknow@u.washington.edu>

31 Zuidema, 'Bureaucracy and Systematic Knowledge', p. 425.

32 Jan Douwe van der Ploege, 'Potatoes and Knowledge', in M. Hobart, ed., *An Anthropological Critique of Development*, (London: Routledge, 1993), pp. 209–27. See also Brian Wynne, 'May The Sheep Safely Graze?', in S. Lash, B. Szerszynski and B. Wynne, eds., *Risk, Environment and Modernity: Towards a New Ecology*, (London: Sage, 1996), pp. 44–83.

33 Denis Wood, 'Maps and Mapmaking', *Cartographica*, Vol. 30, 1, (1993), pp. 1–9.

34 Fred R. Myers, *Pintupi Country, Pintupi Self: Sentiment, Place and Politics among Western Desert Aborigines*, (Washington, London, Canberra: Smithsonian Institution Press and Australian Institute of Aboriginal Studies, 1986).

35 Kingsley Palmer, 'Knowledge As a Commodity in Aboriginal Australia', in D. Turnbull, ed., *Knowledge, Land and Australian Aboriginal Experience*, (Geelong: Deakin University Press, 1991), pp. 6–10.

36 This section draws on Helen Watson, with the Yolgnu community at Yirrkala and David Wade Chambers, *Singing the Land, Signing the Land*, (Geelong: Deakin University Press, 1989); Helen Watson-Verran, 'Working Where Knowledge Systems Overlap', *Knowledge and Policy*, Vol. 14, (1993); Helen Watson-Verran and David Turnbull, 'Science and Other Indigenous Knowledge Systems', in S. Jasanoff, G. Markle, T. Pinch and J. Petersen, eds., *Handbook of Science and Technology Studies*, (Thousand Oaks: Sage Publications, 1995), pp. 115–139.

37 Watson, *Singing the Land, Signing the Land*, p. 11.

38 Howard Morphy, *Ancestral Connections: Art and an Aboriginal System of Knowledge*, (Chicago: University of Chicago Press, 1991); Nancy M. Williams, *The Yolgnu and Their Land: A System of Land Tenure and the Fight for its Recognition*, (Canberra: Australian Institute of Aboriginal Studies, 1986).

39 Peter Sutton, *Dreamings: The Art of Aboriginal Australia*, (Ringwood: Viking, 1988). Morphy, *Ancestral Connections*.

40 Luke Taylor, 'Seeing the "Inside": Kunwinjku Paintings and the Symbol of the Divided Body', in H. Morphy, ed., *Animals into Art*, (London: Unwin Hyman, 1989), pp. 371–389.

41 Ian Keen, 'Metaphor and the Meta-Language: "Groups" in Northeast Arnhemland', *American Ethnologist*, Vol. 22 (1995), pp. 502–527.

42 This map was drawn by Davis see S. L. Davis and J. R. V. Prescott, *Aboriginal Frontiers and Boundaries in Australia*, (Melbourne: Melbourne

University Press, 1992). For devastating critiques see Peter Sutton, ed., *Country: Aboriginal Boundaries and Land Ownership in Australia. Aboriginal History Monograph 3*, (Canberra: Aboriginal History Inc., 1995). On Aboriginal mapping see Jane Jacobs, 'Understanding the Limitations and Cultural Implications of Aboriginal Tribal Boundary Maps', *Globe*, Vol. 25, (1986), pp. 2–12; Jane Jacobs, 'Shake 'Im This Country': The Mapping of the Aboriginal Sacred in Australia—The Case of Coronation Hill', in P. Jackson and J. Penrose, eds., *Constructions of Race, Place and Nation*, (London: University College London, 1993), pp. 100–120.

[43] Andrew Barry, 'The History of Measurement and the Engineers of Space', *BJHS*, Vol. 26, (1993), pp. 459–68.

[44] Mike Featherstone, 'In Pursuit of the Postmodern: An Introduction', *Theory, Culture and Society*, Vol. 5, Special Issue on Postmodernism, (1988).

[45] Collins, *Changing Order*.

[46] See for example James Gleick, *Chaos: Making a New Science*, (London: Viking Penguin, 1987).

[47] Nigel Thrift, 'Flies and Germs: a Geography of Knowledge', in D. Gregory and J. Urry, eds., *Social Relations and Spatial Structures*, (London: Macmillan, 1985), pp. 366–403.

[48] Ian Hacking, 'The Self-Vindication of the Laboratory Sciences', in A. Pickering, ed., *Science as Practice and Culture*, (Chicago: University of Chicago Press, 1992), pp. 29–64; Karin Knorr-Cetina, *The Manufacture of Knowledge: An Essay on the Constructivist and Contextual Nature of Science*, (Oxford: Pergamon Press, 1981); Rouse, *Knowledge and Power*.

[49] van der Ploege, 'Potatoes and Knowledge', p. 212.

[50] Andrew Pickering, ed., *Science as Practice and Culture*, (Chicago: University of Chicago Press, 1992), p. 8.

[51] Haraway, *Symians, Cyborgs and Women*.

[52] Robin Horton, 'African Traditional Thought and Western Science', *Africa*, Vol. 37, (1967), pp. 50–71 and 155–87 and Robin Horton, 'Tradition and Modernity Revisited', in M. Hollis and S. Lukes, eds., *Rationality and Relativism*, (Oxford: Blackwell, 1982), pp. 201–260. This position is typical of many development theorists who while encouraging the use of indigenous knowledge nonetheless see it as closed and local as opposed to the open universality of science. For example Eugene Hunn, 'What is Traditional Ecological Knowledge?', in N. Williams and G. Baines, eds., *Traditional Ecological Knowledge: Wisdom for Sustainable Development*, (Canberra: Center for Resource and Environmental Studies, 1993); Michael Howes and Robert Chambers, 'Indigenous Technical Knowledge: Analysis, Implications and Issues', *Institute of Development Studies (IDS) Bulletin*, Vol. 10, Jan 2, (1979), pp. 5–11; D. Brokensha, D. M. Warren, et al., eds., *Indigenous Knowledge Systems and Development*, (Lanham: University

Press of America, 1980); D. M. Warren, J. Slikkerveer, et al., eds., *Indigenous Knowledge Systems: The Cultural Dimensions of Development*, (London: Kegan Paul International, 1991). For critique see Arun Agrawal, 'Dismantling the Divide Between Indigenous and Scientific Knowledge', *Development and Change*, Vol. 26, 3, (1995), pp. 413–439.

[53] S. L. Star, 'The Structure of Ill-Structured Solutions', p. 46. Adi Ophir and Steven Shapin, 'The Place of Knowledge: A Methodological Survey', *Science In Context*, Vol. 4, (1991), pp. 3–21, p. 15.

[54] Bruno Latour, 'Visualisation and Cognition: Thinking With Eyes and Hands', *Knowledge and Society*, Vol. 6, (1986), pp. 1–40, p. 7.

[55] Steven Shapin and Simon Schaffer, *Leviathan and the Air Pump: Hobbes, Boyle and the Experimental Life*, (Princeton: Princeton University Press, 1985).

[56] Ophir, Shapin 1991, 'The Place of Knowledge', p. 15.

[57] Harry Collins, *Changing Order: Replication and Induction in Scientific Practice*, (London: Sage, 1985), pp. 55ff.

[58] Rouse, *Knowledge and Power*, p. 72.

[59] P. Hunter, 'The National System of Scientific Measurement', *Science*, Vol. 210, (1980), pp. 869–74, discussed in Bruno Latour, *Science In Action*, (Milton Keynes: Open University Press, 1987), p. 251.

[60] Clarke, and Fujimura, *The Right Tools For the Job*; John Law, 'Power, Discretion and Strategy', in J. Law, ed., *A Sociology of Monsters: Essays on Power, Technology and Domination*, (London: Routledge, 1991), pp. 165–191; Pickering, *Science as Practice and Culture*.

[61] Wiebe Bijker, Thomas Hughes, and Trevor Pinch, eds., *The Social Construction of Technological Systems; New Directions in the Sociology and History of Technology*, (Cambridge: MIT Press, 1987); Wiebe Bijker and John Law, eds., *Shaping Technology/Building Society: Studies in Sociotechnical Change*, (Cambridge: MIT Press, 1992); Michel Callon, John Law, and Arie Rip, eds., *Mapping the Dynamics of Science and Technology; Sociology of Science in the Real World*, (London: MacMillan, 1986).

[62] Giles Deleuze and Felix Guattari, *A Thousand Plateaus; Capitalism and Schizophrenia*, (Minneapolis: University of Minnesota Press, 1987), p. 90.

[63] John Law, 'Technology and Heterogeneous Engineering: The Case of Portugese Expansion', in W. Bijker, T. Hughes and T. Pinch, eds., *The Social Construction of Technological Systems; New Directions in the Sociology and History of Technology*, (Cambridge: MIT Press, 1987), pp. 111–34.

[64] Michel Foucault, *Power/Knowledge: Selected Interviews and Other Writings 1972–77*, (New York: Pantheon Books, 1980), pp. 71ff.

[65] Clifford Geertz, *The Interpretation of Cultures: Selected Essays*, (New York: Basic Books, 1973).

[66] James Clifford, *The Predicament of Culture; Twentieth-Century Ethnography, Literature and Art*, (Cambridge: Harvard University Press, 1988).

[67] G. E. Marcus and M. M. J Fischer, *Anthropology as Cultural Critique: An Experimental Moment in the Human Sciences*, (Chicago: University of Chicago Press, 1986).

[68] Katherine Hayles, *Chaos Bound: Orderly Disorder in Contemporary Literature and Science*, (Ithaca: Cornell University Press, 1990), pp. 213–4.

[69] Edward Said, *Orientalism: Western Conceptions of the Orient*, (New York: Pantheon Books, 1978).

[70] Ian Adam and Helen Tiffin, eds., *Past The Last Post; Theorising Post-Colonialism and Post-Modernism*, (New York: Harvester Wheatsheaf, 1991).

[71] Among the exceptions are Steve Fuller, *Social Epistemology*, (Bloomington: Indiana University Press, 1988); Pickering, *Science as Practice and Culture*; Sal Restivo, 'Modern Science as a Social Problem', *Social Problems*, Vol. 33, (1988), pp. 206–25; Bob Young, 'Science *is* Social Relations', *Radical Science Journal*, Vol. 5, (1977), pp. 165–129. An example of this quietism is Barry Barnes and David Edge, eds., *Science in Context*, (Milton Keynes: Open University Press, 1983), General Introduction, p. 11. This is further discussed in the conclusion.

2 TALK, TEMPLATES AND TRADITION: HOW THE MASONS BUILT CHARTRES CATHEDRAL WITHOUT PLANS

Bringing Chartres into the Present

In this chapter I want to pursue a more detailed exploration of the ways in which the assemblages of local, messy practices coproduce a knowledge space. The Gothic cathedrals have been chosen because they are a premodern European example of knowledge in practice. By looking at a period where much of what we now take for granted about innovation, construction and design was not yet established, it is possible to undo some preconceptions about science and technology. We can consider some of the ways in which the technoscientific world we now inhabit came into being with the formation of a particular kind of knowledge space.

The construction of Gothic cathedrals such as Chartres poses a number of questions. How were they designed? What was the role of the architect, of plans, drawings and of scientific knowledge? How were innovations like flying buttresses possible in the absence of a theory of structural mechanics? How were large numbers of un-differentiated stones assembled into an organised structure? How was the labour and skill of large numbers of men and women coordinated? As a consequence of their presuppositions about the nature of the design process and about the nature of scientific and technical knowledge, many authors answer these questions in a way that on the one hand makes the construction process seem mysterious and radically different from 'modern' construction and design, and on the other obscures the historical emergence of such technical devices as plans. Plans are now a prerequisite for complex building and along with maps have become synonymous with organised, systematic knowledge. Yet, as will become apparent in this and subsequent chapters on navigation and maps, they are culturally and historically contingent devices for assembling knowledge. Important questions in understanding the formation of our technoscientific world are when, where and how plans and maps started to play a formative role in shaping our modes of understanding. The auxiliary question asks when plans and maps became synonymous with scientific understanding, thereby obscuring the messy practices that underlie them.

The accounts of medieval architecture given, for example, by Jantzen, an historian of art, Bernal, a historian of science, and Heyman, an architectural and engineering historian, create a great divide between then and now. They portray science as an abstract and entirely modern phenomenon and cathedral building as mere technical craft unguided by theoretical or scientific understanding. Hence they are drawn to make an inexplicable mystery out of the Gothic cathedrals. Jantzen writes, 'an insuperable barrier indeed separates [the medieval] approach to building from ours'.[1] Correspondingly, Bernal argues that:

> Architecture was indeed the greatest and most characteristic expression of medieval thought and technique. It was however, a purely technical rather than a scientific achievement. The marvellous construction of vault and buttress, far more daring than anything the Romans or the Greeks attempted, was the result of a series of ad hoc solutions to practical difficulties. Theory did not enter into them at all, nor could it, for the theory of the arch, apart from working knowledge of it, was only discovered in our time. For the same reason medieval architecture contributed little, directly or indirectly, to the advance of science.[2]

Likewise Heyman claims:

> It is almost certain that the builders [of Gothic cathedrals] were incapable of even the simplest structural analysis. One of the classic medieval problems was that of the parallelogram of forces, not solved until the end of the sixteenth century; without any rules for the composition of forces, or, indeed, any clear formulation of the notion of a force and of its line of action, it is difficult to see how any calculations can have been done to determine for example the line of thrust in a buttress.
>
> There can, however be no doubt of the practical abilities of the master builders; a cathedral which survives almost intact for 800 years is clearly a work of genius. Equally clearly, the structural system employed, measured by almost any yardstick is almost perfect. Certainly advances must have been made by trial and error, by experiments with the actual structure as well as with models. But, looking at, for example, the complete glass curtain-walls of the Sainte Chappelle in Paris, one is tempted to sense a mastery of building technique greater than any that can be ascribed to mere trial and error.[3]

In creating these dichotomies between technology and science, between the medieval and the modern, between the ad hoc and the theoretical, such analysts are perpetuating what are now taken as self-evident distinctions, but it forces them into making the construction of the cathedrals a mystery requiring the invocation of such imponderables an 'insuperable barrier' or 'genius' or a long-forgotten secret building technique.

These dichotomies can be resolved and the construction of the cathedrals demystified if a more performative approach is taken and the Gothic cathedrals are conceived as sites of experimental practice—literally as 'laboratories'. The power of laboratories derives from their being sites at which people, practices and the diverse but amorphous materials can be shaped, manipulated, assembled, and transmitted beyond the laboratory.[4] There are three essentials components in the transmission of the mix of knowledge involved in the construction process: talk, tradition and templates. Talk and tradition were vital to the interaction between the mason and clerics and between groups and generations of masons. I shall come back to these seemingly mundane but vital components of communication later on.

The key technological component in the transmission of knowledge and in the creation of a manipulable system with respect to the construction of the Gothic cathedrals is the template. A template is a pattern or mold, usually outlined on a thin piece of wood, that a stone mason uses to cut a stone to a particular shape. This small item of representational technology has much of the power of a scientific theory: it manifests the integration of science/technology and theory/practice, and it is a solution to the central problem of knowledge transmission. It was the use of templates, along with constructional geometry and a relatively small range of simple tools—compasses, straight edge and string—that, in an experimental context, enabled the building of extremely high, radically innovative buildings. It was a construction process that lacked a common system of measurement, and in the early Gothic period probably lacked drawn plans and a continuity of architects or design. In the later part of the cathedral building period the use of plans became commonplace and the role of master mason changed to that of architect. Both of these transitions have served to reinforce a distinction between science and technology, and have resulted in the modern over-emphasis on the role of theory at the expense of practice. This distinction and over-emphasis characterising the traditional view of scientific knowledge derive from epistemological presuppositions that conceal the local and messy practices that are typical of the production of technoscientific knowledge in all eras. The differences between the building of Chartres cathedral, for example, and modern technoscientific practice lie not in the possession of some secret or mysterious skill, nor in some essential difference between science and technology on the one hand and theory and practice on the other. As we saw in the previous chapters, both science and technology, now and in the past, are the product of local and tacit knowledge. The differences between them lie in the social and technical means by which local and messy knowledge/practices, are made robust, coherent and mobile,[5] that is, in the ways in which the site-specific or even problem-specific products are added to the work of previous individuals or groups of workers, or are transmitted to another site.

(Re)constructing Chartres

After a disastrous fire, Chartres Cathedral was rebuilt between 1194 and 1230, with a spire 345 feet high, the equivalent of a thirty-storey skyscraper.[6] It has stood for nearly 800 years and to modern eyes is a breathtakingly beautiful example of Gothic architecture. Yet in the seventeenth century, the period when the major positivistic myths about science had their beginnings, such buildings were abhorred. Sir Christopher Wren, for example, followed Vasari's dismissive use of the term 'Gothic', which literally meant the product of uncivilised tribal barbarians:

> Goths, Vandals and other barbarous tribes subverted and demolished their Greek and Roman art introducing in their stead a certain fantastical and licentious manner of building which we have since called modern or Gothic: congestions of heavy dark melancholic and monkish piles without any just proportion, use or beauty, compared with the truly ancient.
>
> They set up these slender and misshapen pillars, or rather bundles of staves and other incongruous props to support incumbent weights and ponderous arched roofs without entablature.
>
> For proof of this I dare report myself to any man of judgement, after he has looked awhile upon King Henry VII's Chapel at Westminster, gazed on its sharp angles, narrow lights, lame statues, lace and other cutwork and crinkle-crankle and then shall turn his eyes on the Banqueting House built at Whitehall by Inigo Jones after the ancient manner.[7]

The question of how Chartres was built becomes more acute when the enormous volume of construction in the period is taken into account. So massive a transformation did all this building produce in Europe that it has been called the thirteenth-century industrial revolution, of which the central dynamic was the 'cathedral crusade'.[8] Over one and a half centuries, a population of two and half million people built fifty major religious buildings, three thousand five hundred churches, numerous abbeys and retreats, military works, palaces and houses.[9] But not only were the Gothic cathedrals huge, complex and ubiquitous, they were structurally radical and innovative, combining great height with thin walls and huge windows. In fact masonry buildings, with rare exceptions such as St Peter's in Rome and St Paul's in London, were never to reach such heights again. It was not until the use of iron framing in the nineteenth century that they could be emulated and surpassed.[10] Inside the Gothic cathedrals, walls were transformed into curtains of glass, pillars became slender columns and ceilings delicate traceries of stone. Outside, they reached prodigious heights, seeming to be simultaneously supported and restrained by the dramatic flying buttresses. How was all this possible in the early thirteenth century?

This question has been given a variety of answers by architectural historians, art historians, and economic historians, though curiously few historians of technology and virtually no historians of science have addressed the problem.[11] Yet a brief consideration of the analysis of Chartres cathedral by the architectural historian John James makes it apparent that many important issues are at stake. The question 'how were they built' is not a simple technical matter but is complex and multi-faceted with political, social, religious, geometrical, economic, aesthetic, organisational, communicational, educational and constructional aspects, only some of which is there space to deal with here.

For those raised on the traditional accounts, James' analysis of Chartres is full of surprises. He finds that 'the design is not a well controlled and harmonious entity, but a mess'.[12] (see Fig. 8). The building has a bewildering variety of buttresses, fliers, roofs, doors and windows. The bays and more importantly the axes in the nave and transepts are completely irregular, the only regularity being in the interior elevation.[13] According to James, Chartres' style cannot be explained as the result of a coherent Gothic aesthetic nor even in terms of gradual transition from Romanesque to Gothic. Altogether there were nine different contractors or master masons[14] who took between twenty-five and thirty years to build the cathedral in thirty distinct campaigns.[15] There were thirteen major design and structural changes in that thirty year period but there was no overall designer, just a succession of builders.[16] James concludes that 'Chartres was the ad hoc accumulation of the work of many men.'[17] (see Fig. 9). John Harvey has a similar view about English cathedrals.

There is not a single English cathedral, except the Renaissance St. Paul's, which was built from start to finish under the supervision of its original architect. Nor is there any medieval cathedral save the last, Bath, which was in essentials finished according to the intentions of its designer, and still retains those essentials unchanged. Most of our cathedrals resemble that other homely product of England, the patchwork quilt.[18]

Figure 8 The messiness of Chartres. Photo D. Turnbull.

Figure 9 'Work of many men' adding collectively to the work of the predecessors. With the permission of the Austrian National Library, Vienna, cod. 2549.

The Question of Plans

While James' and Harvey's conclusion corresponds quite remarkably with my own sociological perspective, it is contested by architectural historians, though usually on presumptive grounds of what must have been. For example, Mark disagrees with James about the lack of an overall scheme,[19] as does Kostof, who argues that 'buildings of substantial scale or a certain degree of complexity must be conceived by someone before construction of them can begin', and again, 'The notion that Gothic cathedrals were the triumph of anonymous team work or the conjuring of scholarly churchmen cannot be seriously entertained.'[20] Similarly Shelby rejects James' thesis that there was a succession of contractual crews and no overall architect.[21] There is, however, no clear agreement about how the cathedral was built, though Murray's analysis broadly confirms James' account of cathedral building as a discontinuous process.[22]

James' account is indeed provocative; it is not surprising that many analysts have taken exception to it. The principal objections levelled against it are rational or logical ones based on the supposition that a building as complex as Chartres could not have been built without a plan or a designer. To the modern mind the design argument in architecture seems self-evident just as an analogous argument in biology used to seem self-evident until its displacement by evolutionary theory. The world is a very complex place full of intricate mechanisms like the eye, therefore they had to have had a designer. Arguably the design argument derived its self-evidence from what is popularly still believed about science and architectural practice. Science is held to be the product of great thinkers/designers using laws and theories/plans, and all large buildings are designed by architects and require detailed plans so that the intentions of the architect can be passed on to the builder. Just as the self-evidential character of the argument from design for the existence of God has been displaced by alternative explanations, so the necessity for an architect for Chartres may also become less self-evident in the light of a plausible explanation of how it was built. Concomitantly, the pre-eminent role of theory and genius in science may also be called into doubt.

All analysts are agreed that there are no extant plans for Chartres and the architect is unknown; but it is anachronistic to assume, as some historians have, that they *had* to exist. The nature and usage of plans and the role of the architect have changed over time and underwent a transition in the very process of building the cathedrals. The question of the existence of plans, when they came into common usage, and the nature of their role is extremely controversial, just as it is with the curiously separate question of the emergence of map usage. The only current certainty is that apart from the plan of the monastery at St. Gall dated 820 BC, there are no extant plans from the Western medieval period before 1225. Beyond that we can only survey the controversy among the experts who are sharply divided.

According to art historian Robert Branner: '... it was Gothic Architecture with its emphasis on linearity that seems to have called modern architectural drawing into being ... [and] Project drawings—those from which buildings could be constructed—were made by Roman and Byzantine architects, but contrary to current belief, it is highly questionable whether they were used in the early medieval west.'[23] According to architectural historians Mark and Clark, the earliest evidence of the use of drawings to record and transmit architectural ideas dates from about 1225, almost at the time when Gothic construction began to decline.[24] The continental historian Scheller argues rather conservatively that there are 'few if any drawings pre 1350'[25]. Lon Shelby argues that 'architectural drawings were only just coming into use as controlling documents in the design process when Chartres was built'.[26] He also points out 'in medieval building practice, plans and elevations did not possess the supreme importance they do in modern times, but during the later Middle Ages drawings came to be more and more widely used',[27] a conclusion that is accepted by John Harvey.

> The mere fact that surviving drawings in England are extremely rare has led to the sweeping conclusion that technical *working* drawings were not made. This is countered by the continental material ... Study of the continental drawings ... [confirms] that detailed drawings were usual—and indeed essential—for the execution of all major works from about the middle of the thirteenth century if not before.[28]

This conclusion largely fits with that of the map historians Skelton and Harvey, who come at the question from a very different perspective. In their view 'the very concept of a map was unknown' before the late fourteenth century and the 'idea of repesentation in plan suddenly became generally known', perhaps because of the use of maps in civil law but more likely because it was in the late fourteenth century that 'for the first time the building trade began as a regular practice to use plans drawn on parchment or paper and not simply marked out on the ground or on special drawing floors.'[29]

However, earlier writers have taken a more performative view:

That the medieval builder frequently began operations with little else pre-arranged than the general scheme of the building, may be quite safely affirmed. They appear to have had but few drawings of any sort, and those that they had, when compared with the work they allege to have forecast, are difficult to reconcile or even understand because of their crudity and incompleteness.

And

... no individual designer *qua* architect was existent and *per se* he was not necessary.[30]

Blomfield doubted 'that the necessity for working drawings was seriously felt by the Gothic builders.'[31] Spiro Kostof confirms the view of these earlier writers despite his claim that:

There are extant architectural drawings from as far back as Ancient Egypt and Mesopotamia. Indeed, it is hard to see how any structure but the simplest and most traditional could be built without the benefit of such preliminaries.[32]

He goes on to agree with James when he argues that:

A cursory sketch plan was enough to record these [initial geometric] choices. All details would be designed on site and executed individually. The architect supervised every step; he provided templates for every twist of tracery. Improvisation and on-the-spot reversal during the building process were not uncommon.[33]

Obviously absence of evidence is not evidence of absence. A plausible position in the controversy is to accept the distinction made by the French architectural historian Erlande-Brandenburg between site drawings and architectural plans without accepting his outright rejection of James' claims.[34] Indeed there are good reasons *not* to expect site drawings to survive. They would, in all likelihood, have been drawn by the master mason on scraps of wood and paper as detailed explanations of particular structural problems, just as they are on building sites today. Even if they were more substantial, site drawings are subject to the vicissitudes of wind, rain and wear, and though on occasion they may have been drawn on velum, it was a commodity of some scarcity. Even when heavily degraded through re-use, velum was still sought after for making glue.[35] The architectural plans which would have been the documents on which the prelates and the architect based their design discussions were, according to Erlande-Brandenburg, assiduously preserved along with templates in the vestry. In this way the vestry came to act as the 'site's memory'.[36] The question is then, at what point did such plans become part of the design process?

The assumption that the essential requirement for the construction of organised complex structures, like Chartres, is a design, a plan, a set of rules or even a genetic code to specify the whole and its parts, by virtue of making the process algorithmic, explains too little and too much. It does not explain how the cathedrals were structurally achieved and attributes powers to rules that they cannot have. I want to argue that a plan or design is too strong a requirement; a minimum requirement is some means of transporting knowledge within the structural site, or between different sites. So can such an explanation be developed for the Gothic cathedrals? The achievement of the order of complexity and structural innovation involved in their construction required a high degree of precision in the production of the stones as well as requiring larger numbers of workers and types of workers. In addition theological and religious concerns had to be integrated with the mundane and the practical. These factors create organisational difficulties which turn crucially on a fundamental problem—communication. Knowledge and instructions had to move between many participants. For a given building there had to be clear communication between the ecclesiastical client and the master mason, and between the master and other masons on and off site, since some stones were cut at the quarry. Masons had also to communicate with other teams of masons and workers, principally carpenters, who were responsible for the invisible but nonetheless essential scaffolding and form work as well as the roof and all the heavy lifting equipment. In addition, knowledge had to be transmitted between sites and across successive generations of masons.

Talk, Tradition and Templates

The architectural historian Lon Shelby posed the question of who designed the cathedrals in just these terms: knowledge transmission and assemblage. In the absence of plans how did the scholastic and the craft traditions work together? The patron scholar couldn't build and the master mason couldn't read so how did the spiritual and intellectual values of the day become integrated in the building?

Figure 10   Master mason and client talking. By permission of The British Library (ms Cotton Nero D1 fol 23v).

Shelby's deceptively simple but profoundly important answer is—talk. (see Fig. 10)

'Frequent sometimes daily consultations between the master mason and the patron or his representative were the normal routine in medieval building.' It was 'this symbiotic relationship' which provides the essential clue to who designed the medieval churches.[37] The dynamic interaction between patron and mason and between masons and other craftsmen enabled the radical innovations as well as the constant design changes. Innovations and changes that individual masons were able to manifest as design decisions through the use of constructive geometry in the drawing of the templates.[38]

Masonry as a knowledge tradition, while not having any secrets, did differ in two important ways from other organised trades whose skills and practices were similarly handed on through guilds and apprenticeships, both of which made masonry, literally, an 'ad hoc' profession. Firstly, they seldom practised their profession in one place; the job did not come to them, they went to the job.[39] This exposure to new sites and the work of others was a constant spur to innovation. Secondly, the construction site was essentially an experimental laboratory in which the masons were able to see whether an innovation was successful. Talk, tradition, and templates provided for a distributed, heterogeneous, design process strongly analogous to the scientific theory building described earlier by Star:

> ... different viewpoints are constantly being adduced and reconciled ... Each actor, site, or node of a scientific community has a viewpoint, a partial truth consisting of local beliefs, local practices, local constants, and resources, none of which are fully verifiable across all sites. The aggregation of all viewpoints is the source of the robustness of science.[40]

This heterogeneity is also reflected in the discontinuous character of the cathedral building process. The building of all churches and cathedrals in the Paris basin in this period tended to be conducted in short campaigns.[41] The mortar they used was slow setting and possibly subject to shrinkage; work may have had to stop whenever a certain number of wall courses had been laid or when the formwork for an arch was removed in order to allow the mortar to dry and the stonework to settle. The erection of scaffolding, centring and roofs made for delays in the cutting and laying of stone. The cycle of fundraising through donation and tithing followed by expenditure also made financing a discontinuous process. Hence James concludes that 'the essential reality behind the inventiveness of [the thirteenth] century resides in the short term campaign'.[42]

From our modern, representationalist vantage-point, the construction time constraints and the unequivocal transmission of instructions could only be achieved with drawing.[43] However, the introduction of architectural plans did not occur overnight but was itself the result of a developmental process of coproduction. Experimentation with more sophisticated and demanding construction techniques brought with it a need for more detailed modes of representing the parts of the building. In all probability the first full-scale drawing of Chartres, like that of Rheims Cathedral, was the ground-plan that the master mason laid out on the ground. Prior to that he might only have had a preliminary model produced as the result of initial discussions with the church authorities.[44] Drawing of some kind is a necessity for instructing the other masons how to cut the stones and where to lay them. Indeed the beginnings of the technology of representation that is involved in the modern system of architectural drawings may have come about in conjunction with the development of cathedral building. The first reference made to a tracing house attached to a construction site is in an English text of 1274.[45] It is thus only at the zenith of the Gothic period that there is any evidence of the use of architectural project plans from which site drawings could be traced or derived.

However, the use of plans in the modern sense is only possible with a standardised system of measurement; in the thirteenth century masons had no such common measure. Moreover, of 5,000 medieval drawings that have been examined only ten have measurements on them at all.[46] Drawings were used, but at full-scale, like those still extant incised into the stone in the ambulatory at Clermont Ferrand.[47] More commonly they would have been laid out on sheets of plaster or wood. But regardless of whether there were 'plans' in the modern sense or full-scale drawings, a key device is the template, a pattern or mold that permits both the accurate cutting and replication of shaped stone and the transmission of knowledge between workers.[48]

Cathedrals as Laboratories

Wilson, an American physicist, was one of the first to see a parallel between cathedrals and laboratories:

As an accelerator builder, I have found great satisfaction in relating to the men who built cathedrals in the thirteenth century. When Ernest Lawrence built his cyclotrons with a dedicated passion he was not different from Suger, also with a dedicated passion, building the cathedral St Denis. The Abbot Suger was expressing a devotion to the church with his exalted structure, a structure that transcended all contemporary knowledge of strength of materials. And Lawrence too expressed, in his fashion, a devotion to the discovery of truth. He too transcended contemporary technology in attaining his dizzying heights of energy. I am sure that both the designers of the cathedrals and the designers of the nuclear accelerators proceeded almost entirely on educated intuition guided by aesthetic considerations ... Of course, building, even designing, a large accelerator is a complex team activity—just as it was for the cathedral.[49]

How the cathedrals were built becomes clear if we take Wilson's metaphor seriously and recognise that the cathedrals were comparable to modern laboratories in three important ways. Firstly, their very construction constituted a series of full-scale experiments. Close observation of the drying mortar enabled the builders to detect areas of stress in the fabric and to take appropriate remedial measures through the placement of buttresses, pinnacles or reinforcement.[50] Intuitively, it may seem that one needs laboratories to perform experiments rather than the other way round. However, laboratories are not simply built by architects, they are constituted through the performance of experiments. Secondly, laboratories are the spaces in which the local, tacit and messy knowledge/ practices of groups of practitioners are transformed through collective work into a coherent tradition. Thirdly, cathedrals just like twentieth-century laboratories are powerful loci of social transformation, absorbing large amounts of capital and concentrating resources, skills and labour.[51] Through this process of heterogeneous engineering, machinery, instruments, skills, techniques, theory, raw materials, and social relations are interrelated and assembled. This combination of social and material factors constitute a manipulable system, the establishment and maintenance of which may be considered an essential function of modern laboratories.[52] Such a system in a modern laboratory enables two orders of manipulation: firstly, of natural phenomena in order to generate data and secondly, of that data into the literature. Similarly the 'cathedral laboratory' provides for the manipulation of unshaped rocks into precision-cut stones and their subsequent assemblage into a stable whole. In both cases the focus is on getting the experiment to 'work' through the process of collective practice.

Answering the question 'how were the cathedrals built?' involves seeing them as knowledge spaces analogous to experimental laboratories in which the key elements were templates, talk, and tradition. The power of the template lies not only in the way in which it facilitates accurate mass production, but also in the fact that simple geometrical rules of thumb will often suffice for the template itself to be accurately reproduced as often as required.[53] Templates help to make possible the unified organisation of large numbers of men with varied training and skill over considerable periods of time.

> On them were encapsulated every design decision that had to be passed down to the men doing the carving in shop and quarry. Through them the work of all the masons on the site was controlled and coordinated. With them dozens, and in some cases hundreds, of men were guided to a common purpose. They were the 'primary instruments' of the trade.[54]

In addition to the power to organise the work of large numbers of workers, templates have the power to allow for great exactness of stone cutting and enabled a 'robust', enduring, coherent structure, despite a discontinuous process, and radical design and structural changes. Three major 'reversals of forces'[55] are achieved with this one small piece of representational technology; one person can get large numbers of others to work in concert; large numbers of stones can be erected without the benefit of a fully articulated theory of structural mechanics or a detailed plan; and incommensurable pieces of work can be made accumulative.

The template makes possible the transformation of amorphous masses of stone into an enduring stable structure whose stability is achieved despite the lack of what we would take to be the basic essentials for producing the specifications for a particular component in a building: a common and precise mode of measurement, a knowledge of structural mechanics, and a detailed scale plan. James' analysis shows that each successive contractor had their own individual measure.[56] Masonry buildings like Chartres are dependent on stability rather than strength in order to stand. It is possible to achieve stability through proportional rather than structural analysis, hence in large part structural analysis was not required.[57] According to Pacey:

> though the masons lacked the knowledge of a modern engineer ... it is clear that [they] usually knew very precisely where the buttresses ought to be and at what height their counter pressures were needed. To this extent, then, their experiments were guided by knowledge. Their trial and error was not just groping in the dark, for they had a considerable insight into what shape a building should be: insight which was aided by geometrical rules of design ... As it turns out, the successful design of masonry structures

depended more on getting the shape, that is the geometry, than on calculating the magnitude of forces in the modern way.[58]

Construction with Geometry and String

Thus another essential ingredient is geometry. In the absence of rules for construction derived from structural laws problems could be resolved by practical geometry, using compasses, a straight-edge, ruler, and string (see Fig. 11). The kind of structural knowledge which was passed on from master to apprentice related sizes to spaces and heights by ratios, such as half the number of feet in a span expressed in inches plus one inch will give the depth of a hardwood joist. These rules of thumb were stated and learnt as ratios, for as the span gets larger the depth of the joist will too.[59] This sort of geometry is extremely powerful; it enables the transportation and transmission of structural experience, makes possible the successful replication of a specific arrangement in different places and different circumstances, reduces a wide variety of problems to a comparatively compact series of solutions, and allows for a flexible rather than rigid rule-bound response to differing problems.[60]

The sort of geometry required is not that of Euclid, but rather a set of rules for deriving ratios and proportions through the division of squares and circles using compasses—what Shelby calls 'constructive geometry'.[61] Essentially it enables a dimensionless analysis precluding the need for a common measure. Geometrical techniques in this case provide a powerful mode of communication that dissolve problems of incommensurability that the use of individual measurement systems might otherwise have.

However, geometry alone is not enough; it has to have a material manifestation, in this case the template. Templates could either be derived from an exposed section of earlier work or set out directly by the master mason using his knowledge of geometry and then used by a mason to cut stones to specification. While simple stones could be cut without them, complex irregular stones would require several templates, and many hundreds would have to be cut in the course of construction. Templates, in their more durable form, were valuable possessions and master masons may have taken them from job to job. Different geometrical techniques could be used to make them, which allowed for the possibility of individual stylistic variation; but as those techniques were themselves relatively simple, master masons could show ordinary masons how to prepare them for particular tasks.[62]

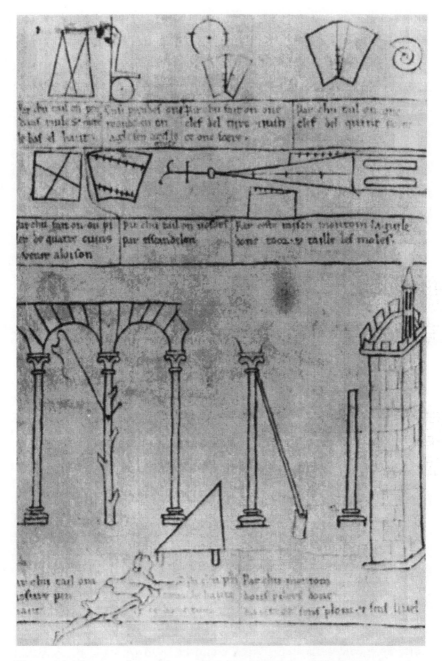

Figure 11 The use of geometry and string. Sketch by Villard de Honnecourt.
Reproduced with the permission of Bibliothèque Nationale, Paris.

Templates are models or patterns; that is, accepted concrete, local or indexical solutions that can be applied to other problems (see Fig. 12). Functionally they perform the role of exemplars, in the more restricted sense of Kuhn's paradigms. This use of portable solutions as opposed to fully articulated and consistent plans to build cathedrals and transmit knowledge is reflected in the 'model books' of the time, like that of Villard de Honnecourt. Printing not having been invented, the only way to compile and transport knowledge, in addition to the tacit knowledge of the master mason and his templates, was via the collections of drawings of model solutions known as model books. 'In an age when no other reproduction methods were known it was the drawing book which transmitted iconographic and formal elements from place to place, from atelier to atelier, from generation to generation.'[63] These books have some interesting characteristics. They seem to our modern eye completely unsystematic, putting together drawings of human figures with machines and architectural details; nor do they ever show anything in its totality, providing only partial views or at best particular elevations.[64] Hence, it seems that they do not presuppose the kind of ordering we take for granted, instead they assume that order can be created out of the aggregation of model solutions or paradigms.

The point of this examination of the role of plans, geometry, and templates is two-fold. It shows that the building of the cathedrals is neither mysterious nor a merely practical matter. What it takes is the establishment of a laboratory, and the joint deployment within it of both a mode of proportional analysis and a small innovation in the technology of representation, the template. By analogy, modern technoscience, which is a large complex structure requiring the integration of the local knowledge and skills of a wide range of people, may also succeed in constructing a unified edifice without the benefit of anything so intangible as the scientific method or fully articulated theory. The local, contingent and theory-independent nature of modern technoscientific practice is illustrated by the remark of Peter Brooke, the architect of a 39-storey skyscraper in Melbourne:

> The principles of the shape and structure are well known, but the detailed solutions always vary. Actually building it is rather like a gigantic experiment and you are never really sure what it will end up looking like.[65]

Form and Function

Contemporary technoscience is often portrayed as being governed solely by the dictates of its own internal logic. An aphoristic version of

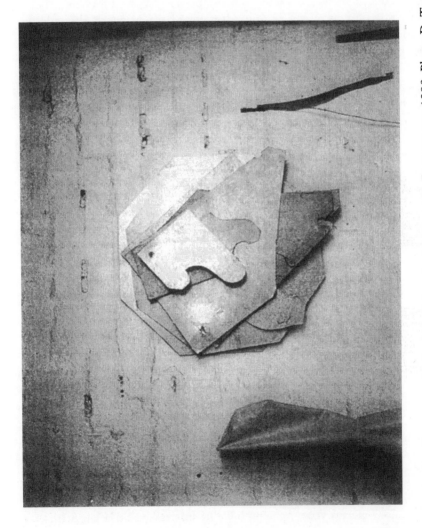

Figure 12 Contemporary templates in use. Melbourne University Maintenance Department, 1990. Photo D. Turnbull.

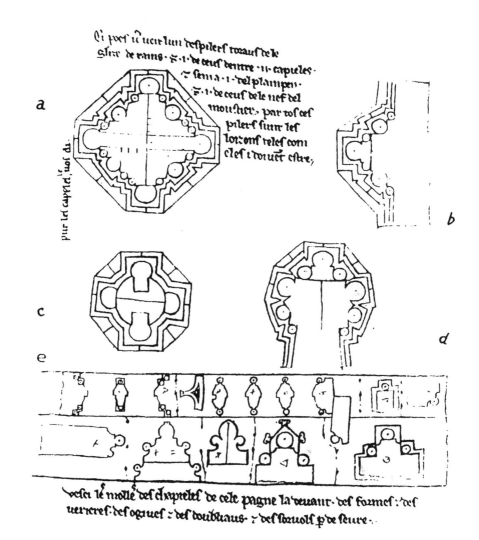

Figure 13 Thirteenth century sketch of templates by Villard de Honnecourt. Reproduced with the permission of Bibliothèque Nationale, Paris.

this technoscientific determinism is 'form follows function'. Augustus Pugin the nineteenth-century English architect argued that all features should reflect the purpose and materials and that 'it is in pointed architecture alone that these principles have been carried out.'[66] It was Pugin's articulation of this principle in his precipitation of the Gothic revival that led to the virtual equation of modernity and good design with the idea that function and technology have aesthetic and social primacy. Since Pugin derived the concept from his understanding of Gothic architecture, we can now go back to the Gothic cathedrals and re-examine the question; is the structural form of the Gothic cathedrals dictated by the requirements of high stone buildings? The rationalists, like Viollet-le-Duc who was responsible for much of the restoration of the French cathedrals in the mid-nineteenth century, argued that such characteristic Gothic features as flying buttresses, ribbed vaulting and pointed arches, are the consequence of functionalist minimalism, that they are the optimal structural bones. The illusionists on the other hand would have it that they are dictated by stylistic considerations rather than by necessity.[67] Recent evaluation of Gothic structures suggests that neither of these understandings holds true, but that a degree of rational functionalism is employed in the service of a higher aesthetic.[68] Buildings of that height would not be feasible economically, nor would the foundations take the weight unless they used techniques that optimised the use of stone, hence the functional and economic necessity of the slim 'misshapen' pillars abhorred by Evelyn. Equally such tall buildings had to be able to resist high wind loading; hence the flying buttresses were functionally required as props. In turn the vertical buttresses on which the fliers depended had to be able to resist the shear loading, hence the otherwise apparently redundant pinnacles. Contrariwise, the much vaunted ribs serve no structural function, the thickness of the walls is deliberately concealed, and the flying buttresses were not always maximally effective. In the case of Laon Cathedral the buttresses were added later to conform to the thirteenth-century aesthetic, and some of the Gothic cathedrals, like Beauvais, may even exceed the structural limits.[69] Simson has argued that, 'We find it necessary to suppress the symbolic instinct if we are to understand the world as it is rather than as it seems. Medieval man conceived the symbolic instinct as the only reliable guide to such an understanding.'[70] Medieval man integrated form, function and geometry as a 'graphic functionalism' in the attempt to create a literal 'image of heaven'.[71]

Thus, in the case of the Gothic cathedrals, the idea that 'form follows function' only has any cogency when abstracted from the interests of the builders and from the 'technoscience world' in which it is embedded. The pointed arch, the flying buttress, and the ribbed vault all make possible certain forms which otherwise be difficult or impossible, but these functional elements can only constrain rather than determine the actual outcome, the realised form. There is no deterministic, internal logic of function or form. The structure of the cathedrals results from the combination of religious beliefs and aesthetic values, a developing but limited set of building practices, economic opportunities, modes of communication, and the work of others. These factors all interact as a whole to produce a particular form. The 'Gothic style', as such, was not in the minds of the cathedral builders. They had no theory of the 'Gothic', nor could they have had. The notion of a particular style implying a unifying set of rules or principles is a construct of contemporary analysts and critics. The fact of the enduring existence of the Gothic cathedrals creates an impression of an irreversible process driven by a determinate logic. That impression serves to deny the contingent and ad hoc way in which the cathedrals were actually built. 'Medieval architecture followed no predetermined course and there was in the line of its development no immanent necessity. It is only the irreversibility of what has happened that, after the fact, turns accident into necessity.'[72]

Theory and Practice

This contextualisation of the form/function relationship also opens up the question of the relationship between theory and practice and between science, technology and design. If form rigorously followed function it would imply that the form of a building is determined by the physical laws governing the behaviour of the structure, that the builder had some understanding of the forces at work, and that technology follows science being applied knowledge whether tacit or otherwise. On the face of it this seems unlikely in the case of the Gothic cathedrals. There are two kinds of reasons for thinking this to be the case; one is historical, the other derives from an analysis of contemporary structural practice which throws fresh light on this fundamental issue.

There is no written evidence of an adequate understanding of basic structural mechanics until Galileo's *Two New Sciences* in 1638, but this does not imply, as some commentators have suggested, that the cathedral builders had *no* knowledge of structural mechanics.[73] Galileo did not create his laws out of whole cloth. In the very period when the cathedral builders had to resolve some profound structural problems, Jordanus Nemorarius and others were starting to develop theoretical statics.[74] Hence, it seems highly likely that the development of the theoretical laws of structural mechanics had its beginnings in the very process of their application, in building the cathedrals and schools in which scholars, monks and masons were trained.

The representationalist conception of science has led to an emphasis on theory, written law-like knowledge and its transmission through texts. However, the issue at stake is not one of understanding the development of general theory, but rather of how knowledge created in one circumstance is made to work in another. In other words the problem, in both science and technology, is not one of putting theory into practice but of the transmission of practices. It is small social and technical variations which, in effecting that transmission, account for differences in knowledge systems.

The issue of knowledge transmission and the site specific character of scientific knowledge are also reflected in the practice of contemporary engineers. David Billington, in a recent analysis of the 'new art of structural engineering', argues that science tries to produce general unifying theories, whereas engineering aims for solutions with a limited range of application. He has extensively explored the work of Robert Maillart, the Swiss bridge designer:

> ... who developed in 1923 a limited theory for one of his arched bridge types that violated in principle the general mathematical theory of structures and thereby infuriated many Swiss academics between the wars. But Maillart's limited theory worked well for that special type of form. Within that category type Maillart's theory was useful and had the virtue of great simplicity; he developed the theory to suit the form, not the form to suit the theory.[75]

By contrast, Billington claims, the American bridge designers of the early twentieth century were convinced that effective bridge design should be derived from general theory. This obscured their familiarity with the tradition, that is their knowledge of the success and failure of particular bridges in the past, as is shown by the defective design of many major bridges in the 1930s and the Tacoma Narrows Bridge collapse of 1940.

Thus it seems reasonable to suppose that the Gothic cathedral builders, like the builders of today, did not need a generalised theory in order to achieve successful practice, but case-specific solutions, or exemplars. So the question then is how those solutions were transmitted.

Knowledge can be transmitted in a variety of ways. It can be by word of mouth. It can, as Bachelard suggests,[76] be 'frozen' into the technique, in this case the technique of using geometry and compasses, being materialised in the form of portable templates. It can also be transmitted through education and the establishment of a tradition. A tradition may or may not include theories and texts but always includes training, development of skills and the knowledge and observation of other structures and solutions. As Billington has argued, a 'tradition' is essential in engineering, that is, an historical awareness of previous successes and failures.[77] Which is, of course, exactly what Mark and James have argued for the Gothic cathedrals.

Building on the work of others sounds like a recipe for dogmatism and stasis. How can you use the work of your predecessors or peers and build things that the world has never seen before? Further, how can you do it without theory or plan, without a permanent overseer, and without a common measure? The answer in the case of cathedrals is that it is done with communication, precision-cut stones, geometry and experiment. Provided that the stones are sufficiently well cut according to a system of proportion and are assembled in a way that contains all the thrusts within vertical columns of stone as revealed in previous building, then accumulation and innovation is possible, given one other factor—namely motivation or interest, in this case the religious and aesthetic urge to create heaven on earth.

This characterisation of cathedral building resonates very strongly with Holton's description of modern science.

> ... the scientists' chief duty [is] not the production of the flawlessly carved block, one more in the construction of the final Temple of Science. Rather it is more like participating in a building project that has no central planning authority, where no proposal is guaranteed to last very long before being modified or overtaken, and where one's best contribution may be one that furnishes a plausible base and useful materials for the next stage of development.[78]

The Technoscientific Knowledge Space Coproduced with Cathedrals

The cathedrals were both the focus and the motor of the thirteenth-century industrial and agricultural revolutions. They were a direct expression of the resurgent integration of the commercial and religious life that accompanied the development of cities and the influx of capital in Europe following the crusades, along with a transformation of agriculture brought on by the horse collar, the mold board plough, the horseshoe and the three-field rotation system.[79] While the cathedrals were dependent on the availability of finance, and the growth of cities, they in turn produced a massive transformation of the organisation of labour, resources and knowledge. Communities comprised of a huge variety of tradesmen, masons, sculptors, carpenters, glaziers, smiths, and tilers began to develop. As White has pointed out, the Gothic cathedrals 'are the first vast monuments in all history to be built by free—nay unionised—labour'.[80] A massive development of resources and trades took place; quarries opened up, roads and transport expanded, glass making and window making were transformed, as were metal working, stone working and carpentry.

> At Chartres, the building of the cathedral attracted numerous artisans. Work on this enterprise ... undoubtedly transformed the upper part of the town into one immense building site that occupied, directly or indirectly, an entire population of workers.[81]

But the biggest transformations were in the organisation and integration of all this money, resources, skill and religious fervour, principally in the form in which knowledge was produced, used and transmitted. Along with the cathedral came not only the emergence of the role of the master mason, the master carpenter, glazier and sculptor, but also the lodge or guild and the itinerant tradesman who took the whole of Europe as his workshop. The lodge was originally a temporary building on the construction site to shelter the masons while they carved the stones. Eventually it became the cooperative institution whereby knowledge and skills were transmitted through apprenticeship, mutual exchange and accumulation, as manifested, for example, in the lodgebooks.

At the same time, cathedral schools and universities began to develop. The close integration of commerce, tradeskills, religion and classical education is not only manifested in the fabric of Chartres, which has windows and chapels devoted to the guilds and the seven liberal arts as well as the major religious figures, but also in the social institution it housed. It was at Chartres that Bishop Thierry set up the cathedral school that was one of the first in the West to study natural phenomena. It was also where many master masons received their education, in keeping with the school's policy of bringing together men of the liberal arts and men of the mechanical arts, the intellectuals and the highly skilled workmen, science and technology.[82] This attitude is reflected in the writing of some of the founders of experimental science in this period—Robert Grosseteste, Roger Bacon, and Peter of Maricourt—who said in his treatise on magnetism *Epistolae de Magnete*:

> You must realise, dearest friend that while the investigator in this subject must understand nature and not be ignorant of the celestial motions, he must also be very diligent in the use of his own hands, so that through the operation of the stone he may show wonderful effects. For by his industry he will then in a short time be able to correct an error which he would never do in eternity by his knowledge of natural philosophy and mathematics alone if he lacked carefulness with his hands. For in investigating the unknown we greatly need manual industry without which we can usually accomplish nothing perfectly. Yet there are many things subject to the rule of reason which we cannot completely investigate by the hand.[83]

The cathedrals were thus a site at which a range of social, religious and technical roles and activities were assembled, while at the same time the process of cathedral building served to transform and develop those roles and activities. The cathedrals simultaneously created and were produced in a knowledge space.

From Master Mason to Architect

In the middle of the thirteenth century, the acme of the Gothic period, science and technology were one in Chartres cathedral, and theory and practice were uniquely synthesised in the knowledge and skills of the master mason. However, as the role of the master mason evolved into that of architect, so theory became divorced from practice and skill became expertise. Eventually the structural principles of Gothic architecture were lost, never to be recaptured. In 1568 Philibert de l'Orme could still describe the Gothic as 'the modern way of vaulting'. By 1711 it had been forgotten. Louis X1V ordered a gothic clock tower to be built, but despite the concerted efforts of five architects it collapsed. In the end tie bars and supplementary arches and floors had to be used, exactly the kind of artificial prop the Gothic technique eschewed.[84]

Most commentators agree that the role of the mason began to change around the middle of the thirteenth century[85] after the completion of Chartres and around the time when the masons' lodges started up.[86] Whether there is a causal connection is debatable, but it is in this period that the preacher Nicholas de Biard complains:

> The masters of the masons, carrying a baguette (measuring rod) and gloves, ordered others to 'cut it there for me', and worked not at all, although they received a larger payment; it is this way with many prelates.[87]

By the sixteenth century a fundamental shift had occurred in the role of the mason. As the social and professional status of the architect rose, the mason dropped gradually into serving merely as builder for the architect. As execution and design became separate, the education and training of the mason and the architect became distinct. A new style of gentleman architect emerged who did not serve an apprenticeship but learnt from books, thereby avoiding the taint of being, or associating with, craftsmen.[88]

The split between theory and practice, an essential characteristic of the process of the division of labour had been rather atypically disavowed by Vitruvius, the Roman architect and military engineer whose text *De Architectura* was one of the very few to be available throughout the Middle Ages, though it was unlikely that it was read by or known to any masons. Vitruvius defined architecture as a discipline consisting of both practice (*fabrica*) and reason (*ratiocinatio*).[89] In antiquity it had been commonplace to deprecate handiwork and separate it from theory and mathematics.[90] This practice was again commonplace by the fifteenth century—as can be seen in the work of Alberti, the first Renaissance architectural writer, who separated design from construction—and has remained so till now. Interestingly, contemporary bridge building may, like the Maillart example, show a countervailing trend. The most recent advances in which cable-stayed bridges are being built across unprecedented spans are not due to any breakthrough in materials or design. Rather, 'the construction industry ... has been able to extend the boundaries of bridge technology by getting its designers, builders and computer specialists to work together more closely.'[91]

At the height of the Gothic cathedral building 'crusade', theory and practice were firmly integrated in the activities of the master masons, in their training and in their texts. But, as theory became divorced from practice, the master masons became architectural 'experts', and it was experts who were commonly consulted whenever difficulties arose. The building of Milan Cathedral, begun in the late fourteenth century, is an example of the decline associated with these transitions. Following the laying of the foundations, the Italians became uncertain of how to proceed and called in a succession of foreign experts to resolve a fundamental dispute over what system of proportion to use, the square or the triangle, and what should be the basic units of measurement. After the French expert Jean Mignot arrived, the consultative process degenerated into an acrimonious debate in which the Italians claimed 'scientia est unum et ars est aliud'—theory is one thing, practice another—to which Mignot gave his famous retort, 'ars sine scientia nihil est'—practice is nothing without theory.[92] Though this may sound like a scientific expert scoring a blow for rationality over dogmatic traditionalism, the discredits are evenly distributed. Mignot, under the guise of 'scientia', was in fact trying to impose on the Milanese the system of proportion based on the square which was more familiar to his northern colleagues, although he had little understanding of its use in practice. The Milanese themselves were so removed from the principles of Gothic architecture that they claimed the pointed arch exerted no thrust on the buttresses.[93] In the end the Milanese viewpoint prevailed; nonetheless the cathedral stands to this day. By this point theory had become completely sterile and almost totally divorced from practice.

Conclusion

The Gothic cathedrals constitute a potent and illuminating example of the ways in which technoscientific knowledge was produced in the twelfth and thirteenth centuries. They were in effect large-scale laboratories where knowledge spaces were coproduced through a process of contingent assemblage. Cathedral raisings were sites of experimental practice where the collective work of skilled specialists was aggregated, producing a manipulable system and a working experiment—the cathedral itself. This was possible in the absence of fully articulated structural theory, specified design or plans, or even of common measure, because the builders developed ways in which their local and tacit knowledge and their disparate practices could be combined and transmitted to other sites in the form of skills, geometric method and templates. This constituted a tradition of shared solutions and skills in which theory and practice were integrated and no strong distinctions were made between science and technology.

The example of the Gothic cathedrals undermines some of the great myths about science and technology. There is no great divide between the past and the present or between science and technology. Technoscience then and now results from site-specific, contingent and messy practices.[94] It can be, and often has been, ad hoc, disunited, atheoretical, lacking in a common measure, yet still results in robust structures and traditions. Technoscience, like the cathedrals, is the product of collective practice based on the earlier work of others.

Notes

[1] H. Jantzen, *High Gothic*, (London: Constable, 1962), p. viii.

[2] J. D. Bernal, *Science in History,* Vol. 1, (Harmondsworth: Penguin, 1965), p. 310.

[3] Jacques Heyman, 'The Stone Skeleton', *International Journal of Solids and Structures,* Vol. 2, (1966), pp. 249–79, p. 249.

[4] Terry Stokes and David Turnbull, 'Manipulable Systems and Laboratory Strategies in a Biomedical Research Institute', in H. L. Grand, ed., *Experimental Inquiries: Historical, Philosophical and Social Studies in Science,* (Dordrecht: Kluwer Academic Publishers, 1990), pp. 167–192. See also Latour, 'Visualisation and Cognition'.

[5] On the achievement of robustness see Leigh Star, *Regions of Mind: Brain Research and the Quest for Scientific Certainty,* (Stanford: Stanford University Press, 1989); Susan Leigh Star, 'The Sociology of the Invisible: The Primacy of Work in the Writings of Anselm Strauss', in D. Maines, ed., *Social Organisation and Social Processes: Essays in Honour of Anselm Strauss,* (New York: Aldine de Gruyter, 1990).

[6] Jean Gimpel, *The Cathedral Builders,* (New York: Grove Press, 1961), p. 6. This comparison was first drawn by Henry Adams one of the early celebrants of modernism in architecture as technology, and has been frequently repeated ever since; Henry Adams, *The Education of Henry Adams,* (New York: New York Modern Library, 1931), pp. 342ff; see also Robert Branner, *Gothic Architecture,* (New York: George Braziller, 1965), p. 25.

[7] Christopher Wren, *Life and Works of Sir Christopher Wren from the Parentalia or Memoirs by His Son Christopher,* (London: 1750 reprinted 1903), pp. 174–5. 'Then new architects arose who created that style of building for their barbarous nations which we call Gothic and produced some works which are ridiculous to our modern eyes but appeared admirable to theirs' Giorgio Vasari, *The Lives of the Painters, Sculptors and Architects vol 1,* (New York: Everyman's Library, 1550 reprinted 1963), p. 12.

[8] Gimpel, *The Cathedral Builders.*

[9] John James, *The Contractors of Chartres 2 vols,* (Wyong: Mandorla Publications, 1979), p. 11 and John James, 'An Investigation into the

Uneven Distribution of Early Gothic Churches in the Paris Basin, 1140–1240', *The Art Bulletin*, Vol. March, (1984), pp. 15–46.

10 Carl Condit, *The Chicago School of Architecture: A History of Public Buildings in the Chicago Area 1875–1925*, (Chicago: University of Chicago Press, 1964), p. 79.

11 A. C. Crombie, *Medieval and Early Modern Science; Vol. 1 Science in the Middle Ages V-X111 Centuries*, (New York: Doubleday, 1959), pp. 205–6 who allows that 'Thirteenth century architects must have had a greater ability to generalise the problems of stress and weight lifting involved than the poverty of theoretical writings might suggest.'

12 John James, *Chartres: The Masons Who Built a Legend*, (London: Routledge and Kegan Paul, 1982), p. 9.

13 According to Spiro Kostof, *The Architect: Chapters in the History of the Profession*, (New York: Oxford University Press, 1977), p. 91 the slight irregularities which accurate surveys reveal can be accounted for by the fact that the cords used to lay out the building were stretched bay by bay.

14 James, *Chartres: The Masons Who Built a Legend*, p. 26.

15 Ibid, p. 60.

16 Ibid, p. 60.

17 Ibid, p. 123.

18 Harvey, J. 1974, *Cathedrals of England and Wales*, B. T. Batsford, London, pp. 32–3.

19 Robert Mark, *Experiments in Gothic Structure*, (Cambridge: MIT Press, 1982), p. 16, n. 10.

20 Spiro Kostof, *The Architect: Chapters in the History of the Profession*, (New York: Oxford University Press, 1977), p. v and p. 77.

21 Lon R. Shelby, 'The Contractors of Chartres, [review]', *GESTA*, Vol. XX, (1981), pp. 173–8. See also S. Murray, 'Contractors of Chartres, [review]', *Art Bulletin*, Vol. 63, (1981), pp. 149–52 and more recently Charles Radding and William Clark, *Medieval Architecture, Medieval Learning: Builders and Masters in the Age of the Romanesque and Gothic*, (New Haven: Yale University Press, 1992), p. 138.

22 J. Van der Muelen, 'Recent Literature on the Chronology of Chartres Cathedral', *Art Bulletin*, Vol. 4, (1967), pp. 152–72. S. Murray, *Building Troyes Cathedral: The Late Gothic Campaign*, (Bloomington: Indiana University Press, 1987) see especially pp. 5–7.

23 Robert Branner, 'Villard de Honnecourt, Reims and the Origin of Gothic Architectural Drawing', *Gazette des Beaux-Arts*, Vol. 61, (1963), pp. 129–46, p. 129.

24 Robert Mark and W. W. Clark, 'Gothic Structural Experimentation', *Scientific American*, Vol. 25, (1984), pp. 144–153, p. 251.

25 R. W. Scheller, *A Survey of Medieval Model Books*, (Haarlem: De Erven F. Bohn, 1963), p. 1.

26 Shelby, 'The Contractors of Chartres', p. 175.

27 Lon R. Shelby, 'Medieval Masons' Tools. 11. Compass and Square', *Technology and Culture*, Vol. 6, (1965), pp. 236–248, p. 242.

28 John Harvey, *The Mediaeval Craftsmen*, (London: Wayland Press, 1975), p. 119.

29 R. A. Skelton and P. D. A. Harvey, *Local Maps and Plans from Medieval England*, (Oxford: Clarendon Press, 1986), pp. 35–6.

30 Francis B. Andrews, *The Mediaeval Builder and His Methods*, (Wakefield and Ottowa: EP Pbl and Rowman and Littlefield, 1925 reprinted 1976), p. 2 and p. 8.

31 Reginald Blomfield, *Architectural Drawing and Draughtsmen*, (London: Cassell and Co., 1912), pp. 13–18.

32 Spiro Kostof, *A History of Architecture: Settings and Rituals*, (New York: Oxford University Press, 1985), p. 4.

33 Ibid, p. 408.

34 Alain Erlande-Brandenburg, *The Cathedral: The Social and Architectural Dynamics of Construction*, (Cambridge: Cambridge University Press, 1994), pp. 257ff.

35 Kostof, *The Architect: Chapters in the History of the Profession*, p. 75 and Branner, 'Villard de Honnecourt', p. 135.

36 Erlande-Brandenburg, *The Cathedral*, p. 257.

37 Lon R. Shelby, 'The Education of Medieval English Master Masons', *Medieval Studies*, Vol. 32, (1970), pp. 1–26, p. 18, fn 48.

38 Lon R. Shelby, 'The Contractors of Chartres, [review]', *GESTA*, Vol. XX, (1981), pp. 173–8.

39 Lon R. Shelby, 'The "Secret" of the Medieval Masons', in B. Hall and D. West, eds., *On Pre-Modern Technology and Science*, (Malibu: Undena Publications, 1976), pp. 201–222.

40 Susan Leigh Star, 'The Structure of Ill-Structured Solutions: Boundary Objects and Heterogeneous Distributed Problem Solving', in L. Gasser and N. Huhns, eds., *Distributed Artificial Intelligence*, (New York: Morgan Kauffman Publications, 1989), pp. 37–54, p. 46.

41 James, *The Template-Makers of the Paris Basin*, pp. 2–6.

42 Ibid, p. 6.

43 See for example John Harvey, *The Medieval Architect*, (London: Wayland Press, 1972), p. 101.

44 See Branner, 'Villard de Honnecourt', p. 130.

45 Ibid, p. 131.

46 F. Bucher, *Architector: The Lodgebooks and Sketchbooks of Medieval Architects vol 1*, (New York: Abaris Books, 1979), p. 10.

47 Branner, 'Villard de Honnecourt', pp. 131 and 134.

48 Harvey, *The Medieval Architect*, pp. 119 and 174.

49 R. R. Wilson, 'The Humanness of Physics', in D. M. Borchert and D. Stewart, eds., *Being Human in a Technological Age*, (Athens Ohio: 1979), pp. 25–36, pp. 29–30.

[50] Mark, *Experiments in Gothic Structure*, p. 56.

[51] A. Touraine, 1973, *Production de la Societe*, cited in Michel Callon, John Law, and Arie Rip, eds., *Mapping The Dynamics of Science and Technology; Sociology of Science in the Real World*, (London: MacMillan, 1986) p. 4.

[52] Terry Stokes and David Turnbull, 'Manipulable Systems and Laboratory Strategies in a Biomedical Research Institute', in H. L. Grand, ed., *Experimental Inquiries: Historical, Philosophical and Social Studies in Science*, (Dordrecht: Kluwer Academic Publishers, 1990), pp. 167–192.

[53] See James, *Chartres: The Masons Who Built a Legend*, p. 34; James, *The Contractors of Chartres*, Vol. 11, p. 543, and John Harvey, *Cathedrals of England and Wales*, (London: B. T. Batsford, 1974), pp. 119 and 174.

[54] James, *The Template-Makers of the Paris Basin*, p. 2.

[55] On the reversals of forces see Latour, *Science in Action*, p. 221ff.

[56] James, *Chartres: The Masons Who Built a Legend*, pp. 34 and 40.

[57] Heyman, 'The Stone Skeleton', p. 251.

[58] Arnold Pacey, *The Maze of Ingenuity: Ideas and Idealism in the Development of Technology*, (London: Allen Lane, 1974), p. 48.

[59] James, *The Contractors of Chartres*, vol. 11, 543–549.

[60] F. Bucher, 'Design in Gothic Architecture: A Preliminary Assessment', *Journal of the Society of Architectural Historians*, Vol. 27, (1968), pp. 49–71, p. 71.

[61] Lon R. Shelby, 'The Geometric Knowledge of the Medieval Master Masons', *Speculum*, Vol. 47, (1972), pp. 395–421. See also Sergio Luis Sanabria, 'From Gothic to Renaissance Stereotomy: The Design Methods of Philibert de l'Orme and Alonso de Vandelvira', *Technology and Culture*, Vol. 31, (1989), pp. 266–299.

[62] Shelby, 'The Contractors of Chartres', p. 174 argues that it is this last factor that may explain the uniformity within sections of Chartres and the discontinuities between sections that James' analysis suggests, without having to accept James' proposal that it was built by a series of completely unconnected contractors.

[63] Scheller, *Survey of Medieval Model Books*, p. 3

[64] Gerhard Rosenberg, 'The Functional Aspect of the Gothic style', *Journal of the Royal Institute of British Architects*, Vol. 43, (1936), pp. 273–90 and 364–71, p. 364.

[65] Sian Watkins, 'Sky-high Jigsaw', *Age*, (Melbourne: 1990), p. 7.

[66] A. W. Pugin, *The True Principles of Pointed or Christian Architecture*, (London: 1841), p. B.

[67] Mark, *Experiments in Gothic Structure*, p. 3.

[68] Ibid. See also Heyman, 'The Stone Skeleton'; Rosenberg, 'The Functional Aspect of the Gothic Style'; David P. Billington and Robert Mark, 'The Cathedral and the Bridge: Structure and Symbol', *Technology and Culture*, Vol. 25, (1984), pp. 37–52; Carl Condit, 'Another View of "The Cathedral

and the Bridge"', *Technology and Culture*, Vol. 25, (1984), pp. 589–594; David P. Billington and Robert Mark, 'In Response to "Another View of the Cathedral and the Bridge"', *Technology and Culture*, Vol. 25, (1984), pp. 595–601; and Robert Mark and David P. Billington, 'Structural Imperative and the New Form', *Technology and Culture*, Vol. 30, (1989), pp. 300–329.

69   Mark, *Experiments in Gothic Structure*, p. 60.

70   Otto Von Simson, *The Gothic Cathedral*, (New York: Pantheon Books, 1956) p. xix.

71   Ibid, p. 6–8.

72   Jean Bony, 'The Genesis of Gothic: Accident or Necessity?', *Australian Journal of Art*, Vol. ii, (1980), pp. 17–31, p. 29.

73   Mark, *Experiments in Gothic Structure*, p. 3.

74   Crombie, *Medieval and Early Modern Science; Vol. 1*, p. 203.

75   David Billington, *The Tower and the Bridge: The New Art of Structural Engineering*, (Princeton: Princeton University Press, 1985), pp. 8–10.

76   Gaston Bachelard, *The New Scientific Spirit*, (Boston: Beacon Press, 1985), p. 13.

77   David P. Billington, 'History and Esthetics in Suspension Bridges', *Journal of the Structural Division, Proceedings of the American Society of Engineers*, Vol. 130, (1977), pp. 1655–72.

78   Gerald Holton, 'Do Scientists Need a Philosophy?', *Times Literary Supplement*, Vol. Nov 2, (1984), pp. 1231–4.

79   Robert Mark, 'The Structural Analysis of Gothic Cathedrals', *Scientific American*, Vol. 227, Nov, (1972), pp. 90–99; Lynn White Jnr, ed., *Medieval Religion and Technology: Collected Essays*, (Berkeley: University of California Press, 1978).

80   Lynn White Jnr, 'The Medieval Roots of Modern Technology and Science', in L. White Jnr, ed., *Medieval Religion and Technology: Collected Essays*, (Berkeley: University of California Press, 1978), pp. 75–92, p. 63.

81   Simson, *The Gothic Cathedral*, p. 170.

82   Jean Gimpel, *The Medieval Machine: The Industrial Revolution of the Middle Ages*, (London: Victor Gollancz, 1977), pp. 141ff.

83   Quoted in ibid, p. 176.

84   Rosenberg, 'The Functional Aspect of the Gothic Style', p. 274.

85   Simson, *The Gothic Cathedral*, p. 220.

86   Ibid, p. 222.

87   Gimpel, *The Cathedral Builders*, p. 136.

88   Lon R. Shelby, *Gothic Design Techniques: The Fifteenth Century Design Booklets of Mathes Roriczer and Hans Schmuttermayer*, (Carbondale: Southern Illinois University Press, 1977), pp. 3ff.

89   Pamela O. Long, 'The Contribution of Architectural Writers to a "Scientific" Outlook in the Fifteenth and Sixteenth Centuries', *Journal of Medieval and Renaissance Studies*, Vol. 15, (1985), pp. 265–98, p. 267.

90 Arthur T. Geoghegan, *The Attitude Towards Labour in Early Christianity and Ancient Culture*, (Washington D.C.: Catholic University of America Press, 1945), p. 229.

91 Bill O'Neill, 'Bridge Design Stretched to the Limits', *New Scientist*, Vol. 132, Oct 26, (1991), pp. 28–35, p. 32.

92 P. Frankl, *The Gothic: Literary Sources and Interpretations Through 8 Centuries*, (New Jersey: Princeton University Press, 1960), p. 79.

93 Ibid, p. 72. See also Harvey, *The Medieval Architect*, p. 162 and J. Ackerman, '"Ars Sine Scientia Nihil Est": Gothic Theory of Architecture at the Cathedral of Milan', *Art Bulletin*, Vol. xxxii, (1949), pp. 84–111.

94 A conclusion confirmed by Mikael Hård, 'Technology as Practice: Local and Global Closure Processes in Diesel-Engine Design', *Social Studies of Science*, Vol. 24, (1994), pp. 549–85.

3 TRICKSTERS AND CARTOGRAPHERS: MAPS, SCIENCE AND THE STATE IN THE MAKING OF A MODERN SCIENTIFIC KNOWLEDGE SPACE

Two of the major themes pursued in this book are the way knowledge spaces are created out of the messy motley of practice, and the 'great divide' between science and other knowledge traditions. Nowhere are these two themes better exemplified than in the synergistic relationship of science and cartography. That relationship is now so self-evident and yet so complex that it is best explored by going back to basics and asking what maps are, what they do and how they come to be so embedded in modern consciousness. The seemingly trite question, 'what is a map'? is hard to answer because maps are the paradigmatic examples of the kind of spatial knowledge that is produced in the knowledge space we inhabit. Not only do we create spaces by linking people, practices and places, thus enabling knowledge to be produced, we also assemble the diverse elements of knowledge by spatial means. Unpacking such a transparent, lived-in, dual spatiality necessitates a fairly difficult reflexive exploration since it involves the attempt to understand the spatiality of knowledge from within the knowledge space that has been coproduced with that knowledge.

In this chapter I revisit the great divide to set up the possibility of recognising other ways of assembling knowledge, thereby gaining the perspective of an alternative space. Some of the recent discussions about the spatiality of knowledge then open up a discussion of the socio-historical origins of our knowledge space in early attempts by the state to assemble cartographic knowledge in sixteenth-century Iberia. While these were ultimately unsuccessful, they were a precursor to the know-ledge space that came with the integration of the state, science and cartography that began with the French national survey in the eighteenth century. Because all this raises profound reflexive difficulties, I have adopted the role of the jester—an approach suggested by the Fool's Cap Map, one of the most revealing of cartographic images.

Being a Trickster

Although the author and origin are unknown, the Fool's Cap Map (see Fig. 14) dates from the late sixteenth century, probably post-1587,

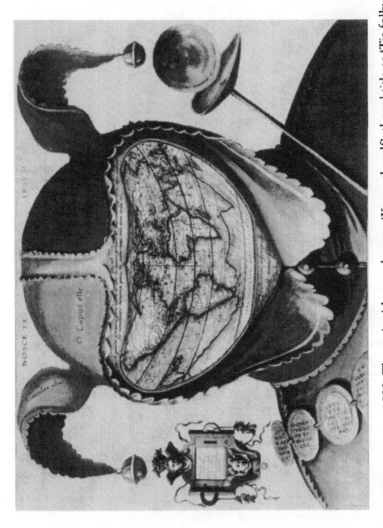

Figure 14 'Fool's Cap' Map, anon c. 1590. The main title translates as 'Know thyself', the subtitle as 'Tis folly to be wise'. The cartouche suggests it was drawn by Epicthonius Cosmopolites, translated as 'Everyman indigenous to himself'. By permission of the Bodleian Library, University of Oxford, Douce Portfolio 142 no 92.

given the Ortelius map projection. It is referred to in Burton's *Anatomy of Melancholy* where it is suggested that the author is Epicthonius Cosmopolites. The left-hand cartouche claims Democritus laughed at it, Heraclitus wept over it and Epicthonius Cosmopolites portrayed it. Rodney Shirley, having failed to identify any personage of that name, translates it as 'everyman indigenous in this world of ours'.[1] The title is roughly translatable as ''tis folly to be wise'. There are several variants of this image but they all bear the Delphic injunction 'know thyself'. One way of reading the image would suggest that all seemingly universal truths, all apparently trustworthy knowledge or authoritative maps, are partial and untrustworthy in that they conceal a hidden social ordering. This may be seen in the analogous role of the jester who confirms the king's power through mocking him. The jester's costume is of course the origin of the term motley. Just as the jester's motley is an assemblage of heterogeneous components, so, too, is our mapping of the world. The moral is that we need to remind ourselves of the role of the jester or the trickster in order to avoid taking our knowledge for truth—thus becoming victims of our own folly.

But the jester is also the trickster, a mythological figure in a vast range of cultures: the monkey god in India; the spider in Africa; the coyote in America; Loki in Scandinavia are some examples. The trickster is the spirit of disorder, the enemy of boundaries. The function of the trickster myth, according to Kerényi 'is to add disorder to order and so make a whole, to render possible within the fixed bounds of what is permitted, an experience of what is not permitted.'[2] A classic example of the kind of ordering through the establishment of boundaries is the 'great divide' between 'us and them', 'then and now',[3] the 'we' who use and make maps, and the 'they' who don't, the 'then', when maps were relatively uncommon and the 'now', when they are taken for granted. The trickster warns us to be wary of such boundaries and divides. The trickster is also a performer and should remind us that history telling is also a performance; we in the academic West make too much of representation and neglect the performative side of knowledge making and knowing the world. We who purport to be historians, sociologists, or cultural critics, are also tricksters.[4]

Maps as the 'Hard Case'

Maps are indeed important representational devices that have changed modes of thought. Internally, through the spatial arrangement of information, maps allow for enhanced connectivity. Externally maps allow for the assemblage of information at centres of calculation.[5] However, maps are the important 'hard case' since they appear to provide a counter to the claim that knowledge spaces are the result of contingent assemblage. Maps are often taken as emblematic of scientific knowledge; just as, scientific theories are often taken as inherently maplike.

In attempting to explore what maps are and why they appear to be so fundamental to our thinking, we need to go back to what has sometimes been called the cartographic revolution—the complex socio-historical processes beginning around 1600 whereby the state, science and cartography became so strongly intermeshed that in effect they coproduced one another. Modern cartography is the product of joint processes of cognitive and social ordering resulting in the establishment of the knowledge space within which scientific knowledge is assembled and the state is organised, as is now taken for granted in Western culture. It is from an examination of that 'taken-for-grantedness' that I want to work my way backwards.[6]

I argue that there has not been an 'epistemological break' or 'cartographic revolution'. Instead there has been a rather heterogeneous, locally contingent process in which maps have become integrated with science and the state. In that process the space that we have taken for granted has been produced. Space is a contingent assemblage, though we find this hard to see because we live in a knowledge space in which maps are a mimetic reflection of external objective space. But just as there is more than one way to navigate, there are many ways of mapping; different cultures, different periods and different groups within a given culture have produced differing knowledge spaces or ways of assembling knowledge which have simultaneously shaped those cultures, eras and people.

The Pacific is where the single best example of radically different ways of assembling knowledge and space can be found; in the next chapter I shall look at the navigation system of Pacific Islanders. But it was in Portugal and Spain that the first attempt to assemble cartographic knowledge scientifically took place. Explaining why this first effort was ultimately a failure leads me to look at the French national survey and the social labour involved in producing the knowledge space we now inhabit. But first I want to examine our modern map consciousness.

Maps and the Modern Mind

We are largely unconscious of the centrality of maps in contemporary Western life precisely because they are so ubiquitous, so profoundly constitutive of our thinking and our culture. We are bombarded by maps in our newspapers, on our televisions, in our books, and in our getting around in the modern world. The cartographic trope is all pervasive. We talk of cognitive maps, mental maps, genetic maps, or of mapping the mind and mapping the human genome. Minds, languages, cultures, laws and social environments are described as maps.[7] Postmodernists constantly resort to the cartographic figure in their explorations of the contemporary landscape.[8] A salient example is a recent newspaper article that portrays the scientific description of the grammatical structure of English as a process of mapping comparable with the mapping of the world's flora and fauna into phyla and species.[9] Ludwig Wittgenstein indirectly invoked the cartographic metaphor to characterise the whole philosophical enterprise when he said 'A philosophical problem has the form "I don't know my way about."'[10]

The cultural theorist Stephen Hall claims that if there is one thing that best represents the ways in which we as human beings perceive, represent, measure, know and understand reality, it is the map.[11] This cogent suggestion is but one which, in its universalising assertion, focuses on much of what I want to investigate. The mode of perceiving, representing, measuring, knowing and understanding reality that best represents contemporary Western technoscience is indeed the map. Our 'form of life' is so intensely cartographic that it is tempting to accept Denis Wood's description of modern Western society as 'map immersed'.[12] However, whilst scientific maps predominate they have not yet provided one universal form of knowledge space.

The past twenty years have seen a vast increase in the range of spatially portrayed domains.[13] Scientists are currently mapping everything from the cosmos to the atom, from the brain to society, from physical objects to the laws of physics. At the same time there are moves to expand our linear, individual and causal explanations to include spatial, relational and systemic explanations. This transition to spatial explanation has occurred not only in the physical and biological sciences, as Hall's *Mapping the Next Millennium* so amply illustrates, but is also underway in the social sciences:

> Understanding how history is made has been the primary source of emancipatory insight and practical political consciousness, the great variable container for a critical interpretation of social life and practice. Today, however, it may be space more than time that hides consequences from us, the 'making of geography' more than the 'making of history' that provides the most revealing tactical and theoretical world.[14]

So comprehensive is this spatialisation of knowledge that it is now possible to dream of the ultimate archive in which all knowledge can be brought together as a 'fuzzy cognitive map'.[15]

Maps as Scientific Theories

However, just as we have come to expect in this ever more reflexive world, there is also a concomitant transformation in progress reshaping both what it is we take maps to be and what we take science to be. One of the most important themes that has emerged in the revised understanding of cartography and science was proposed by Brian Harley, whose extensive but unfortunately curtailed writings have displayed the ways in which maps are texts that can be deconstructed to reveal their concealed power.[16] Denis Wood in his iconoclastic and penetrating book *The Power of Maps* has gone even further to argue that maps are 'weapons in the fight for social domination.'[17] Similar themes are of course prevalent in the sociology of scientific knowledge. Joseph Rouse argues that 'the experimental and theoretical practices of science are themselves forms of power'.[18] Likewise Bruno Latour holds that science's power and domination is to be explained through the examination of the practice of scientists and technologists in constructing and elaborating social networks.[19]

An essential step in this exploration is to reconsider the ways in which maps are equated with scientific knowledge. Scientific theories and their 'maplikeness' have been commented on by such philosophers as Michael Polanyi, in whose view 'all theory may be regarded as a kind of map extended over space and time',[20] and Thomas Kuhn, who extended the point:

> ... as a vehicle for scientific theory, the paradigm functions by telling the scientist about the entities that nature does and does not contain and the ways in which those entities behave. That information provides a map whose details are elucidated by mature scientific research. And since nature is too complex and varied to be explored at random, that map is as essential as observation and experiment to science's continued development. Through the theories they embody, paradigms prove to be constitutive of the research activity. They are also, however, constitutive of science in other respects ... paradigms provide scientists not only with a map but also with some of the directions essential for map making. In learning a paradigm the scientist acquires theory, methods, and standards together usually in an inextricable mixture.[21]

But it is between cartography and science conceived as total systems of knowledge that there is an especially powerful symbiotic and symbolic synergy. Not only is the commonest image of scientific knowledge or theories that of the map, but the strongest theme running through the history of cartography is that of maps becoming increasingly scientific and ever more accurate mirrors of nature. The development of 'scientific maps' has come to be identical with a progressive, cumulative, objective and accurate representation of geographic reality, synonymous with the growth of science itself.[22] Hence, the map/science relationship is not simply metaphoric. Through the process of knowledge assemblage we have created a naturalised space amenable to being mapped; we now equate scientific knowledge with maps. (see Fig. 15).

An instance of the ways in which the processes of science and mapping are jointly embedded is the concept of 'discovery' and 'exploration'. Territorial discovery and scientific discovery are both conflated with, and mediated by, maps and have often been used to create the classic example of the great divide between the oral and literate cultures. A recent example of this genre is David Olson's *The World on Paper*. He quotes approvingly Walter Ong:

> Only after print and the extensive experience with maps that print implemented would human beings, when they thought about the cosmos or universe or 'world', think primarily of something laid out before their eyes, as in a modern printed atlas, a vast surface or assemblage of surfaces ready to be 'explored'. The ancient oral world knew few 'explorers', though it did know many itinerants, travellers, voyagers, adventures and pilgrims.[23]

Thus Olson builds his great divide between the scientific explorers with maps and the indigenous voyagers without. 'The Inuit map serves only as a mnemonic for the already known; the world map of Columbus or Cook served as a theoretical model for thinking about the unknown.'[24] Olson agrees with Skelton on the other divide that 'Cook's may without exaggeration be called the first scientific voyages of discovery. They mark an epoch no less in the mapping of the world than in its exploration.'[25] His conclusion is that:

> The paper world, therefore, did not simply provide a means for accumulating and storing what everyone knew. Rather it was a matter of inventing the conceptual means for coordinating the bits of geographical, biological, mechanical and other forms of knowledge acquired from many sources into an adequate and common frame of reference. This common frame of reference became the theoretical model into which local knowledge was inserted

Figure 15 Louis XVI giving instructions to La Perouse. By permission of the Musée National du Château de Versailles.

and reorganised. This is the sense I believe in which Western science of that period acquired the distinctive property of being theoretical science.[26]

Captain Cook and the supposed difference between accidental and deliberate voyages is a key issue in the consideration of Pacific Islander navigation in the next chapter, but for the moment I want to focus on the relationship between cartography and science.

The Suppressed Question

Thirty years ago, Marshall McLuhan made a claim while simultaneously throwing out a challenge:

> Maps are a prime vehicle for repositioning, reframing, rethinking science because theories are maps, maps are science instantiated, without maps science would not have been possible.
> The art of making pictorial statements in a precise and repeatable form is one that we have long taken for granted in the west. But it is usually forgotten that without prints and blueprints, without maps and geometry, the world of modern science would hardly exist.[27]

In order to meet McLuhan's challenge and rethink the self-evident rationality of science and the map/science relationship, we jesters need to ask, 'what is it that we are disposed not to question about maps'? We must be especially careful to bear this question in mind when such cartographic theorists as Robinson and Petchenik ask 'what can there be about the map which is so profoundly fundamental? Why should a representational system for space be so basic?' For their answer to their own question is, 'the problem in analysing maps as communication is that the universal metaphor turns out to be the *map* itself' because 'maps are surrogates of space'.

> As we experience space, and construct representations of it, we know that it will be continuous. Everything is somewhere, and no matter what other characteristics objects do not share, they *always* share relative location, that is spatiality; hence the desirability of equating knowledge with space, an intellectual space. This assures an organisation and a basis for predictability, which are shared by absolutely everyone. This proposition appears to be so fundamental that apparently it is simply adopted a priori.[28]

The geographers Chorley and Haggett claim a common link in language to argue that 'it is characteristic that maps should be likened to language and scientific theories.'[29] Malcom Lewis, an historical geographer, has similarly argued for an evolutionary relationship between language and spatial consciousness.[30] Denis Wood finds a Piagetian development in mapping paralleling the cognitive development of children.[31] Michel de Certeau locates the centrality of space in human consciousness in the more pedestrian but no less vital role of walking in our everyday lives.[32] Much of the essence of these sorts of claims is summed up in the view of the anthropologist Robert Rundstrom in his work on Inuit maps, that 'mapping is fundamental to the process of lending order to the world'.[33] Wood agrees that mapping, in the sense of deploying mental maps, is a common human trait but argues that it is not the same as mapmaking, which for him is largely restricted to societies with a high degree of social complexity.[34]

A claim for the most fundamental role of maps in our understanding comes from recent work in neurophysiology, which suggests that the role of the human neocortex is to create and store memories as maps.[35] The ethologist Talbot Waterman even goes as far as to argue that many animals, birds and insects have a 'map sense'.[36]

Such claims, while seemingly attractive, are more likely to reflect the pervasiveness of the map metaphor in our scientific culture and in questions we are not, therefore, disposed to ask, than the existence of maps in animal or human brains. Whatever the aetiology of the spatial in our knowledge, these researchers all assume the metaphysically self-evident spatiality of knowledge. This assumption seems to capture the essence of why it seems so natural to think of knowledge in terms of maps. Robinson and Petchenik's position suggests an argument that might be sketched out along the following lines: maps are surrogates of space; knowledge is in some sense spatial in virtue of its being structured; organised knowledge or theories are therefore like maps. Likewise Lewis' claims for a link between spatiality and linguistic structure are extremely suggestive. However, both arguments fail to pose the question of how we came to accept our modes of spatiality because they cede too much to another seemingly plausible self-evident intuition; that the underlying reality is the topographical relation of objects, that they *'always* share relative location'. It is this taken-for-granted understanding of objects, their relations, and our ability to represent those relations that in part constitutes the forms of life underlying Western contemporary thought and science. Indeed our representations of spatial relations are coproduced with our understanding of what spatial relations consist in. Given this dialectic how do we break into the apparent circle?

Maps as Lies

In order to render visible, vocalisable and questionable that which is otherwise transparent, silent and unquestioned in regard to spatial representation, it is necessary, as Shapin and Schaffer suggest, to bring into focus the hidden labour, social organisation and discursive formations that make the mode of knowledge production map-like. One way to do that is to focus on the contradictions inherent in maps as representations. Maps suffer acutely from such contradictions in so far as they claim accuracy, scientificity and authority. Of necessity, they cannot avoid the use of some mode of representation which is not itself also a representation, that is to say maps are inherently conventional in that they employ arbitrary symbol and classification systems. Equally, they cannot achieve a full one to one correspondence with what they represent, that is to say they are necessarily selective. Whatever pragmatic resolution of these problems is adopted it is bound to be incompatible with total truth preservation and consequently, as Monmonier has pointed out, all maps are lies.[37] For analogous reasons, as we saw in Chapter 1, Nancy Cartwright argues that the laws of physics are also lies.[38] The problem is that explanation and truth, the joint aims of scientific inquiry, cannot be simultaneously satisfied.[39] This trade-off between explanation and truth can be seen as a dynamic tension and the source of change,[40] but more typically the potential for incoherence that it generates is handled by suppression of the conditions under which a given representation, explanation or truth claim is produced.

At one level the selectivity and conventionality of maps are non-problematic: we all accept that we cannot represent everything at once and that some mode of representation is necessary. But at another level we are seldom aware of the ways in which our views of the world are ordered by suppressed social constructs. We are blind to the processes by which the social is naturalised. Maps have boundaries, frames, spaces, centres and silences which structure what is and is not possible to speak of.[41] Maps are the product of such transparent processes as 'compilation, generalisation, classification, formation into hierarchies, and standardisation of geographical data.'[42] We are in danger of being 'prisoners in [their] social matrix. For cartography as much as for other forms of knowledge, "all social action flows through boundaries determined by classification schemes."'[43] Escape from the prison of such seemingly natural boundaries is problematic since they are taken for granted. But as soon as the social construction of such boundaries is made apparent, what were once bars become potential sites of resistance.

The generally suppressive effects and silences of cartographic representations have been brought out by Jose Rabasa, for whom 'the effect of universality or totality is only achieved through blindness to the subjective reconstitution of the fragments. The map is a palimpsest subject to ironic reconstitution through bricolage.'[44] Similarly Michel de Certeau critiques the map as a 'totalising device' and argues that the application of mathematical principles produces 'a formal ensemble of abstract places' and 'collates on the same plane heterogeneous places, some received from tradition and others produced by observation.' The map is, in effect, an homogenisation and reification of the rich diversity of spatial itineraries and spatial stories. It 'eliminates little by little' all traces of the 'practices that produced it.'[45]

De Certeau's characterisation of the map as a homogenised assemblage that eliminates the local practices that produce it is extremely apposite. But why is it held that a scientific representation of the world needs to be abstract and geometric? According to the French historian of cartography Christian Jacob:

> Maps allow the assemblage of a multitude of heterogeneous inputs in order to subject them to the same mathematical logic and to erase their differences through the coherence of the visual codes. They delocalise knowledge, and thus render it accessible, in a condensed and synoptic form, to future generations of unknown researchers, who can reproduce it according to the same design.[46]

Thus, it is claimed that in the pursuit of the aims of accuracy and objectivity all locations need to be rendered equivalent and connectable in a mathematiseable framework; subjectivity and error can be eliminated and all new information about the world can be accumulated systematically.

Put this way the self-evident necessity of abstract geometrisation seems quite compelling and there appears to be a natural coincidence of internal logics between science and cartography. However, there are three broad kinds of considerations that militate against that compulsion. Firstly, there are alternative ways of creating geographic assemblages. Secondly, such modes of representation cannot be achieved purely scientifically, for large amounts of social work are involved in creating the connections between the heterogeneous elements. Without such work those elements have no natural relationship; self-assembly cannot be achieved by logic or structural necessity. Finally, the connections that maps establish with the social life in which they are embedded are also not natural or self-evident and have power effects that pervade the whole society. Indeed, it is through the social work of creating the assemblages that science and society co-produce each other.

Was There a Cartographic Revolution?

These three considerations can be approached by addressing the question: what brought about the cartographic transformation in sixteenth-century Europe? How were local knowledge, people and practices assembled to produce the 'universal' and objective knowledge that we now equate with science and cartography? This is the second focus of this chapter, to try to disassemble the apparent naturalness of the 'science is a map' metaphor.

It has been noted by many historians of cartography that there was a marked increase in map production and use in the last half of the sixteenth century. Buisseret, for example, claims that around the year 1600 maps suddenly start to be 'essential to a wide a variety of professions'.[47] Skelton and Harvey see a sudden dramatic increase in maps after 1550 and argue that 'the maplessness of the Middle Ages is hard for us to grasp',[48] hence the temptation to label this apparent transformation of epistemological break as a 'cartographic revolution' and to see in it the origins of modern map consciousness. Such a Kuhnian inclination is, I think, to be resisted.

Though map usage increased rapidly at this time, the use of maps was by no means uniform or ubiquitous.[49] (see Fig. 16) The adoption of mapping as a mode of knowledge assemblage was a local and contingent matter and was not uniform in, for example, estate management and land transfer, where one might have expected its universal adoption. Alain Pottage points out that in the case of English estates:

> ... what mattered were the economic qualities of the estate, and not its geometric extent ... the technology of cartography was not rapidly or wholeheartedly embraced by the agencies of land transfer, so that the traditional scheme of narrative description survived the extension of 'linear' space for longer than it might otherwise have done.
>
> [It was] in the course of the nineteenth century, [that] maps, and in particular the model of what was described as a 'cadastral' map did come to be

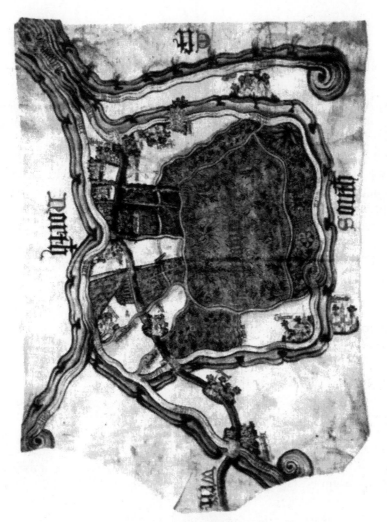

Figure 16 Late fifteenth-century local estate map, Inclesmoor, Yorkshire.

seen as somehow 'obvious' or indispensable ... A cartographic description was seen as the perfect measure of the identity of land. To some, it seemed that the certainty of property could be assumed only by delineating 'land' on a proper surface of description.[50]

Certainty that could only be achieved by reference to a common standard provided by the technology of the Ordnance Survey. Previously, property had been irredeemably uncertain but nonetheless unproblematic, a contractual construct embedded in literary and oral practices for assembling local knowledge, social expectations, trust and memory. What property was and how it was known was the product of a different knowledge space from the one with which we are now familiar.

The question of property maps is also particularly interesting because Peter Barber locates the first use of sketch plans in legal disputes in England at about 1400, when they were used to 'illustrate and when possible to clarify, disputes over rights, ownership and jurisdiction'.[51] This indicates how very variable the use of maps can be, even within a fairly restricted domain such as land ownership, reflecting the different contexts for establishing conditions of trust and knowledge assemblage.

By contrast, as we saw in the last chapter, the use of architectural drawings in the building of cathedrals seems to have developed around the mid-thirteenth century at the zenith of the Gothic cathedral construction era, and sketch plans were almost certainly used from at least the twelfth century. While the building of such complex and innovative structures was thus possible without detailed plans, the very process of construction created a knowledge space within which the role of the mason evolved into that of the architect and plans began to be used as control documents. In the context of naval shipbuilding and the massive Dover harbour project the use of accurate plats or plans was only taken up in the late sixteenth century. Shipbuilding and fortification, like the Gothic cathedrals, had a long history of large-scale, complex projects without the use of detailed drawings. The reason for their introduction seems to have lain in the facility of maps for bringing together otherwise disparate techniques, interests and needs for control by the state.[52]

The integration of cartography with the affairs of state gained some of its impetus from the political revolutions of the 1530s. According to Peter Barber, 'maps were to become one means by which Cromwell's (and later, Burghley's) objective of enhancing royal authority could be achieved, and it was thus that they made their most profound contribution to Tudor government.'[53] The military building program that brought about the modernisation and expansion of England's defences under Henry VIII was 'once and for all, to establish maps and plans as one of the English government's everyday tools in the formulation of policy and in the process of administration'.[54] However, this revolution was based, in Barber's view, on the 'humble and frequently inelegant manuscript plats'.[55] Though scales had started appearing on these plats by 1547,

> The sort of precision to be found in scale maps was often not required by decision makers who could make do perfectly adequately on most occasions with rough and ready picture or position maps lacking scale or standardised conventional signs. These continued to be produced and used for decades and centuries to come.[56]

Hence it may be that the kind of calculative rationality we associate, thanks to Weber, with the modern state is a matter of degree of complexity. Wood, for example, argues that mapmaking

> ... characterises a degree of organisation in society which is not just a function of size but of differentiation and hierarchical integration ... the need to keep written records occurs when control of the social process in rapidly expanding groups is at stake ... The state in its pre-modern and modern forms evolves together *with* the map as an instrument of polity to assess taxes, wage war, facilitate communications, and exploit strategic resources.[57]

He concludes that map use did not come about through the renaissance discovery of Ptolemy, the scientific revolution, painterly realism, rationalised land management, or the emerging nation state. Projections, realism, and quantification were secondary: mapmaking 'emerges as a rationalising tool of state control during periods of relative prosperity in capitalist state economies' around the world.[58]

Wood's arguments, though cogent, are incomplete because they overlook the problem of assemblage. While maps did start to become important tools in government policy making during the Tudor period, the modern state and the scientific map did not emerge until appropriate modes of assemblage were created. In Tudor times maps, surveys, plans and plats were accumulated by individuals like Lord Burghley, Elizabeth I's secretary of state between 1550–1553 and 1558–1570.[59] Whenever he wanted to assemble his maps he took whatever was to hand, of whatever scale or dimension and simply had them bound together; a classically messy motley. The first glimmerings of a need for a more formalised mode of assemblage was recognised with the establishment of the State Paper Office in 1610, but it had a turbulent beginning, with powerful individuals using it as an opportunity to pillage maps for their own private collections.[60] So, an increase in map making alone does not indicate a change in consciousness or a revolution. Many other things had to be set in place before maps were fully integrated with state and scientific knowledge making.

The First Attempt at Map Assemblage

An ideal site for a close examination of such processes is the very first attempt to assemble cartographic knowledge systematically in the interest of the state, which occurred in Spain and Portugal early in the sixteenth century when they established the Casa de la Contratación and the Casa de Mina. These Boards of Trade housed the first scientific institutions—hydrographic offices that held the Padron Real, a master template map, on which all the knowledge of the New World was to be assembled. This attempted assemblage was ultimately a failure. There is a complex of reasons for this, but a contributing factor was that the Padron Real and all the maps utilised by ship's captains were portolan charts. (see Figs 17 and 18). The most obvious feature of portolan charts is the network of rhumb lines which give them the deceptive appearance of having a fixed, mathematically determined grid. In fact the rhumbs are actually lines joining the named points of direction generated by drawing one or two large circles so placed as to cover most of the chart, each circle being subdivided into sixteen or thirty-two equidistant points. The ad hoc way in which these assemblages of geographical information were achieved is emphasised by the fact that the rhumb lines on different charts do not coincide, each chart having its own starting point.

The means of locating a port or coastal feature on portolan charts was not by reference to a mathematical grid but to distance and direction. Originally conceived in terms of wind direction and represented as a wind rose, it was later translated into a compass direction through subdivision of the horizon circle into thirty-two colour-coded but not numbered points. In short it was directionality—the attribution of direction to the observational and experiential phenomena in analogue rather than digital form—which allowed for the process of assemblage of the heterogeneous elements of the portolan charts. Portolan charts

Figure 17 A portolan chart, the Cantino Planisphere, 1502. By permission of the Minestero per i Beni e le Attività Culturali.

were essentially 'catalogue[s] of directions to follow between notable points' and mnemonics for recalling lists of ports.[61] As we shall see in the next chapter, this way of ordering knowledge spatially is common to all early seafaring traditions, and enabled navigators as disparate as the Pacific Islanders and the medieval sailors of the North Sea to have a dynamic cognitive map in their heads. The problem for the state was not just that portolan charts lacked a grid, projection, or a common measure, but that they were rooted in a maritime tradition. That tradition enabled ships' masters to navigate autonomously, using their own experience and charts from a variety of non-official sources. Portolan charts were too local.

To bring all the knowledge of the new world together, the Iberian governments were attempting to construct a 'general system of metrication'[62] and to regularise the old nautical tradition, in a number of ways: by training and licensing the captains; encouraging the development and improvement of instruments including the compass and the astrolabe; commissioning new tables for calculating distances, giving latitudes and the sun's declination; and by establishing new techniques like latitude sailing and new forms of social organisation. In this way they hoped to be able to assemble and standardise all the new information by bringing it under one roof.

The Casa de la Contratación de las Indias was founded by Royal decree in January 1503. On August 8, 1508 a separate geographical or cosmographical department was created, 'perhaps the first Hydrographic Office in history'.[63] Within that office the government ordered that a master chart of the new territory, the Padron Real, be compiled under the supervision of a commission of pilots headed by Amerigo Vespucci, the Pilot Mayor. The Padron Real was a huge wall chart that embraced 'all the lands and isles of the Indies then discovered and belonging to the crown'. All pilots were instructed to trace on their charts 'every land, island, bay, harbour and other thing, new and worthy of being noted' and to report these findings after returning from their voyages.[64]

Disciplining the Master Map

However, the standardisation and accumulation of knowledge could not be achieved by decree or by representations alone. Keeping stable all the components of an assemblage or network—people, instruments, and data—required constant effort and discipline.[65] In order to stop their maps unravelling, the Casa had to establish the boundaries of the

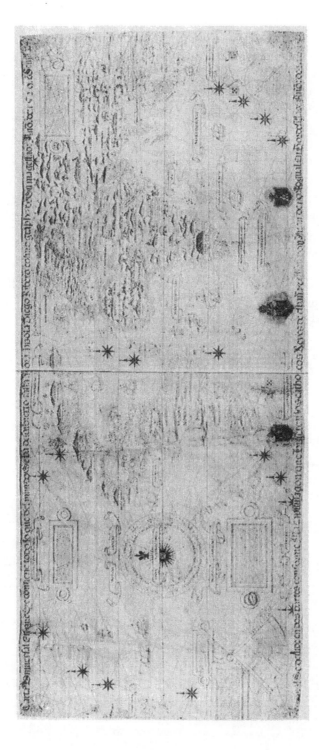

Figure 18 Diogo Ribeiro's Plansiphere 1529. With permission of the Biblioteca Apostolica Vaticana.

knowledge space and to police the inputs and outputs as they moved across the boundaries. What kinds of persons could contribute new knowledge, how that knowledge was to be expressed and evaluated, how it should be stored and reproduced, how disputes over conflicting evidence should be settled, and what were appropriate techniques for adjudicating ownership and control all had to be established. What was to count as knowledge was as much a political and moral problem as it was an epistemological one.

The social, moral and political nature of establishing the process of standardisation and stabilisation is reflected in a series of disputes focused on the Padron General. One such dispute reveals the basic difficulty of establishing 'the facts of the matter' in correcting the Padron General: who was the proper authority, what was the proper technique for determining which piece of information was correct in a case of disagreement? In 1543, the Pilot Mayor Sebastian Cabot and the cosmographer Alonso de Chaves went to court over corrections to the Padron.[66] Chaves complained that the instruments he was provided with were faulty and that the Padron was not kept up to date because pilots did not know how to collect data to give to the cosmographers. Other noted pilots also agreed the Padron was useless.

But what was an appropriate authority on which to resolve disputed claims? The visitor appointed by the Casa to hear the case was a good committee man who believed in consensus and argued that truth would be established by everyone agreeing to sign the Padron. Gutierrez, a chart and instrument maker, revealed that the form of his charts was determined by the demands of his customers. Cabot claimed that he did what was required by law. Others appealed variously to the authority of the crown and God. The visiting Portuguese cartographer Francisco Falero took the modern, but as yet unestablished, empirical position, and called for observation, description and experiment, while also pointing out the inherent flaws of the portolan charts' projectionless plane chart mode of representation.

In 1563 the Casa was still concerned about errors in the Padron and, in one of the earliest examples of sociological investigation, the pilots were given a questionnaire asking their opinion on how to correct it. The majority of respondents agreed that the charts were in error, but perhaps reflecting their adherence to the tradition of the portolan charts, they thought that the best solution was not to change it, but to let individual pilots carry on using whatever techniques they found best. Those who liked compasses should carry several, those who liked astrolabes could try bigger ones.[67]

The cosmographer Alonso Santa Cruz, who was initially employed along with Sebastian Cabot in the 1530s to try to resolve the difficulties the Casa had with the Padron, pursued similar sociological techniques, developing the plan to map the New World territories by questionnaire. The project, incomplete at his death, was taken over by Juan Lopez de Velasco, who proposed a solution to the key problem in assembling knowledge in space and time—longitude. No one at this point was able to establish with any accuracy where the New World was with respect to the old. In 1577 Lopez sent out instructions to local officials to observe the lunar eclipses of September 26, 1577 and September 15, 1578, from which he hoped to be able to work out the longitudes of each place. In addition to the eclipse measurements Lopez attempted to assemble more detailed territorial knowledge of the New World by sending out a questionnaire.[68] This questionnaire asked a large number of very detailed questions, including a request to each official to draw a map of his town and its adjacent area. Barbara Mundy has analysed the sixty-nine maps that were painted by Mayan officials and sent to Spain in response to this request.[69] The maps were left to the local artists, who used the opportunity to advance their own interests, blending their traditional modes of representation with those demanded by the Spanish:

> Far from providing the simple boundaries expected of them, they took the initiative of offering a territorial synthesis of their jurisdiction that conformed to local tradition by packing their maps with pre-Hispanic features.[70]

The resulting hybrid maps made Lopez' project impossible. The results of the questionnaire were equally incapable of assemblage. Many failed to answer; those that did often misunderstood the question or the instructions on making observations, or gave inaccurate responses. Lopez was unable to establish the conditions of simultaneity and homogeneity required to create his planned knowledge space. However, the maps resulting from the encounter, while not ethno-cartographically pure, do reveal a profound cartographic ability and engagement. The Mayans were able to graphically represent their interests and local knowledge, their sense of history, memory and place. Rather than being passive recipients of Western scientific cartography, they were agents of knowledge, and according to the French historian Serge Gruzinski, their 'maps became the basis of a new legality ... colonial geography was born of the fusion of notions of pre-Hispanic territory and Spanish occupation.'[71]

A Fifth Continent?

Ultimately the knowledge space that the Spanish tried to construct proved too hard to sustain. The navigational tradition of the portolan charts was immune to the state's demands. But just as the difficulties of controlling the inputs were proliferating, so too were the problems of controlling the outputs. There were other centres of calculation; Seville was only briefly a compulsory passage point. In Dieppe, for example, French cartographers under the leadership of the armateur Jean Ango set up a chart production house that had a network of informants sending information from all over the world.[72] (see Fig. 19). However, the Dieppe School also had difficulties with assembly of that information, as is evidenced by the so called 'Java la Grande' problem or the 'Portuguese Discovery of Australia.'

Figure 19 A section of a 'Dieppe' World Map showing Java La Grande. Pierre Descalliers, 1550. By permission of The British Library (Shelfmark: 1000008.011).

From the publication in 1547 of the Dauphin map, the first of the Dieppe series of world maps, charts started to show a fifth continent labelled Java La Grande. This emergent land mass has long intrigued historians of Renaissance cartography who are unable to decide whether it was 'a pseudo Borneo, or a misplaced and duplicated Java'.[73] Whether it might be partly Vietnam,[74] pure imagination or a hoax,[75] the claim that has attracted the most attention and the most criticism is that Java La Grande in fact represents Australia[76] and that the distortions of the outline are the consequence of a misassemblage, by the French cartographers at the Dieppe School, of charts drawn by the original Portuguese discoverers.

Jean Rotz' *Boke of Idrography* (1542) is the earliest surviving work of the Dieppe school, all the source materials—navigators' charts, journals, sailing directions and drawings—having been destroyed in the English bombardment of Dieppe in 1694.[77] Rotz was probably on Jean Parmentier's expedition to Sumatra in 1529–30. According to the historian of cartography, Helen Wallis, it was this Sumatra voyage which provided the opportunity for Rotz to obtain information on Christovao de Mendonca's ill-fated expedition to the south in 1521, from which only one of the three original caravels returned to Sumatra. Rotz took to Dieppe copies of the charts that Mendonca brought back to Malacca showing sections of the Australian coast.

An explanation, advanced by the proponents of the Portuguese discovery of Australia, for the peculiar shape of Australia on these maps is that the Dauphin map of 1536, the Rotz map of 1542, the Vallard Map of 1547 and the Desceliers map of 1550 are compilations from separate charts of what were taken to be sections of the Australian coast from Darwin to Tasmania. The difficulty for Rotz and the other French cartographers was how to assemble them. They had no direct experience of the voyage themselves, they had no grid, and no indication of scale or orientation. Hence, even though the charts had returned to a centre of calculation, something in addition to the inscriptions was needed in order to assemble them. Commenting on a similar misassembly in early Canadian cartography, W. F. Ganong remarked:

> Cartographically myopic as the first explorers often were, even blinder were the cartographers at home, who had to piece together and reconcile, without the slightest means of testing their conclusions, the diverse records and maps that explorers brought back.[78]

Bringing the World Back Home

Many of these difficulties in creating a knowledge space that could embrace the world are held to have been resolved with the advent of Mercator's projection of 1569. This projection provided a grid and the possibility of representing loxodromes, that is courses of a constant bearing, as a straight line. Its absence had previously been a severe drawback, as Pedro Nunes had pointed out, since loxodromes on plane charts as on portolan charts, though drawn as straight lines, were in fact curves. When perspective, geometry, and the grid of latitude and longitude were combined, it was possible to calculate accurately the location of any spot on earth. It was this calculative framework, this space within which to assemble knowledge that, according to some historians of the Renaissance and the scientific revolution, provided the essential precondition for the possibility of modern science.[79] Such a framework had, of course, been initially proposed by Ptolemy in his *Geographia*, which reached Europe by way of the Byzantine Empire in the thirteenth century, though it did not achieve wide circulation until its Latin translation in the fifteenth century. While it had the potential to contain the world and bring it to the desktop, considerable social and technical difficulties had to be resolved before a knowledge space of this kind could be fully established. Moreover, as late as 1753, Tobias Mayer published his state of the art 'Mappa Critica' of Germany, which portrayed the location of 200 places despite the fact that 'only 33 were fixed by astronomical determinations of latitude' and none were apparently well fixed by longitude'.[80] Mayer's map serves to show that cartographers were not completely dependent on fixed, mathematically determined spatial structures to assemble knowledge.

To achieve the integrated assemblage of geographical knowledge that we now take for granted, science, cartography and the state had to be aligned as they became, for the first time, through the process of the triangulated surveys of France and England. By the mid-seventeenth century the problem of the bureaucratic regulation and taxation of the French state had become recognised as one susceptible to cartographic solution, and the problem of assembling cartographical knowledge was treated as being essentially linked to the astronomical and geophysical sciences. The French Academie Royale was set up in 1666 with the explicit purpose of correcting and improving maps and sailing charts, in light of the recognition that the solution of the major problems of geography, chronology and navigation lay in astronomy. In 1667 work was begun on the Royal Observatory at Faubourg St Jacques.

The World on the Third Floor

As head of the leading French observatory, Jean Dominique Cassini was in correspondence with astronomers all over Europe and was deluged with astronomical data. He had to devise a new way to assemble it. Though he did use a map—his famous Planisphere Terrestre—it was a markedly different way of assembling data cartographically from that which we take for granted today. Cassini started by drawing a 24 foot circle on the floor on the third level of the west tower of the new observatory, which had been oriented by compass and quadrant when the foundations were laid. The map employed an azimuthal projection with the north pole at the centre, from which meridians radiated at ten degree intervals, with the prime meridian being drawn from the centre passing through the midpoint between the two south windows of the octagonal tower and with the parallels of latitude forming concentric circles.

This floor map attracted a great deal of attention and was considered a major achievement. James II and Louis XIV both came to see it. Being on the floor, it was subject to a good deal of wear and though it was restored in 1690, by the turn of the century it had become effaced.[81] What is striking is that Cassini's first impulse was like that of the Iberian monarchs, though somewhat more primal: to build a physical space in which to assemble knowledge. He felt that accurate assemblage of information about the world from different observatories could only be stabilised by being locked onto the world, by being given the same geophysical orientation. However, in 1682 Cassini transferred the determination of 40 locations onto a sketch map that was issued as an engraved world map in 1694.[82] (see Fig. 20).

Tying France Together

Arguably, if there is anything resembling a turning point in map consciousness, at least in the scientific community, it is marked by the abandonment of the Planisphere project. From that point on, the rational way to represent the whole world scientifically was on a sheet of paper, which was to be achieved not by bringing different astronomical sites into one central space but by the creation of a new space in which the distributed sites were linked with the invisible bonds of social labour.

But Cassini was not the only one with a problem. Until the late Middle Ages, French territory, as in England, was known in a 'literary

Figure 20 Cassini's Planisphere Terrestre 1696. Reproduced with the permission of Bibliothèque Nationale, Paris.

mode', through itineraries, journeys and lists; which assembled local knowledge in written descriptions.[83] The literary form of spatial knowledge began to prove less adequate to the needs of the state in the mid-seventeenth century, when it became the task of the secretary of home affairs, Jean Baptiste Colbert, to restore the floundering French economy and ensure an ever increasing income to provide for the lavish expenditures of Louis XIV. Colbert set out to develop the nation's resources and build an infrastructure of roads and canals, but he was stymied by the lack of a map of the whole of France which, like everywhere else in Europe at this time, was a country that operated almost entirely on local knowledge. All the systems of

Figure 21 Triangulation of France with the base line running through Paris. Reproduced with the permission of Bibliothèque Nationale, Paris.

weights, measures and taxes were local, there was no centralised uniform system of mensuration, and there was virtually no collective topographical knowledge.[84]

The lack of an accurate, large-scale map of the kingdom prevented Colbert from gaining an overview of the extent and variety of the country's resources. His first attempt was to assemble all the provincial maps and ensure their commensurability through the use of a common scale and criteria of accuracy.[85] To this end he instructed the field commissioners of the provinces to evaluate their maps and send their amended versions to Paris, a discipline that was impossible to impose. That provincial maps already existed was not sufficient in itself to ensure their assemblage at a centre of calculation. To achieve such an assemblage two problems had to be solved: one social and one technical. The Provincial administrators had to be persuaded to cooperate in a national project which they saw as organising their resources for the benefit of the King. At the same time all those provincial maps, as Colbert had recognised, could not be assembled unless and until they were rendered commensurable. In the face of these political and technical problems of assemblage the response of Cassini, Jean Picard and the Académie was to propose the creation of a network of surveyed triangles that would encircle the whole country and thereby enable the drawing of a unified map of the whole of France on one grid (see Fig. 21).

The network of triangles could provide a solution to the general technical problem of assembling all the separate topographic surveys of the whole of France. A centralised, Académie-based approach would also provide a political solution if the King could be sufficiently diverted from his military ambitions to fund the project. Ultimately the national map could only be achieved by bringing into line not only the King, but also the satellites of Jupiter, pendulum clocks, telescopes, surveying chains, trigonometry, quadrants, new printing techniques, all the provinces of France and the earth itself. In aligning all these places, practices, people and instruments a new space was created, a space that we now take for granted, but one which did not come into existence naturally or even easily, requiring as it did the physical and social labour of tying France together with surveying chains.

The first discussions of the project were held in 1683 and it was proposed that J. D. Cassini survey a line from Dunkerque to Barcelona. (see Fig. 22) This would have the co-dependent purpose of enabling the measurement of the circumference of the earth and providing the base line for all future surveying operations in France. A hitherto independent geodetic problem of the day concerned the sphericity of the earth. Was it a perfect sphere, a prolate spheroid elongated at the poles or an oblate one flattened at the poles and bulging at the equator? Once again the question arose that had bothered the Portuguese and Spanish navigators and cartographers for a century and a half, what is the length of a degree of latitude? Did it vary with distance from the pole and if so did it increase or decrease? Consequently, not only did the shape of Earth have to be aligned, so did French and English science. Newton's theory of gravity indicated an oblateness of the earth while French theory and early measurements seemed to indicate a prolate spheroid. The disagreement created yet more pressure for greater accuracy in measuring the length of a degree. Eventually Louis XV ordered a decisive test: two arcs were to be measured, one near the Equator, in

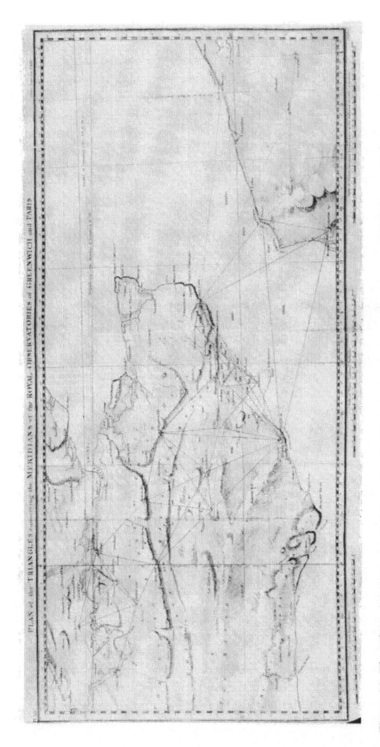

Figure 22   The 'Plan of the Triangles' linking the Meridians of Paris and Greenwich across the Channel. With the permission of the Ordnance Survey.

Peru (1735–1744) and one near the Arctic, in Lapland (1734–37). These 'tests' were the rationale for what were arguably the first purely scientific expeditions and involved vast amounts of work and commitment.[86]

By 1739 'France was enclosed by an uninterrupted chain of 400 triangles surveyed from 18 fundamental bases.'[87] In 1744 the first outline map was produced, but the complete topographic survey resulting in the publication of the *Carte de Cassini* was not finished until 1789.[88] Altogether it took 121 years of arduous labour by vast numbers of people at a cost of 700,000 *livres* to produce the first national map.[89] The *Carte de Cassini* was important historically not just because it was the first thorough topographical survey of a whole country—'it [also] taught the rest of the world what to do and what not to do.'[90] It established the practice, adopted in all national mapping projects ever since, of linking topographic surveys with a chain of great triangles. Just how difficult it is to achieve this enlightenment project of the ultimate survey is nicely revealed in Matthew Edney's account of the survey of India.[91] Edney found that the technological fix offered by triangulation served to intensify the Enlightenment's 'cartographic illusion' of the 'mimetic map'. But totalising archives are impossible in practice. The British could only make their general maps of South Asia by combining multiple surveys based on local knowledge and techniques within a framework of latitude and longitude—a motley assemblage just like the Padron Real.

France and England Bound as One

Similar social processes were also central to what, in 1783, was to be the first international cooperative mapping venture. The initial pressure for this transformation of international space did not come from either military or economic forces, as Wood has argued. Rather it came largely from the demands of a rapidly internationalising science. The technical problem was to measure precisely the difference in latitude and longitude between the Paris and Greenwich observatories.[92] (see Fig. 23) The English and French astronomers disagreed by a matter of 11 seconds of longitude and 15 seconds of latitude which, on the ground, amounts to roughly 500 metres.[93] Such technical questions are not, of course, *sui generis*, but are coproduced with the instruments and practices that make possible both their formulation and their solution. Concomitant with that process is the creation of the kind of homogeneous and unified space in which science's universalised forms of knowledge become

Figure 23 The Greenwich (above) and Paris (below) observatories, sketched in the eighteenth-century.

possible through the linking of local knowledge spaces. In turn, the creation of such a scientific knowledge space generates a different social space.

César François Cassini III suggested that the astronomical problem could be solved by a trigonometric survey from Greenwich to Dover and a triangulated connection to the French National survey, thereby expanding the isolated spaces of the observatories into one homogeneous space. In 1787 England and France were invisibly but indissolubly linked. The connection between the two national spaces was established by trigonometric triangulation using lights and the new theodolite at night to span the Channel. However the problem of creating equivalences between all the pieces of heterogeneous information was not so easily resolved. It was necessary first of all to convert the French *toise* to the English league. Then, having established an agreed linear distance between the meridians of Paris and Greenwich, there were difficulties converting this value into degrees since, once again, this depended on agreement about the precise length of a degree and the shape of the earth. In addition there were problems in establishing the difference in clock time between the meridians. Only when social means could be found to solve these seemingly technical problems could the astronomers measure the differences between their observatories, thereby creating one unified knowledge space and hence a new international and political space. The establishment of this new international space would set in motion the process whereby the whole of the Earth's territory could be mapped as one, all sites would be rendered equivalent, and all localness would vanish in the homogenisation and geometrisation of space. To this day, the project remains incomplete; even though the international geoid system was accepted in 1980, the conversion of national surveys to this common reference surface still produces local difficulties. In Australia, for example, the Geodetic Datum is based on a local ellipsoid whose centre of mass differs from that of the internationally defined ellipsoid by 200 metres to the north east. All maps are having to be redrawn with details being changed by an average of 1 mm.[94]

Cook Adrift

What this journey through the sixteenth and eighteenth centuries has done is to put back the traces that have been erased and show that in order to achieve the kind of 'universal' and 'accurate' knowledge that constitutes modern science and cartography, local knowledge, personnel, and instrumentation have to be assembled on a national and international scale. This level of organisation is only possible when the state, science and cartography become integrated. The first scientific institutions in Europe, the hydrographic offices in the Casa da Mina and the Casa de la Contratación went a long way towards achieving such a degree of integration. Though ultimately a failure, they were examples of the kinds of organisation that were later developed in the integration of science, cartography and the interests of the state in the triangulation of France and the subsequent linking of the French and English national surveys.

This linking created a transnational knowledge space whose ramified bureaucratic structure, in providing the conditions for the possibility of modern science and cartography, has the appearance of determining all our knowledge. However, such a knowledge space is not and cannot be entirely hegemonic as is shown by the example of Captain Cook, who some have claimed as 'the first scientific explorer'.[95] Cook was sent to Tahiti to observe the transit of Venus which would provide a measure of solar parallax and hence determine the dimensions of the solar system, an astronomical problem directly related to the 'great problem of the day'—the determination of longitude. Cook found Tahiti 'scientifically' by using a map and calculating longitude by the method of 'lunar distances', Tahiti's longitudinal position having been fixed previously by its 'discoverer', Captain Wallis. This canonical tale of scientific discovery and mapping now stands in need of deflation by appropriate application of the jester's bladder.

As we have already seen, the problem of determining longitude was crucially dependent on the resolution of the uncertainties involved in fixing the relative positions of the Greenwich and Paris observatories. So that Cook, despite having calculated his way to the Pacific, was 4 degrees adrift by the time he reached New Zealand, demonstrating that maps and scientific discovery can only be maximally effective when set in a social network. His predecessors, without such advantages, should perhaps be denied the title of explorers or 'deliberate discovers'. But when Cook was in Tahiti he took on board the Polynesian navigator Tupaia who was able draw him a map covering an area of the Pacific as large as the United States and giving the position of 74 islands. (see Fig. 24) Tupaia and his predecessors had systematically explored and colonised the entire Pacific, making two-way deliberate voyages without the use of paper maps. Clearly, though there are significant differences between Polynesian and European modes of knowledge assembly, there is no great cartographical divide. The salient point is that the Polynesian methods were basically performative, not representational. To the extent that we too, do not know the world simply through maps and representations, but through practice and performance, we can resist the dominance of maps and of science. Not only do maps carry within themselves the seeds of their

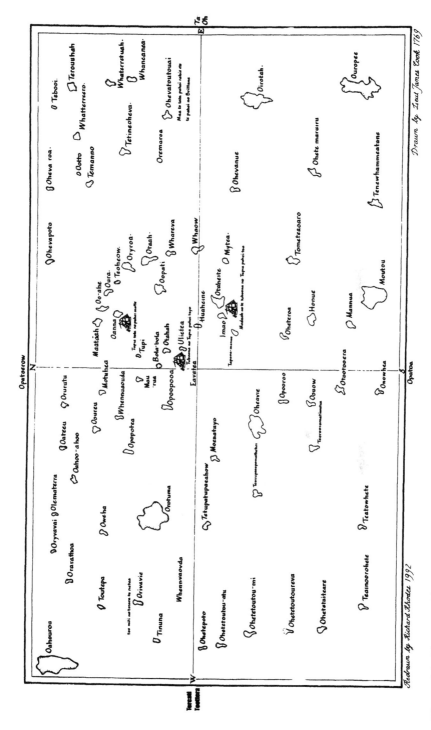

Figure 24 'Tupaia's Chart'. By permission of The British Library (Shelfmark: 1008767.011).

alternatives, but they are not the only way of knowing the world or of assembling knowledge, as is shown by the example of Pacific navigation.

Notes

1 Rodney Shirley, 'Epicthonius Cosmopolites: Who Was He?', *Map Collector*, Vol. 18 (March), (1982), pp. 39–40.

2 Karl Kerényi, 'The Trickster in Relation to Greek Mythology', in P. Radin, ed., *The Trickster: A Study in American Indian Mythology*, (New York: Schocken Books, 1972), p. 185.

3 On the great divide and the theoretical position that informs this chapter see the classic article Latour, 'Visualisation and Cognition'.

4 On the necessity of being a trickster see Haraway, *Simians, Cyborgs and Women*.

5 On centres of calculation see Latour, *Science In Action*.

6 Cf the discursive strategy of Shapin and Schaffer, *Leviathan and the Air Pump*.

7 B. De S. Santos, 'Law: A Map of Misreading. Toward a Postmodern Conception of Law', *Journal of Law and Society*, Vol. 14, 3, (1987), pp. 279–302, p. 282. Edmund Leach, *Culture and Communication: The Logic by Which Symbols Are Connected*, (Cambridge: Cambridge University Press, 1976), p. 51.

8 Elizabeth Ferrier, 'Mapping Power: Cartography and Contemporary Cultural Theory', *antithesis*, Vol. 4, 1, (1990), pp. 35–52; Rosalyn Diprose and Robyn Ferrell, eds., *Cartographies: Poststructuralism and the Mapping of Bodies and Spaces*, (London: Allen and Unwin, 1991).

9 Lucy Sullivan, 'Language Map Gives Few Wrong Directions', *The Australian*, (Melbourne: 1994), p. 29.

10 Wittgenstein, *Philosophical Investigations*, p. 49.

11 Stephen S. Hall, *Mapping the Next Millennium: The Discovery of New Geographies*, (New York: Random House, 1992), p. 3.

12 Denis Wood, *The Power of Maps*, (New York: The Guilford Press, 1992), p. 34.

13 Hall, *Mapping the Next Millennium*, p. 4.

14 Edward W. Soja, *Postmodern Geographies: The Reassertion of Space in Critical Social Theory*, (London: Verso, 1989), p. 1.

15 Daniel McNeill and Paul Freiberger, *Fuzzy Logic*, (Melbourne: Bookman Press, 1993), p. 230.

16 J. Brian Harley, 'Maps, Knowledge and Power', in D. Cosgrove and S. Daniels, eds., *The Iconography of Landscape*, (Cambridge: Cambridge University Press, 1988), pp. 277–312; J. Brian Harley, 'Silences and Secrecy: The Hidden Agenda of Cartography in Early Modern Europe',

Imago Mundi, Vol. 40, (1988), pp. 57–76; J. Brian Harley, 'Deconstructing the Map', *Cartographica*, Vol. 26, (1989), pp. 1–20; J. Brian Harley and David Woodward, eds., *The History of Cartography, Vol. 1 Cartography in Prehistoric, Ancient and Medieval Europe and the Mediterranean*, (Chicago: University of Chicago Press, 1987).

[17]   Wood, 1992, *The Power of Maps*, p. 66.

[18]   Rouse, *Knowledge and Power*, p. 248.

[19]   Latour, 1987, *Science in Action*.

[20]   M. Polanyi, *Personal Knowledge: Towards a Post-critical Philosophy*, (London: Routledge & Kegan Paul, 1958), p. 4.

[21]   Kuhn, *The Structure of Scientific Revolutions*, p. 108.

[22]   Harley, 'Deconstructing the Map', p. 4. See also Matthew Edney, 'Mathematical Cosmography and the Social Ideology of British Cartography 1780–1820', *Imago Mundi*, Vol. 46, (1994), pp. 101–116.

[23]   David Olson, *The World on Paper: The Conceptual and Cognitive Implications of Writing and Reading*, (Cambridge: Cambridge University Press, 1994), p. 205; Walter Ong, *Orality and Literacy: The Technologizing of the Word*, (London: Methuen, 1982), p. 73.

[24]   Olson, *The World on Paper*, p. 216.

[25]   Ibid, p. 212. R. Skelton, *Explorer's Maps: Chapters in the Cartographical Record of Geographical Discovery*, (London: Routledge & Kegan Paul, 1958), p. 243.

[26]   Ibid, p. 232.

[27]   Marshall McLuhan, *Understanding Media: The Extensions of Man*, (New York: McGraw-Hill, 1964), p. 157.

[28]   A. H. Robinson and B. B. Petchenik, *The Nature of Maps: Essays Towards Understanding Maps and Mapping*, (Chicago: University of Chicago Press, 1976), p. 4.

[29]   R. J. Chorley and P. Haggett, *Models in Geography*, (London: Methuen, 1967), pp. 48–9.

[30]   Malcom Lewis, 'The Origins of Cartography', in J. B. Harley and D. Woodward, eds., *The History of Cartography, Vol.1 Cartography in Prehistoric, Ancient and Medieval Europe and the Mediterranean*, (Chicago: University of Chicago Press, 1987), pp. 51–2.

[31]   Barbara Belyea, 'Amerindian Maps: The Explorer as Translator', *Journal of Historical Geography*, Vol. 18, (1992), pp. 267–77; Barbara Belyea, 'Images of Power: Derrida/Foucault/Harley', *Cartographica*, Vol. 29, (1992), pp. 1–9; Barbara Belyea, 'Review Article of Denis Wood's *The Power of Maps*, and the Author's Reply', *Cartographica*, Vol. 29, 3&4, (1992), pp. 94–99; Barbara Belyea, 'Inland Journeys, Native Maps', *Cartographica*, Vol. 33, 2, (1996), pp. 1–16; Denis Wood, 'How Maps Work', *Cartographica*, Vol. 29, 3&4, (1992), pp. 66–74; Wood, 1992, *The Power of Maps*.

[32]   Michel de Certeau, *The Practice of Everyday Life*, (Berkeley: University of California Press, 1984), pp. 91ff.

33   Robert A. Rundstrom, 'A Cultural Interpretation of Inuit Map Accuracy', *Geographical Review*, Vol. 80, (1990), pp. 155–68, p. 155.

34   Wood, 'Maps and Mapmaking', p. 2.

35   See for example the work of Treisman and Allman cited by Hall, *Mapping the Next Millennium*, p. 17.

36   Talbot H. Waterman, *Animal Navigation*, (New York: Scientific American Library, 1989), pp. 175ff.

37   Mark Monmonier, *How to Lie With Maps*, (Chicago: University of Chicago Press, 1991).

38   Cartwright, *How the Laws of Physics Lie*.

39   Helen Longino, 'Hard, Soft, or Satisfying', *Social Epistemology*, Vol. 6, (1992), pp. 281–7, p. 284.

40   Thomas Kuhn, *The Essential Tension*, (Chicago: University of Chicago Press, 1977).

41   Harley, 'Silences and Secrecy'.

42   J. Brian Harley, 'Power and Legitimation in the English Geographical Atlases of the Eighteenth Century', in J. Wolter and R. Grim, ed., *Images of the World: The Atlas Through History*, (Washington: Library of Congress, 1997), pp. 161–204.

43   Robert Darnton, *The Great Cat Massacre and Other Episodes in French Cultural History*, (New York: Basic Books, 1984) cited in Harley, 'Deconstructing the Map', p. 13.

44   Jose Rabasa, 'Allegories of the *ATLAS*', in F. Barker, ed., *Europe and Its Others*, (Colchester: University of Essex, 1985), pp. 1–16, p. 2

45   de Certeau, *The Practice of Everyday Life*, p. 121.

46   Christian Jacob, *L'Empire des Cartes: Approche Théorique de la Cartographie à Travers l'Histoire*, (Paris: Albin Michel, 1992), p. 464, my translation.

47   Buisseret, D., ed. 1992, *Monarchs, Ministers and Maps: The Emergence of Cartography as a Tool of Government in Early Modern Europe*, University of Chicago Press, Chicago, p. 1; P. D. A. Harvey, *Maps in Tudor England*, (London: The Public Record Office and The British Library, 1993), p. 65; Sarah Tyacke, ed., *English Map-Making 1500–1650: Historical Essays*, (London: British Library, 1983), p. 18.

48   R. A. Skelton and P. D. A. Harvey, *Local Maps and Plans from Medieval England*, (Oxford: Clarendon Press, 1986), p. 4.

49   Catherine Delano Smith, 'The First English Maps', in C. D. Smith and R. Kain, eds., *La Cartografia Anglesa*, (Barcelona: Institut Cartografic de Catalunya, 1997), pp. 39–54.

50   Alain Pottage, 'The Measure of Land', *Modern Law Review*, Vol. 57, (1994), pp. 361–84, p. 374.

51   Peter Barber, 'England 1: Pageantry, Defense, and Government: Maps at Court to 1550', in D. Buisseret, ed., *Monarchs, Ministers and Maps: The Emergence of Cartography as a Tool of Government in Early Modern Europe*, (Chicago: University of Chicago Press, 1992), pp. 26–56, p. 27.

[52] Stephen A. Johnston, *Making Mathematical Practice: Gentlemen, Practitioners and Artisans in Elizabethan England*, (London, 1994).

[53] Barber, 'England 1', p. 33.

[54] Ibid, p. 34.

[55] Ibid, p. 33.

[56] Ibid, p. 38.

[57] Wood, 'Maps and Mapmaking', p. 5.

[58] Denis Wood, 'Mapmaking', in H. Selin, ed., *Encyclopedia of the History of Science, Technology and Medicine in Non-Western Cultures*, (New York: Garland, 1995).

[59] Barber, 'England 1' p. 48.

[60] Ibid, p. 43.

[61] Denoix in Michel Mollat du Jourdin and Monique de La Roncière, *Sea Charts of the Early Explorers: 13th to 17th Century*, (London: Thames and Hudson, 1984), p. 15.

[62] John Law, 'Technology and Heterogeneous Engineering: The Case of Portugese Expansion', in W. Bijker, T. Hughes and T. Pinch, eds., *The Social Construction of Technological Systems; New Directions in the Sociology and History of Technology*, (Cambridge: MIT Press, 1987), pp. 111–34; Law, 'On the Social Explanation of Technical Change', p. 244.

[63] Lloyd A. Brown, *The Story of Maps*, (Boston: Little Brown & Co. reprint Bonanza Books, 1949), p. 142.

[64] Henry Harrisse, *The Discovery of North America: A Critical Documentary, and Historic Investigation. Rep. 1961*, (Amsterdam: N. Israel, 1892), pp. 258–67 cited in Brown, *The Story of Maps*, p. 143.

[65] On stability see John Law and Wiebe Bijker, 'Postscript: Technology, Stability, and Social Theory', in W. Bijker and J. Law, ed., *Shaping Technology/Building Society: Studies in Sociotechnical Change*, (Cambridge: MIT Press, 1992), pp. 201–224.

[66] Ursula Lamb, 'Science by Litigation: A Cosmographic Feud', *Terrae Incognitae*, Vol. 1, (1969), pp. 40–57 and Ursula Lamb, 'The Spanish Cosmographic Juntas of the Sixteenth Century', *Terrae Incognitae*, Vol. 6, (1974), pp. 51–64.

[67] Ibid, p. 59.

[68] Clinton R. Edwards, 'Mapping by Questionnaire: An Early Spanish Attempt to Determine New World Geographical Positions', *Imago Mundi*, Vol. 23, (1969), pp. 17–28.

[69] Barbara Mundy, *The Mapping of New Spain: Indigenous Cartography and the Maps of the Relación Geográficas*, (Chicago: University of Chicago Press, 1996).

[70] S. Gruzinski, *Painting the Conquest: The Mexican Indians and the European Renaissance* (Paris, Flammarion, 1992). See also Dana Leibsohn, 'Mapping Metaphors: Figuring the Ground of Sixteenth Century New Spain', *Journal of Medieval and Early Modern Studies*, Vol. 26, 3, (1996), pp. 497–523.

71 Gruzinski, *Painting*, fn 48, p. 201.

72 Helen Wallis, 'Java La Grande: The Enigma of the Dieppe Maps', in G. Williams and A. Frost, eds., *Terra Australis to Australia*, (Melbourne: Oxford University Press, 1988), pp. 39–81, p. 40.

73 Helen Wallis, *Did The Portuguese Discover Australia? The Map Evidence*, International Cartographic Association, (Perth, Australia: 1984), p. 203.

74 W. A. R. Richardson, 'Is Java-La-Grande Australia? The Linguistic Evidence Concerning the West Coast', *Globe (Journal of the Australian Map Circle)*, Vol. 19, (1983), pp. 9–46.

75 Lawrence Fitzgerald, *Java La Grande: The Portuguese Discovery of Australia*, (Hobart: The Publishers Pty, 1984).

76 Kenneth McIntyre, *The Secret Discovery of Australia: Portuguese Ventures 200 Years Before Captain Cook*, (Menindie: Souvenir Press, 1977); Wallis, 'Java La Grande', p. 47; Wallis, *Did The Portuguese Discover Australia?*, p. 203.

77 Helen Wallis, ed., *The Maps and Text of the Boke of Idrography Presented by Jean Rotz to Henry VIII, Now in the British Library*, (Oxford: Viscount Eccles for the Roxburghe Club, 1981).

78 Ganong cited in McIntyre, *The Secret Discovery of Australia*, p. 86. On the variability of compilation with sources see Anne Godlewska, 'The Napoleonic Survey of Egypt: A Masterpiece of Cartographic Compilation and Early 19th Century Fieldwork', *Cartographica*, Vol. 25, 1&2, (1988).

79 James Burke, *The Day The Universe Changed*, (London: BBC, 1985).

80 Eric G. Forbes, *Tobias Mayer (1723–62): Pioneer of Enlightened Science in Germany*, (Gottingen: 1980), p. 63.

81 C. Jacob, 1992, *L'Empire des Cartes*, pp. 131–2.

82 Gerald Crone, *Maps and Their Makers*, (Folkstone: Dawson, 1953), p. 88.

83 J. Revel, 'Knowledge of the Territory', *Science in Context*, Vol. 4, (1991), pp. 133–161.

84 Ronald Edward Zupko, *Revolution in Measurement: Western European Weights and Measures Since the Age of Science*, (Philadelphia: American Philosophical Society, 1990); Witold Kula, *Measures and Men*, (Princeton: Princeton University Press, 1986); J. L. Heilbron, 'The Measure of Enlightenment', in T. Frängsmyr, J. L. Heilbron and R. E. Rider, eds., *The Quantifying Spirit in the 18th Century*, (Berkley: University of California Press, 1990), pp. 207–242; Ken Alder, 'A Revolution to Measure: The Political Economy of the Metric System in France', in N. Wise, ed., *The Values of Precision*, (Princeton: Princeton University Press, 1995), pp. 9–71.

85 David Buisseret, 'Monarchs, Ministers, and Maps in France before the Accession of Louis XIV', in D. Buisseret, ed., *Monarchs, Ministers and Maps: The Emergence of Cartography as a Tool of Government in Early Modern Europe*, (Chicago: University of Chicago Press, 1992), pp. 99–123, p. 99.

[86] Mary Louise Pratt, *Imperial Eyes: Travel Writing and Transculturation*, (London: Routledge, 1992). The 'toise of Peru' proved longer than that of Lapland necessitating the resurvey of the Paris meridian see Monique Pelletier, *La Carte de Cassini: L'Extraordinaire Aventure de la Carte de France*, (Paris: Presses de l'Ecole Nationale des Ponts et Chaussées, 1990), p. 67.

[87] Lloyd A. Brown, *The Story of Maps*, (Boston: Little Brown & Co. reprint Bonanza Books, 1949), p. 252.

[88] Pelletier, M. 1990, *La Carte de Cassini*, p. 69.

[89] Brown, *The Story of Maps*, p. 254.

[90] Ibid, p. 255.

[91] Matthew Edney, *Mapping an Empire: The Geographical Construction of British India*, (Chicago: University of Chicago Press, 1997), pp. 17ff.

[92] Sven Widmalm, 'Accuracy, Rhetoric and Technology: The Paris-Greenwich Triangulation, 1784–88', in T. Frängsmyr, J. L. Heilbron and R. E. Rider, eds., *The Quantifying Spirit in the 18th Century*, (Berkeley: University of California Press, 1990), pp. 179–206.

[93] W. A. Seymour, ed., *A History of the Ordnance Survey*, (Folkstone: Dawson, 1980), p. 14.

[94] Auslig Website <http://www.auslig.go.au>

[95] See David Turnbull, 'Cook and Tupaia, a Tale of Cartographic Méconnaissance?', in M. Lincoln, ed., *Science and Exploration: European Voyages to the Southern Oceans in the Eighteenth Century*, (London: Boydell and Brewer, 1998).

4 PACIFIC NAVIGATION: AN ALTERNATIVE SCIENTIFIC TRADITION

Speaking of Others' Knowledge

In the last chapter it was argued that the seemingly self-evident co-incidence of the internal logics of science and cartography is under-mined by the fact that there are alternative ways of creating geographic assemblages. Australian Aboriginal mapping, briefly discussed in Chapter 1, is a particularly salient example of a completely different way of knowing the world. But perhaps the most telling counter-example in the context of knowledge spaces, maps and debates over the 'great divide' is the Pacific navigational knowledge tradition. Detailed consideration of this example also raises some of the problems implicit in comparisons between knowledge traditions, and in attempts to establish an equitable dialogue across the gap between knowledge spaces.

To talk of another culture's knowledge is fraught with political and ethical difficulties about rights, ownership and control. Such difficulties are especially acute in Australia, where there is an indigenous culture dominated by a multiplicity of other cultures. While it is an appro-priate political strategy for Aborigines to try to regain autonomy by asserting control over their own knowledge, it is, I think, a mistake to deny anyone else the right to speak of their knowledge at all. On the one hand, taken to an extreme such an attitude leads to cultural solips-ism and, on the other, it denies the possibility of comparing know-ledge traditions. Such comparisons constitute important political strategies for the deflation of the dominant knowledge tradition of science.

In the case of Pacific navigation it would be nice to be able to say quite straightforwardly, 'Pacific navigational knowledge belongs to those who have produced it and they have the right to control it as they see fit.' However, the issue is one of great complexity shot through with irony. The direct relationship between production and ownership no longer prevails, partly because of the destruction wrought by the introduction of Western modes of exchange, and partly by the deliberate suppression of the knowledge by colonial regimes.[1] Yet at the same time its revival has been due in large part to the work of Western anthropologists and the utilisation of Western techniques of replica voyaging. In addition, the knowledge is varied and localised, so the question of who has the right to speak of it is a very complex one. Equally problematically, if the full power of the knowledge is to be recognised it is not enough for it to be valued in its own right, it must also to be understood in a comparative context. Such comparisons would, of necessity, involve people other than the owners of the knowledge being able to speak of it. This chapter aims to provide both a comparison between Pacific navigation and other systems and to deconstruct the great divide between scientific and traditional knowledge systems, open and closed traditions, literate and oral traditions, mapping and non-mapping cultures, deliberate and accidental voyages, explorers and voyagers. Further elaboration of the content and ownership of Pacific navigation must include the Pacific Islanders and should be situated in the broader context of Pacific natural knowledge systems, but I would argue that important social and political insights are to be gained by establishing a dialogue between knowledge systems in general and modern science and Pacific navigational knowledge in particular.[2] Such a dialogue becomes possible when a relativistic and reflexive perspective permits us to see that Western commentators have frequently misunderstood Pacific navigation because they have construed it through the transparent and self-evident metaphor of map-like knowledge; it also allows us to see their commonality in contingent assemblage.

Undoing the Great Divide

The reconceptualisation of science as an assemblage of heterogeneous local practices as examined in Chapter 1, allows for the *unprivileging* of science and serves to undo the great divide between modern science and other knowledge systems. They are, at root, the same, because all knowledge is a local and contingent assemblage. It is this recognition that allows for the possibility of a full and equitable comparison between knowledge production systems. There are, of course, small but significant differences between knowledge systems, which differences lie principally in the methods that have been developed to handle the localness of knowledge. It is to the collective social work and technical devices that constitute those methods of moving and assembling local knowledge that we should look in our explanations of the similarities and differences between scientific traditions.

There has been considerable debate amongst analysts over whether there is one Pacific system of navigation or two (the Micronesian and the Polynesian), whether there is a variety of local systems based on island groups, and further, whether there is a significant difference between schools of navigation on particular islands.[3] The evidence seems to me to suggest that there are significant differences between the systems precisely because they are local in that they incorporate environmental knowledge specific to the region in which they operate. However, they all have a common feature suggestive of a common origin; the use of the rising and setting points of stars to name divisions of the horizon. Since this common feature is the main focus of the chapter, I shall use the term Pacific navigational systems without distinction and only specify a particular system when dealing with local variations, or when my sources do so.

Calculation v. Orientation

A basic methodological problem in understanding Pacific navigation is that Western analysts have worked backwards from what they take to be the fundamentals of navigation, that is chart-based dead reckoning, and have assumed that these fundamentals must have their equivalents in the Pacific system. This, I suggest, is due to their unexamined assumptions about the nature of information and how it can be stored, retrieved and manipulated. Western social and cultural solutions to these problems are so entrenched as to be invisible to us; consequently we assume them to be common to all knowledge systems. The misconstrual of Pacific navigation helps us to see Western science more clearly as an assemblage of local knowledge.

Such an assumption in the case of the Pacific navigation system is manifested in the seemingly self-evident claim that it is a system of dead reckoning. This is a consequence of our equation of scientific knowledge with measurement and calculation. The underlying assumption suggests that a coherent body of knowledge requires all items to be rendered in a form which makes them equivalent and hence connectable, an effect which can only be achieved through abstraction and mathematisation. Thus, we frequently take it to be necessary that in order for knowledge to be assembled into a coherent whole, analogue information has to be translated into digital data. That is to say, direct and incompatible experiences of time, length, direction and so on, have to be quantified or assigned numerical values in order to be assimilated or assembled.

However, in Pacific navigation there is no reckoning in the sense of calculation or manipulation of digits or abstract quantities. There is only reckoning in the analogue sense of integrating information, creating a pattern that connects, telling a story or having a mental map. Edwin Hutchins, in a persuasive analysis of Micronesian navigation which has the dialogical character I mentioned earlier, points out that:

> The tool box of the Western navigator contains scales and compass roses on charts, dividers, sextants and chronometers. These are all A/D and D/A converters. In our tradition, the operations of observation, computation, and interpretation are each a different sort of activity and they are executed serially. The Micronesian navigator's tool box is in his mind. There are no A/D or D/A converters because all the computations are analog. The interpretation of the result (bearing of the reference island for example) is embedded in the computation (construction of the horizon image) which itself is embedded in the observation (time of day).[4]

This construal of navigation as an abstract task of calculation is assumed by most commentators, of whom there have been a great many, whether they are ethnographers like Åkerblom and Goodenough, cognitive psychologists like Gladwin or practising navigators like Lewis and Thomas.[5] It has lead them to make the claim that the three main practical skills of the Pacific navigator are the ability: 1) to determine direction and maintain a course at sea; 2) to keep track of one's position by dead reckoning; and 3) to have a system of expanding the island target to augment the chance of successful landfall.[6] Thomas Gladwin, for example, in his classic work on the Pacific navigators, perceptively highlighted some important characteristics of the knowledge system. Their knowledge of the islands and star courses is like a map;[7] it is not an isolated system but an intimate part of 'a network of social, economic and often political ties';[8] and it is not merely practical, 'it adds a measure of meaning and value to every act, on land as well as at sea.'[9] Nonetheless despite his performative approach Gladwin concluded that Puluwat navigation is 'entirely a dead reckoning system' and 'depends upon the features of sea and sky which are characteristic of the locality in which it is used'.[10] By 'local' Gladwin means not only that the system depends on using knowledge and observations specific to an area, but also that the techniques employed are specific to a particular archipelago community. In the Marshall Islands for example they use wave interference patterns to maintain direction, whereas the Puluwatans do not.[11]

If the system is merely one of dead reckoning and local knowledge then it would seem, on Gladwin's account, to be severely constrained. This, however, stands in contradiction to his recognition that the core of the system is a dynamic cognitive map. It is this device that enables the system to move beyond the local and to integrate a wide range of heterogeneous information.

Many of our Western misunderstandings of how this is possible may result from the embeddedness of the concepts of maps and plans, something we have already noted in the case of the cathedrals. Lucy Suchman argues that:

> ... in Micronesian navigation nowhere is there a preconceived plan in evidence. The basis for navigation seems to be instead, local interactions with the environment. The Micronesian example demonstrates how the nature of an activity can be missed unless one views purposeful action as an interaction between a representation and the particular contingent details of the environment.[12]

She concludes that:

> The function of abstract representations is not to serve as specifications for the local interactions, but rather to orient or position us in a way that will allow us, through local interactions, to exploit some contingencies of our environment and avoid others.[13]

Thus Gladwin and others, whilst recognising the map-like character of the Pacific system, have seen the main task of the navigator as determining direction and calculating position rather than as orientation for action. They have conceived of the map as a chart for calculating rather than as a device for establishing connections. The basis of the dynamic cognitive map is the star compass, though compass is once again a misleading Western concept suggesting that the primary task is direction finding and course maintenance, rather than orientation and integration. The basic contradiction in Gladwin's claim that it is entirely a dead-reckoning system is revealed in his assertion that:

> Navigation by dead reckoning means that one's position at any time is determined solely on the basis of distance and direction travelled since leaving the last known location. Put the other way round it means that if

you lose track of how far you have come from where you were, you are lost. In contrast to this, Western celestial navigation, loran, and other techniques make it possible to establish a precise position without any knowledge of where you have been, except in the most general sense of knowing what part of the world you are in.[14]

Clearly if the Pacific navigators were totally dependent on calculating how far they had come in order to avoid being lost, the system would never have been able to accommodate all the setbacks of real ocean voyaging.

Star Compass and *Etak*—A Dynamic Cognitive Map

By designating named and identifiable points on the horizon, the star compass provides the framework or map within which the navigator is able to be continuously aware of his position. It does this by enabling the integration of information from a diverse range of sources which would otherwise be incommensurable. (see Fig. 25) The framework is one of conventional but invariant directions. It is by attributing directionality to all the heterogeneous inputs from the sun, stars, winds, waves, reefs, birds, weather, landmarks, seamarks and sealife, that the navigator is able to be constantly aware of his position and orientation:

> ... a practiced navigator can construct the whole compass mentally from a glimpse of only one or two stars near the horizon... the star compass is an abstraction which can be oriented as a whole by determining the orientation of any part.[15]

Establishing course direction is only a secondary function for the star compass, as Frake has argued in the case of its medieval equivalent, the compass rose.[16] Its primary function is one common to all early seafaring traditions and many other land-based knowledge systems such as those of the Anasazi, the Inca and the Australian Aborigines.[17] That function is to enable local, heterogeneous and asynchronous inputs to be become mobile and to be assembled into a coherent whole. The pattern that connects is not mathematical but directional; in effect, each of the inputs is given a directional analogue.

Most analysts have taken *etak* to be the heart of the system but in so doing have both misplaced it and misunderstood it. This results, once again, from their preoccupation with the primacy of calculation, from

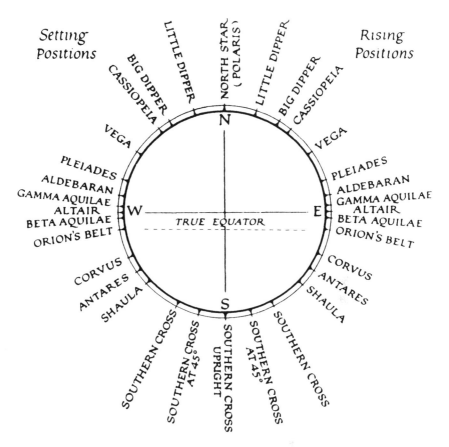

Figure 25 Star compass. By permission of the University of Pennsylvania Museum of Archaeology and Anthropology.

their conception of a cognitive map as a chart, and, according to Hutchins, from their assumptions about motion and voyages. Clearly the star compass alone is not enough for long-distance voyaging in the open ocean. A basic necessity for navigating in addition to establishing position and maintaining a course is to be able to compensate for the effects of current, drift, wind and speed. The Micronesian solution is *etak.* (see Fig. 26). On a given voyage between islands, an island to one side of the seaway is chosen as a reference point. These reference islands are part of the sailing directions learned by the apprentice navigator for each island passage. Given the mental map provided by the rising and setting points of the stars on the horizon it is possible for the navigator to mentally represent the voyage of his canoe against the line

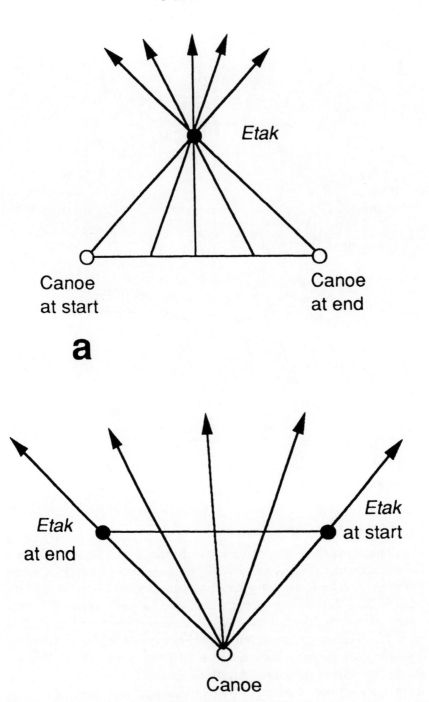

Figure 26 *Etak* according to Hutchins. E. Hutchins, 1996, *Cognition in the Wild*, Cambridge, Mass: MIT Press. With permission of MIT Press.

of the horizon and thence to break it up into conceptual segments. The navigator does this by conceiving his canoe to be stationary and the reference island as moving backwards against the backdrop of the rising and setting points of the stars. As the reference island moves from one such point to another, it completes a segment of the voyage. According to Lewis and Gladwin, 'etak provides a framework "into which the navigator's knowledge of rate, time, geography and astronomy can be integrated to provide a conveniently expressed and comprehended statement of distance travelled." It is a tool "for bringing together raw information and converting it into the solution of an essential navigational question, "How far away is our destination?"'[18]

Contrary to Gladwin and Lewis, Hutchins argues that our Western conceptual representation of a voyage is a bird's-eye view based on the calculation of distance, and as such differs fundamentally from the Micronesian concept of a voyage. He points out that for the Micronesian navigator the conceptual system is egocentric, which seems to fit the ethnographic account. For example, Thomas records Uurupa (a Micronesian navigator) describing etak:

> I keep the star paths in my head wherever I go, even now the paths run through the place where we sit, but I don't think about them very hard because I am on land and am safe. But at sea I have to think very hard. I keep the paths in mind even when we fish Wuligee reef. I don't have to think too hard of course because we can see the island, but I must be prepared in case we get caught in a storm.[19]

This means that the imagined star courses of etak meet at the canoe and not at the reference island as depicted by Lewis and Gladwin.

Just as Gladwin has difficulties reconciling the Western uniform distribution of compass points round the horizon with what seems to him to be sloppiness and irregularity in the Micronesian star compass, he also finds inconsistency in the differing lengths of the etak segments.[20] He is forced to conclude that,

> Although etak has for us much of the quality of a systematic organising principle or even a logical construct, the Puluwat navigator does not let logical consistency or inconsistency, insofar as he is aware of them, interfere with practical utility.[21]

Hutchins points out that this apparent problem results from taking etak segments as units of measurement:

The notion that consistent units of measurement are necessary for accurate navigation is very deeply ingrained in our cultural tradition. So much so in fact, that it is hard for us to conceive of a system of navigation that does not rely on such units and a set of operations for manipulating them. Yet there is no evidence in the record that the *etak* segments perform that function, nor is there any evidence of any set of mental arithmetic operations that would permit a navigator to manipulate *etak* segments as though they were units of distance.[22]

Hutchins claims that the *etak* segments are not units of distance but of temporal duration.

The concern of the navigator is not how far he travels in a particular *etak* segment, but how long he will travel before asserting that the reference island has moved back under the next star bearing.[23]

The apparent inconsistencies of the Micronesian system then drop out because the Micronesian navigator, like all experienced sailors, is able to estimate the speed of the canoe through direct sensory inputs like the sound of the hull in the water.

Whatever the result of this debate, which can only be resolved by the navigators themselves, the key point to recognise is that Micronesian navigation is based on a dynamic integrative conceptual framework. It enables the smooth meshing of the two conceptual devices, the star compass and *etak*, so that the learned body of knowledge of star courses and seamarks can be instantaneously summoned to the task of processing the observations of the moment. The total system forms a 'logical construct or cognitive map.'[24] The sophistication and complexity of this cognitive map is fully realised when the canoe is tacking against the wind requiring constant course changes as well as estimations of the effects of drift and current. Thus the system is more than a map in the Western sense; it is a dynamic spatial organisation of knowledge, but it is also a technical device, albeit a mental one, for assembling and moving local knowledge.

Navigation as Strategy

In addition, the system is also essentially strategic. It is strategic, firstly, in the fairly low-level sense that it deploys techniques for incorporating environmental clues. One such strategy is the technique of 'expanding the target'. Low islands can be easily missed; the target therefore is

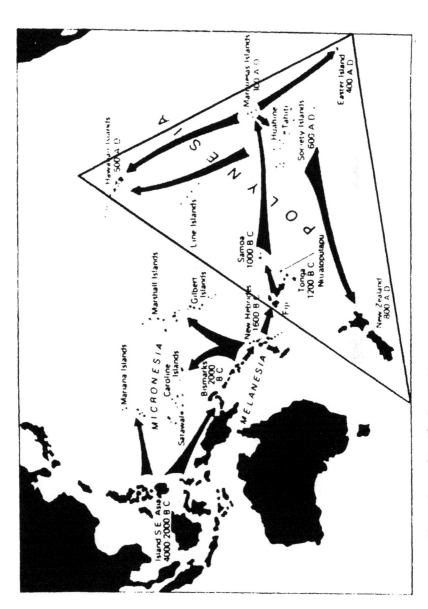

Figure 27 Chronology of Pacific Occupation.

expanded by looking for patterns of ocean swells, flights of birds, cloud formations and reflections on the undersides of clouds. The islands also happen to be in lines or 'chains' as a result of their formation at the edge of crustal plates, so the navigator can orient himself by intersecting a chain at any point.

Another, higher-level strategy is that outlined by Geoffrey Irwin. According to his model, the Pacific navigational system enables the discovery of unknown islands in a vast ocean by aiming to minimise wastage of resources, time and human life. He argues that this is best achieved by sailing against the wind and up the latitude on the outward journey, since it ensures an easy return journey. He claims that this strategy is confirmed

> ... by what we know of Pacific pre-history. The trajectory of earliest settlement is upwind. Melanesia was crossed and settlement pushed on to eastern Polynesia. Then it moved across the wind, and Hawaii is one example. Last of all it was downwind to New Zealand ... The model ... allows learning and requires it. The exploration of the remote Pacific was accompanied by expanding geographical knowledge and increasing navigational skill, especially as it probed the far reaches of Polynesia.[25]

Though this model requires further empirical testing, Irwin nonetheless makes a good case for believing that the 'first exploration of the Pacific was navigationally systematic'.[26] But, most importantly, he provides a performative perspective which portrays Pacific navigation as a set of open-ended practices or strategies for handling uncertainty in contrast to representational perspective of fixed techniques, rules or plans. (see Figs 27 and 28).

Discovery: Accidental or Deliberate?

The strongest manifestation of the great divide is the claim that the finding of the islands in the Pacific by the early voyagers was accidental, as opposed to the 'deliberate' discovery by the Europeans.[27] The Pacific Islanders, on this view, had only a 'traditional' knowledge system inadequate to the complex and difficult task of discovering the unknown whilst the scientific Europeans were able to plot a course and establish the position of unknown islands and were thus able to bring the knowledge back.

The 'deliberate'/'accidental' distinction, despite its constant articulation, is specious, since it would make nearly all discoveries accidental.

A more cogent requirement is the strategic ability to bring the knowledge back and thus enable two-way communication. The ability to make two-way voyages, and have some way of bringing the knowledge back, is the fundamental prerequisite for a knowledge system to transcend the 'merely' local. Two hundred years ago Captain Cook was the first to recognise that the people of the Pacific Islands, despite being scattered over a wide area, had a common culture and language and hence were of one nation.[28] Consequently he posed the question, 'How shall we account for this nation spreading itself so far over this Vast ocean?'[29] There is now a good deal of evidence from archaeology,

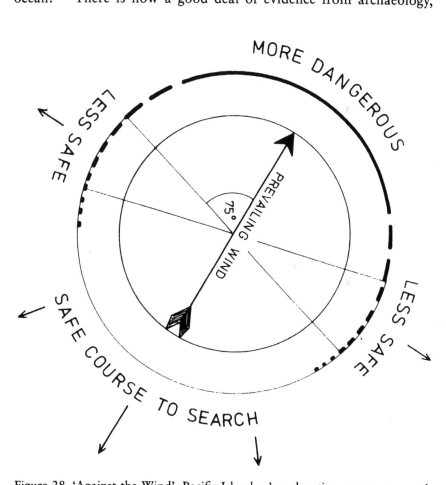

Figure 28 'Against the Wind'. Pacific Islanders' exploration strategy, according to Irwin. Irwin, G., *The Prehistoric Exploration and Colonisation of the Pacific,* Cambridge: Cambridge University Press, 1992. With permission of Cambridge University Press.

linguistics, anthropology, computer simulation of drifting, and experimental voyaging, to show that the Pacific was in fact colonised by people with a complex and common culture.[30] Such cultural integrity could not have been maintained if groups of islanders had drifted off accidentally, unable to return or communicate. Now we have the first archaeological evidence of two-way voyaging in this case: the bringing back of green obsidian flakes from Mayor Island off the coast of New Zealand to the Kermadec Islands, 1200 km to the north.[31] Taking this kind of evidence into account, and reconceiving the nature of the Pacific navigational system as I have discussed above, now makes their colonisation of the Pacific neither a mystery nor an accident but the consequence of the implementation of a sophisticated knowledge system, though a system that differs in important ways from the European one.

The seeming cogency of the opposition between accidental and deliberate discovery turns upon the concept being self-evident and unproblematic. That it is neither can be seen by a brief examination of the way it is handled within the Western knowledge tradition. Science itself is often equated in the lay mind with discoveries, and indeed for many scientists and science analysts, 'discovery is what science is all about'.[32] But what constitutes a discovery can be problematic. Columbus, for example, is said to have 'discovered America', despite the fact that there were American Indians already living there, despite strong evidence that the Basques and the Vikings had settlements there centuries before, and despite the fact that Columbus himself believed that he had found China. Clearly then, 'the discovery of America' is not a straight forward factual matter. It depends on who makes the claim and what sort of evidence they provide to whom in what circumstances—in other words 'discovery' is a retrospective social attribution. For the attribution to have been persuasive, Columbus or his representative had to return to Europe; indeed he had to return with evidence. More importantly, he had to come back with sufficient information to enable himself and others to do it again. The evidence would typically be in the form of documents and maps which would allow the information to be recorded and integrated with previous knowledge. It is this documentary character of scientific discovery that is taken to be one of the significant differences between Western science and Pacific navigation. However, as we have seen in the previous chapter, such an integrated system of knowledge can only be achieved with considerable amounts of social labour; much of the world was 'discovered' without such a system being established. Hence it would be a mistake to suppose that documents are an essential prerequisite to a knowledge system.

The complexities of 'scientific discovery' can be further pursued through a consideration of the arguments of those who hold the discovery of the Pacific Islands to be accidental. The chief proponent of this view was the historian Andrew Sharp.

> The early off-shore voyages of the Old World were in land-locked seas to extended coasts. Crude methods of navigation by the sun, stars, and wind direction were good enough for voyages of no great distance between extended coasts, because a landfall somewhere or other was assured, even if the precise destination was missed. The voyagers could thus maintain a broad course by bearings in relation to the east-west paths of the stars and sun and their rising and setting points, and the north bearing of the Pole star. When they came in sight of the coast, which they could not miss, they could pick their way along it. Ocean islands which are more than 300 miles from the continents or from one another were in an entirely different class. There was no way of finding they existed by crossing between coasts as in land-locked seas and gulfs. The idea of systematic exploration involves the presumption that explorers were prepared to go twice as far as any island they happened to find, and to do so many times without success, for an explorer cannot hope to find new land more than very occasionally, if at all. Above all, unless one can fix the position of the island one finds, and plot a course from it and back to it again, two-way contact is not established.[33]
> ... all the distant ocean islands in the world must have been discovered in the first place by accident, and not by deliberate navigation to those islands. Navigation implies that the existence and location of one's objective is known, and a course set for it. Unless and until the objective has been discovered, navigation is not an issue ... in the case of New Zealand, Hawaii and the other detached Polynesian islands, the prehistoric discoverers had no way of gaining the knowledge necessary for navigation back to their home islands. It will follow that the settlement of these detached islands was contemporaneous with their discovery.[34]

The clear implication of Sharp's remarks is that Pacific navigation is inadequate to the task of deliberate discovery. He pre-empts the argument by claiming that 'all islands must have been discovered by accident in the first place.' Further, he fails to concede to open ocean navigation the strategic approach he allows for land-locked seas. In this he not only undervalues the skills of the Norse and medieval navigators as well as those of the Pacific Islanders, but misses the strategic and performative character of all discovery and navigation.

Discovery in science is seldom purely accidental or purely deliberate. For a discovery to be deliberate in the full sense it would have to be the predicted outcome of a rigorous set of deductions. However, since all the results of science are in some measure equivocal and hence subject to community agreement and negotiation, such deliberateness is ultimately unobtainable. Equally, the truly accidental can have no place since at the very least the scientist has to be able to perceive the connection between the fortuitous accident and the anticipated outcome. In the words of the old adage, 'fortune favours the prepared mind'.

A classic example of an apparently deliberate discovery was Adams' and Leverrier's prediction of the existence of Neptune prior to its observation.[35] This has often been celebrated as a great confirmation of Newton's laws and of the predictive power of modern physics. Adams and Leverrier postulated the existence of the unknown planet in order to explain the perturbations in the orbit of Uranus. However, in their calculations they used Bode's law, a purely arithmetic rule relating the distances of the planets, leading them to assume too large a distance and hence a correspondingly greater mass for the planet. Despite having got the distance and mass wrong, the planet was observed by telescope in the predicted position in the night sky because Adams and Leverrier got the longitude or direction right. Whether or not this constituted an accidental or deliberate discovery is thus open to debate; such distinctions are clearly arbitrary.

Sharp reached his negative conclusions and had them widely accepted, despite presenting no evidence, perhaps because certain presuppositions about the nature of navigation and discovery were taken as self-evident both by him and by subsequent analysts. Lewis, for example, in describing his own re-enactment of the Pacific voyages, points out that:

> Following a sun course as we did, like using any other kind of sailing directions, implies that someone has not only found the destination, but returned home with a report of bearings and distance that would enable others to reach it too. Modern test voyages cannot, therefore, throw any navigational light on original discovery. This must always be a largely accidental event, since the most an explorer could have to suggest the existence and bearing of an unknown land would be the clues afforded by drifting objects, migratory bird flight paths, and the like.[36]

Lewis is correct in arguing that modern voyages cannot repeat the original circumstances of discovery where the destination is completely unknown, a difficulty which reflects a degree of circularity inherent in the notion of replication; what counts as replication cannot become settled until it is agreed that the phenomena exist and what the relevant conditions are.[37] Lewis over-emphasises the accidental by comparing return voyages made in full knowledge of the island's position with the initial voyage supposedly made in ignorance, thereby repeating Sharp's failure to acknowledge the strategic character of all voyages of discovery.

Nonetheless, the performance of a replication can be an extremely powerful form of experiment, as is clearly illustrated by what was to become a very important event in the rebirth of Hawaiian cultural knowledge. In 1976 the Hokule'a was built as a replica 19-metre double canoe; it sailed from Hawaii to Tahiti and back, navigated by the Carolinian navigator Mau Piailug, even though he had no personal familiarity with the route. Mau had briefings on the local geography, sailing conditions and changing skies, which he was able to integrate with his cognitive map; he was completely successful in applying his navigational techniques in what were for him new circumstances. The voyage was repeated, with Mau keeping a watching brief, in 1980, by the Hawaiian navigator Nainoa Thompson, who had to learn to navigate from scratch. He did it by reading Western books on Pacific navigation, using the planetarium at Honolulu's Bishop Museum, and by working with Mau. (The synergy between the knowledge incorporated in the planetarium and Mau's Micronesian knowledge is an interesting instance of the lack of any true divide.) Nainoa succeeded in learning all the star rising and setting positions but had grave doubts he would ever learn to apply the *etak* system successfully and developed his own method of dead-reckoning. Nainoa was able to complete the voyage using non instrumental methods across thousands of miles of open ocean, coping with current changes, variable winds, and the doldrums. Furthermore, the plot of his own estimated position and the actual track of the Hokule'a demonstrate a high degree of accuracy. Interestingly, Finney, in his analysis of the voyage, also found that Nainoa's methods were not solely rule-bound but involved 'intuitive responses based on experience', suggesting that formalistic approaches to knowledge and understanding are inadequate in so far as they omit the tacit, experiential, intuitive and the holistic.[38]

In 1985–6 the Hokule'a sailed again from Hawaii to Tahiti and then to the Cook Islands, New Zealand and Fiji, finally demonstrating that return voyages to all the Pacific islands were within the capacity of the Pacific navigators. This reconstruction of Hawaiian navigational knowledge has brought about a general cultural revival dubbed the 'Hawaiian Renaissance', an instance of a subjugated knowledge fighting back.

Open or Closed?

Another classic exemplification of the great divide between scientific and traditional knowledge is Gladwin's claim that the system is closed and non-innovative. This is especially contentious in that it seems to stand counter to his own account, and is certainly contradicted by the voyage of the Hokule'a. Hence it may indicate that Gladwin has some hidden assumptions about the distinction between Pacific and Western navigation in particular, and other knowledge systems generally.

While it is the case that there are differing schools of navigation in the Carolines and differing techniques across the Pacific, it seems quite clear that the system developed historically from one basic navigational approach. Whatever your view on accidental and deliberate voyaging, there is little reason to deny that Pacific navigators developed and created new techniques and knowledge to accommodate the new circumstances encountered as they spread out across the world's largest ocean. Gladwin however concludes that 'there is no occasion to seek new techniques or strategies or to question the system as it stands. It works, and if at any time it does not work it is not the fault of the system.'[39] Such conservatism is typical of Western navigation. It is also typical, as Kuhn has noted, of science. When a scientist is working within a paradigm in the global sense, what is on trial is not the theory but the practitioner. The necessity to ensure that a body of knowledge is maintained and transmitted intact on the one hand, and on the other that innovation takes place, produces what Kuhn has called 'the essential tension'[40]. Arguably there is a greater requirement for conservatism in an oral tradition to ensure effective transmission, but that conservatism or closedness does not of necessity preclude change any more than it does in Western science.

Canoes—The Key Technological Device

Pacific navigation has a strong theoretical component, just as it has a strong tacit component embodying a wide range of unverbalised skills. But most importantly, navigation is inseparable from all the other aspects of Pacific island life—canoe-building, fishing, economics, politics and religion. Navigation is nothing without canoe-building, which in itself is a highly developed and complex technology requiring great skill.[41] The canoes of the Pacific islanders are remarkably effective machines for oceanic voyaging. (see Fig. 29) They are capable of riding

Figure 29 Puluwatan canoe. With permission of David Lewis.

out the fiercest storms and of enduring the racking strains of continuous pounding by the wind and waves. They are light and shallow-
drafted, capable of being handled in the tricky waters of lagoons and
reefs, while also able to carry large numbers of people and goods over
long distances. The component parts of their construction are of considerable sophistication, despite their slightly ramshackle appearance.
The hulls are shaped asymmetrically for maximum speed and ease of
handling. The sides of the canoes are sown together as smooth, individually cut planks and sealed with coconut paste, enabling them to be
stripped down and reassembled as they age. All the ropes and sails are
made from parts of the coconut palm, the whole process requiring the
integrated activity of most of the men on the islands. The complete
technology of canoe-building, its development and transmission over
time was, like the navigational knowledge, achieved without the benefit
of measurement or plans. Yet it shows systematic development in
response to the demands of long-distance ocean sailing and local conditions. The full story of the evolution of Pacific canoe design has yet
to be written, but suffice it to say that the five basic types are a unique
and sophisticated response to the problems of stability and steerability
that differ radically from those adopted in the West.[42] Without a technology that provided very strong probability of a successful return
voyage in unknown and diverse conditions, there could not have been
any colonisation of the Pacific. Clearly the technology and the navigational system were far from closed, but were developed and adapted
together as the Islanders spread across the Pacific.

The Pacific knowledge tradition is not limited to matters concerned
with canoe construction and navigation. The understanding and
detailed knowledge of the environment is immense. In the case of fish
taxonomies and behaviour, for example, 'the native [Tahitian]
fisherman is possessed of a store of precise knowledge that may be
truly characterised as a natural science'.[43] The Palauans also have a
vast store of sophisticated knowledge about fish. They understand their
breeding cycles, their rhythmic behaviours and how they correlate with
lunar cycles, and have a variety of strategies for both catching and con-
serving the fish. Until recently much of this knowledge was unknown
to Western science. To treat navigation as an isolated body of knowledge is to miss the 'life world' of the islanders, in which everyone
makes a contribution to navigation because it is an intimate part of
their social and economic activities, inextricably interwoven with
meaning and power. It is also to miss the capacity of the system to be
both local and open.

Writing Reconsidered

Jack Goody in *The Domestication of the Savage Mind*, was one of the first analysts to deny the notion of a great divide representing a fundamental difference between 'primitive' and 'advanced' societies. He allowed that there is a difference, but attributed it to the 'effects of changes in the mode and means of communication'.[44] Thus such dichotomies as primitive/advanced, savage/domesticated, traditional/ modern, closed/open, developing/developed, pre-logical/logical, neolithic/ modern, concrete/abstract, magic/science, bricolage/engineering, myth/history, which have been typically used to characterise the Great Divide should, he argues, be explained or replaced by the oral/literate dichotomy. Goody claims that 'the shifts to writing and then to print must be considered of critical importance in both formalising and increasing the flow of information that has been a precondition of many of the features that differentiate the prehistoric societies of the Neolithic and Palaeolithic from the 'modern' civilisations that followed.'[45] But it also crucially changes the kind of thinking and the kind of knowledge that is possible. 'Writing puts a distance between man and his verbal acts. He can now examine what he says in a more objective manner'. Writing accounts for the difference between the open and closed, between the rational and traditional, because it 'permits a different kind of scrutiny of current knowledge'.[46] 'Writing enables you to talk freely about your thoughts.'[47] Writing allows for lists, formulae, classification, record keeping, recipes, logic and formal texts of instruction.

Thus, according to Goody, 'Traditional societies are marked not so much by the absence of reflective thinking as by the absence of the proper tools for constructive rumination.'[48] This is because 'words assume a different relationship to action and to object when they are on paper than when they are spoken. They are no longer bound up directly with 'reality'; the written word becomes a separate 'thing', abstracted to some extent from the flow of speech, shedding its close entailment with action, with power over matter.'[49]

However, it can be argued that Goody assumes in his account that literacy is autonomous, that it will take on it its own structure and significance no matter what the circumstances of its introduction. Historically there are examples where this has not been the case. For example, in medieval England, when written records of land transactions were first introduced, it was far from self-evident that they would be prime guarantors of 'truth' and 'legitimacy'. Many people at the time felt little confidence in written records since they could be subject to forgery. Such people set far greater store by seals and the oral testimony of 'twelve good men and true'. In order to succeed, those groups with an interest in centralisation had to deliberately construct a 'literate mentality'. Literacy could not bring this transition about by itself.[50]

We have already noted a similar transformation in the nature of testimony in the early development of scientific experimentation in Robert Boyle's work on the vacuum pump in the seventeenth century. Shapin and Schaffer have shown that Boyle had to develop a literary technology as a condition for the acceptance of experimental results. 'Experimental reports rich in circumstantial detail were designed to enable readers of the text to create a mental image of an experimental scene they did not actually witness.' The historian of science Steven Shapin calls this process 'virtual witnessing'. 'Its importance was as a means of enlarging the witnessing public. The notion of a "public" for experimental science [he argues] is essential to our understanding of how facts are generated and validated. In these episodes, circumstantial reporting was a technique for creating a public and for constituting authentic knowledge.'[51] The establishment of the authority and credibility of experimental knowledge in the seventeenth century shows that literacy or writing or record-keeping, rather than being an essential precondition for advanced, theoretical, scientific, modern, critical thinking and knowledge, were instead specific forms of literacy coproduced with experimental science that have now come to be taken for granted.

So the question becomes, what sort of devices and techniques are necessary for the preservation and transmission of knowledge in an oral culture? Several characteristics emerge as central to the organisation of the knowledge involved in Pacific navigation. It is heavily dependent on metaphors, narratives, redundancy, concrete models and communal interaction.[52] It is also consciously reflective on the process of preservation and transmission, and therefore much more than a body of rote lore and ritual.

In coming to understand the operations of the organised body of knowledge that constitutes Pacific navigation we can readily discern its inherently spatial character. It not only embodies knowledge of the spatial relations of the islands of the Pacific but, like all knowledge systems, it is also a spatial system in the sense that it has an architecture or structure. The elements of the system are accessed through a dynamic three-dimensional matrix, as well as being set or boxed within one another. There is a sense in which all knowing is like travelling, like a journey between parts of the matrix. Connecting spatially or cognitively distinct and distant elements is a function of metaphor which allows narratives to be seen as journeys and journeys as narratives. Metaphors are therefore the spatial component that enables one to travel through knowledge.

Knowledge Transmission and Access

There are two major problems involved in the learning and use of a complex body of oral knowledge like that of Pacific navigation. The first is the development of techniques to ensure that the vast body of detailed data is accurately retained and passed on over generations. The second is that the body of data must be instantly accessible to the user. It would be of no assistance to the navigator if he had to work through lists of items to get to the desired item. He must be able to access instantly any part of the system. The first problem is solved in the variety of ways described by Farrall, and Goodenough and Thomas, i.e., encoding the knowledge in songs and ritual, having group learning and testing sessions, using mnemonics, having overlapping and redundant ways of connecting the knowledge and constructing material models of the systems, like stick charts and stone arrangements.[53] (see Fig. 30) The second problem is of course largely resolved through constant repetition and practice until the knowledge becomes completely tacit—an unreflective skill. One of the most important components of this tacit knowledge or skill is the navigator's constant awareness of where he is on, or more precisely in, his cognitive map. Significantly, one of the most effective ways in which the navigator achieves that awareness is through the use of metaphor. The sailing exercises of 'Coral Hole Stirring' and 'Breadfruit Picker Lashing' that Goodenough and Thomas describe are examples of the way metaphors can allow mental journeys through the knowledge structure or of how disparate pieces of information can be connected into a meaningful story or narrative. (see Fig. 31)

Narrative structure and use of metaphor are not however defining characteristics of oral knowledge: they are in fact characteristics of all knowledge, including Western science. The key characteristic that is supposed to distinguish oral and written knowledge is permanence. The written record endures over time. This is a profoundly important feature of written knowledge, for it permits, as Latour points out, the accumulation of data at a centre and the transmission of knowledge

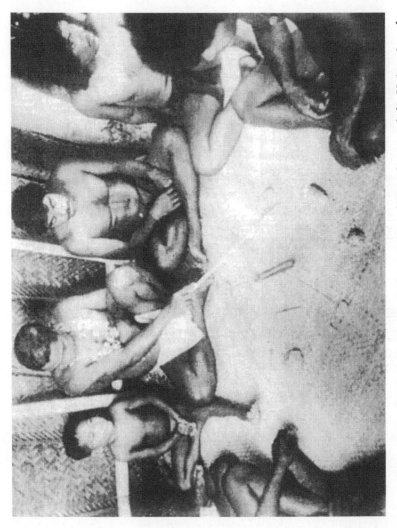

Figure 30 'Teaching the Star Compass'. By permission of *Expedition* and the University of Pennsylvania Museum of Archaeology and Anthropology.

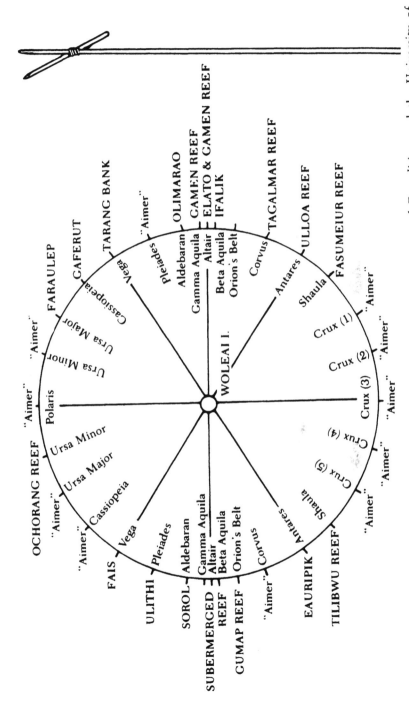

Figure 31 'Breadfruit Picker Lashing' and 'Island Seeing' exercise. By permission of *Expedition* and the University of Pennsylvania Museum of Archaeology and Anthropology.

across space and time. It also allows for criticism and analysis, just as Goody claims. It is, however, salutary to recognise that this distinction is frequently overdrawn.

Pacific navigation is an example of a body of knowledge that has achieved a high degree of permanence. Arguably, this derives jointly from its coherence as a body of knowledge melding into a cognitive map and from its centrality in the life world of the islanders. Once that life world starts to change or break down, the knowledge also becomes destabilised. But one must question how permanent Western science is in that sense. While the records have some permanency, their meaning and significance is dependent on social structures to sustain them. Should the way in which science is taught and reproduced undergo radical transformation that apparent permanency will also evaporate. Science is not autonomous; it has depended on a particular conjunction of political, economic and historical forces which have not prevailed at all times and in all places and may therefore cease at some future time and place. In other words both modern science and Pacific navigation are dependent on tradition for their successful transmission through time and space.

In the Pacific case that tradition or 'talk of the sea', as Stephen Thomas translates it, is obviously a very complex and difficult body of knowledge to master, and is now in grave danger of vanishing because so few are willing to make the life-long commitment to learning it.[54] The existence of the knowledge is crucially dependent on its transmission from the older to the younger generation of men. Written knowledge can have at least some possibility of continued existence independent of being taught, because it can be deposited in texts. Pacific navigation depends on the maintenance of a society that values the knowledge sufficiently for the young men to willingly spend their evenings listening to their elders, singing songs, making rope, or talking of the sea, and their days endlessly learning and practising.

The web of social, economic and political relations that provide for such a valuation of navigational knowledge is quite powerful but not indestructible. Until recently it was the case that, 'The masters of Puluwat are its navigators.'[55] This was in large part because, as Gladwin has shown, the Micronesian islands 'have been linked by their seafaring men and their sailing canoes into a network of social, economic and often political ties without which they probably could not have survived, much less evolved the complex and secure way of life they now enjoy.'[56] But now, twenty-five years after Gladwin found navigation to be flourishing despite the lack, even then, of a practical rationale, the only hope for its survival seems to be as part of the political struggle for autonomy and identity. The power of money as the means of exchange, the decline of fishing, the use of canned food, alcohol, religion, outboard motors, videos, ferry services and tourists have inevitably proved irresistible. The young Pacific Islanders of today no longer regard navigational knowledge as inherently valuable, as the source of meaning and power in their society. As long as everyone saw navigational knowledge as central to their lives, as long as the navigators were the masters—not in the political sense, but as repositories of the knowledge—then it could be the ground of all value in their society. The introduction of another source of value, which has become the means of exchange for highly desirable goods produced outside the society, and which is linked to an education system that demands the acquisition of a completely different but equally complex body of knowledge, seems likely to mark the demise of the former independent and unique knowledge system. The best hope for the survival of the tradition now lies in the new-found recognition of local knowledge and in the renaissance generated by the replica voyages.[57] However, neither of these factors should be isolated from the wider political context of struggles for autonomy, land rights and intellectual property rights on the one hand, and Western cultural and economic domination on the other.

The foregoing account of the social strategies and technical devices for moving and assembling knowledge in Pacific navigation has to be seen in conjunction with the parallel account of knowledge assemblage in the previous chapter, which discusses the establishment of the knowledge space that provides for scientific cartography. Their commonality in contingent processes of assemblage has great importance for both traditions. Modern science has become all too dominant and is producing as many disadvantages as benefits; although an understanding of the social work that underlies its universality should provide possible sites for resistance, for its being other than it is. On the other side of the dialogue, Pacific navigation in particular and island culture generally, are in danger of extinction. If instead of trying to archive Pacific Island knowledge within the corpus of Western knowledge, some of the hidden components of both knowledge systems could be enabled to work together in a third space then there may be, if not a Pacific Renaissance, at least cultural survival. The possibilities of working knowledge systems together are taken up in the Conclusion.

Notes

1 David Turnbull, *Mapping the World in the Mind: An Investigation of the Unwritten Knowledge of the Micronesian Navigators*, (Geelong: Deakin University Press, 1991), p. 3.

2 The sort of dialogue I have in mind is that advocated by so-called dialogical anthropology, of which Anne Salmond's, *Two Worlds: First Meetings Between Maori and Europeans 1642–1772*, (Auckland: Penguin Books, 1991) can be seen as an example, where she enables Maori texts to interrogate and re-evaluate the white accounts of first contact. See also Pam Colorado, 'Bridging Native and Western Science', *Convergence*, Vol. xxi, 2/3, (1988), pp. 49–72. As Lincoln and Slagle put it in the rather awkward way typical of difficult first steps, 'Present tense intercultural understanding is thus a question of granting the *not*-other "other" a voice and place among us ... that is, we can allow the distinctions between cultures to serve positively in our dialogues, and at the same time we can consciously *not* project the exotic "other" across the distances, K. Lincoln and A. Slagle, *The Good Red Road; Passages into North America*, (San Francisco: Harper and Row, 1983), p. xvi.

3 See for example, W. H. Alkire, 'Systems of Measurement on Woleai Atoll, Caroline Islands', *Anthropos*, Vol. 65, (1970), pp. 1–73, and David Lewis, 'Voyaging Stars: Aspects of Polynesian and Micronesian Astronomy', in F. F. Hodson, ed., *The Place of Astronomy in the Ancient World*, (London: Oxford University Press, 1974), pp. 133–48.

4 Edwin Hutchins, 'Understanding Micronesian Navigation', in D. Gentner and A. L. Stevens, eds., *Mental Models*, (New Jersey: Lawrence Erlbaum Associates, 1983), pp. 191–226, p. 223.

5 Kjell Åkerblom, *Astronomy and Navigation in Polynesia and Micronesia: A Survey*, (Stockholm: Ethnographical Museum, 1968); Thomas Gladwin, *East Is a Big Bird: Navigation and Logic on Puluwat*, (Cambridge, Mass: Harvard University Press, 1970); Ward Goodenough, 'Navigation in the Western Carolines', in L. Nader, ed., *Naked Science: Anthropological Inquiry into Boundaries, Power and Knowledge*, (New York: Routledge, 1996), pp. 29–42; Ward H. Goodenough, *Native Astronomy in the Central Carolines*, (Philadelphia: University of Pennsylvania, 1953); David Lewis, *We the Navigators: The Ancient Art of Landfinding in the Pacific*, (Honolulu: University of Hawaii Press, 1994); Stephen D. Thomas, *The Last Navigator*, (New York: Ballantine Books, 1988).

6 For example Gladwin, *East Is a Big Bird*, p. 147.

7 Ibid, p. 34.

8 Ibid, p. 35.

9 Ibid.

10 Ibid, p. 144.

11 Lewis, *We the Navigators*, p. 161.

[12] Lucy Suchman, *Plans and Situated Actions: The Problem of Human-Machine Communication*, (Cambridge: Cambridge University Press, 1987).

[13] Ibid, p. 188.

[14] Gladwin, *East Is a Big Bird*, p. 144.

[15] Hutchins, 'Understanding Micronesian Navigation', p. 195.

[16] Charles O. Frake, 'Cognitive Maps of Time and Tide Among Medieval Seafarers', *Man*, Vol. 20, (1985), pp. 254–70.

[17] Ibid, p. 262 and see Chapter 1.

[18] Lewis, *We the Navigators*, p. 138 and Gladwin, *East Is a Big Bird*, p. 186.

[19] Thomas, *The Last Navigator*, p. 82.

[20] Gladwin, *East Is a Big Bird*, p. 151.

[21] Ibid, p. 189.

[22] Hutchins, 'Understanding Micronesian Navigation', p. 205.

[23] Ibid, p. 214.

[24] Gladwin, *East Is a Big Bird*, p. 181.

[25] Geoffrey Irwin, 'Against, Across and Down the Wind: A Case for the Systematic Exploration of the Remote Pacific Islands', *Journal of the Polynesian Society*, Vol. 98, (1989), pp. 167–206, p. 175.

[26] Ibid, p. 167.

[27] Andrew Sharp, *Ancient Voyagers in Polynesia*, (Sydney: Angus and Robertson, 1963).

[28] Ben Finney, *Voyage of Rediscovery: A Cultural Odyssey Through Polynesia*, (Berkley: University of California Press, 1994), p. 7.

[29] J. C. Beaglehole, ed., *The Voyage of the Resolution and Discovery 1776–1780 Part One*, (Cambridge: Cambridge University Press, 1967), p. cxviii.

[30] Geoffrey Irwin, *The Prehistoric Exploration and Colonisation of the Pacific*, (Cambridge: Cambridge University Press, 1992).

[31] Atholl Anderson and Bruce McFadgen, 'Prehistoric Two-way Voyaging', *Archaeology in Oceania*, Vol. 25, April, (1990), pp. 37–42.

[32] Augustine Brannigan, *The Social Basis of Scientific Discoveries*, (Cambridge: Cambridge University Press, 1981), p. 1 citing Hanson.

[33] Sharp, *Ancient Voyagers in Polynesia*, p. 17.

[34] Ibid, p. 33.

[35] Norwood Russell Hanson, *Patterns of Discovery: An Inquiry into the Conceptual Foundations of Science*, (Cambridge: Cambridge University Press, 1958). Greg Banford, 'Popper and His Commentators on the Discovery of Neptune: A Close Shave for the Law of Gravitation?', *BJHS (British Journal for the History of Science)*, Vol. 27, 2, (1996), pp. 207–233.

[36] Lewis, *We the Navigators*, p. 4.

[37] Collins, *Changing Order*.

[38] Ben Finney, *Hokule'a: The Way to Tahiti*, (New York: Dodd, Mead and Co., 1979), p. 47.

39 Gladwin, *East Is a Big Bird*, p. 204.

40 Kuhn, *The Essential Tension*.

41 W. H. Alkire, 'Systems of Measurement on Woleai Atoll, Caroline Islands', *Anthropos*, Vol. 65, (1970), pp. 1–73.

42 The best account to date is that of Edwin Doran, *Wangka: Austronesian Canoe Origins*, (College Station: Texas A&M University Press, 1981) who has actually done the hard work of assessing their seaworthiness.

43 R. E. Johannes, *Words of the Lagoon: Fishing and Marine Lore in the Palau District of Micronesia*, (Berkeley: University of California Press, 1981), p. viii quoting Handy 1932.

44 Jack Goody, *The Domestication of the Savage Mind*, (Cambridge: Cambridge University Press, 1977), pp. 146ff.

45 Ibid, p. 148.

46 Ibid, p. 150.

47 Ibid, p. 159.

48 Ibid, p. 44.

49 Ibid, p. 46.

50 Brian V. Street, *Literacy in Theory and Practice*, (Cambridge: Cambridge University Press, 1984), pp. 68ff.

51 Steven Shapin, 'Pump and Circumstance', pp. 481–520.

52 Lyndsay Farrall, 'Knowledge and its Preservation in Oral Cultures', in D. Denoon and R. Lacey, eds., *Oral Traditions in Melanesia*, (Port Moresby: Institute of Papua New Guinea Studies, 1981), pp. 71–86.

53 W. Goodenough and S. D. Thomas, 'Traditional Navigation in the Western Pacific: A Search for Pattern', *Expedition* (Published as a pamphlet by the University of Pennsylvania Museum of Archaeology/Anthropology, Philadelphia PA.), Vol. 30, (nd), pp. 4–7.

54 Thomas, *The Last Navigator*.

55 Gladwin, *East Is a Big Bird,* p. 125.

56 Ibid, p. 30.

57 On the recognition of the value of local knowledge in development and the attendant analytical difficulties see Arun Agrawal, 'Dismantling the Divide Between Indigenous and Scientific Knowledge', *Development and Change*, Vol. 26, 3, (1995), pp. 413–439.

5 MAKING MALARIA CURABLE: EXTENDING A KNOWLEDGE SPACE TO CREATE A VACCINE

Earlier chapters focused on the ways in which local knowledge is assembled and the differing kinds of knowledge space that are produced in other eras and cultures. In this chapter I want to look at what is involved in an attempt to create a knowledge space beyond the laboratory. The case in question is a particular attempt to develop a malaria vaccine. As the story unfolds it will become apparent that the value of a vaccine-based approach to combating malaria is contestable, and may work to the disadvantage of some malaria sufferers. This raises very profound questions about the value of this kind of knowledge space and points to its political and moral components. It will also become apparent that a fundamental social strategy in the establishment of a knowledge space is the disciplining of all the actors involved—scientists, malaria sufferers, mosquitos and parasites of all varieties.

This account arises from a visit I made to Papua New Guinea in 1986 as part of an anthropological study of the Walter and Eliza Hall Institute of Medical Research (WEHIMR) in Melbourne.[1] The immunoparasitology unit, one of the most prominent laboratories at the Walter and Eliza Hall, was engaged in a collaborative research effort to develop a malaria vaccine in conjunction with the Institute of Medical Research in Papua New Guinea (PNGIMR), the Queensland Institute of Medical Research (QIMR), the University of Newcastle, Concord Hospital Sydney and the Australian National University.

The starting point of the story was the visit by a team from the United States Agency for International Development (USAID) to Papua New Guinea in 1986. The team's task was to visit half a dozen sites around the world in order to select two that would be suitable for a 'phase three' trial of a malaria vaccine developed by Ruth Nussenzweig's group at New York University's Center for Vaccine Research. 'Phase one' trials test for harmful effects and the ability to produce antibody formation. 'Phase two' trials test for efficacy in immunologically naive individuals. These trials had already taken place using animal models and human volunteers in the USA. The 'phase two' trials were not in fact successful, but had they been so, 'phase three' trials would have begun. It was intended that these trials would constitute the first full-scale attempt to find out whether a malaria vaccine will work in individuals living in a region where malaria is endemic. The scientific and medical significance of such an undertaking would appear obvious, especially when the vaccine produced would be the first against a human parasite, but become less so when looked at from the vantage point of New Guinea, where some basic questions about a malaria vaccine come into focus. Why is there such a push to develop a vaccine? Will it actually help malaria sufferers in the endemic regions? Are there any other approaches to the treatment and elimination of malaria? Is there any local knowledge about malaria treatment? These sorts of questions should always be raised about any scientific or technological development, but they are particularly important when the development is one proposed by the 'First World' for the benefit of the 'Third World'. Such technological 'advances', like the 'green revolution', have often worked to the disadvantage of the poor, or have ignored local knowledge and local social and economic variables, as is evidenced by the failure of the program to eradicate malaria using DDT,[2] the intransigence of schistosomiasis,[3] and the total ineffectiveness in Africa of the vaccine against TB.[4] The world-wide elimination of smallpox is often heralded as the great triumph for vaccination, but smallpox has so far proved to be fundamentally different from malaria, schistosomiasis, and TB in its specificity and variability. Humans are its only host; consequently it is more readily amenable to a laboratory-generated solution and the kind of discipline required is sustainable.

Disciplining the Definition

Malaria is also unlike smallpox in its complex heterogeneity. As a disease, malaria is a classic example of a motley. It is 'a term relating to a ragbag of different strains of the parasite' and of interacting processes.[5] Yet, within the knowledge space of Western laboratory science, malaria is made to appear as a natural entity in the world, it is embedded in a conceptual framework which portrays the discovery and elucidation of its causes as occurring within the gradual unfolding of an emanant scientific logic, which will culminate in a physico-chemical solution to the malaria problem. How malaria is conceived and defined creates different kinds of spaces and vice versa.[6] The definition of malaria that provides for the possibility of a vaccine, is one which focuses on the plasmodium parasite as its cause. But even at this technical level there is room for radically different definitions and approaches. There are, for example, frequent cases of people who have malaria parasites, but who do not have malaria. Their condition is supposedly explained by the argument that the fever is caused by the release of interleukin-1 from macrophages. Such cells can apparently learn to tolerate the stimuli for release; thus the disease is held to be mediated by the host's cells and not by the parasite.[7] Chemotherapy takes another approach and concentrates on producing drugs to kill the parasite in the blood.[8]

On the immunoparasitological account, malaria is caused by a parasite with four major species: *Plasmodium falciparum, vivax, ovale*, and *malariae*. Of these, *falciparum* and *vivax* are the most common and *falciparum* the most lethal. There are three major stages in the life cycle of the parasite: the *sporozoite* stage, where the parasite enters the host's blood by way of the saliva of a biting female anophelene mosquito, and makes very rapidly for the liver; the *merozoite* stage, during which the parasite multiplies and invades the red blood cells, periodically bursting them and releasing toxins which cause the high temperatures usually equated with having malaria; and the *gametocyte* stage, where some of the merozoites divide into male and female preparatory to being taken by the mosquito again and breeding in its gut.[9] At each of these stages the host's resistance to infection is thought to be mediated by antibodies produced by the immune system in response to the parasite's antigens.[10] (see Fig. 32).

In this way malaria can be seen as a natural entity uniquely specifiable as the consequence of parasitic invasion. But it can also be conceived as the interaction of a complex set of processes. Representing it as an interaction of processes enables the constitution of the disease itself to be seen as a social process of selective definition.[11] Historically, the participants in malaria research who have taken the broadest, most inclusive definition of malaria as their disciplinary starting point have been the malariologists. From the malariological perspective, malaria is better understood not as a uniquely specifiable phenomenon, but as an interaction between three factors: the human host, the mosquito vector and the malaria parasite manifested in a particular locale and time.[12] In turn, each of these factors embraces a further set of sub-factors, although perhaps even this definition is too specific in that it depends on some possibly unwarranted assumptions. Could humans be better described as the vector and the mosquito as the host, given that malaria kills human beings? Notwithstanding, a

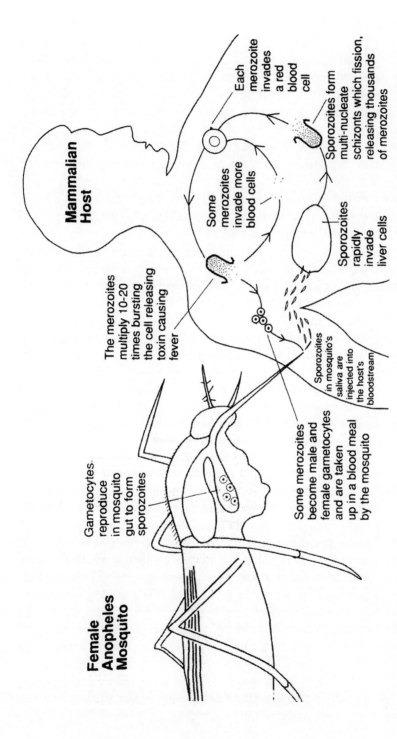

Figure 32 Life cycle of the malarial parasite. From M. Charlesworth, L. Farrell, T. Stokes, and D. Turnbull, *Life Among the Scientists: An Anthropological Study of an Australian Scientific Community*, Deakin University Press, 1992. p. 217. By permission of Deakin University, Australia.

broad malariological perspective, with its emphasis on a complex set of interactions in a specific geographical and socio-economic context, shows that the conditions for the definition of malaria can be assembled in any one of a number of possible ways, depending on which group of factors or interactions is taken as central and consequently which bodies need to be disciplined.

The range of possible definitions is extremely broad. At one end of the spectrum, there have been those for whom malaria is not really a disease at all. In PNG, for example, some of the coastal people in New Guinea describe it as *'samting nating'* (something nothing). There have even been some who have seen it as a saviour. 'Let us give thanks therefore to that little insect, the mosquito, which has saved the land of our fathers for us.'[13] Some critics have defined it as a 'political disease' resulting from the dominance of the Third World by the colonial and mercantile interests of the West.[14] Others have defined it as 'a social problem',[15] an 'administrative problem',[16] a 'military problem',[17] an 'economic problem',[18] an 'ecological problem',[19] or even an 'engineering problem'.[20]

In 1992 Kent Campbell, head of the Center for Disease Control in Atlanta, asked himself ' "what is malaria?" If a population is universally affected, and periodically ill what is the disease we call malaria?'[21] Reversing what seems the more obvious order of things, he answered by saying 'Malaria is a disease that responds to antimalarial drugs.'[22] Garrett following Campbell argues that malaria is 'a disease whose existence was proven by reversing it with drug treatments'. She goes on to claim that, 'At least in the African context when the disease no longer responded to chloroquine treatment because of resistance, it was transformed into a different syndrome.' The Campbell/Garrett position makes malaria a function of the treatment we currently have for it— the ultimate constructivist position. All diseases can be seen as multidimensional and multifactorial, and since the concept of disease 'acts not only to describe and explain but also to enjoin to action',[23] causal definitions of disease and concepts of treatment are typically interdependent and mutually constitutive rather than analytically distinct.

However, the way malaria has been defined or treated does not merely reflect competing interests or differing presuppositions. Certain definitions have tended to predominate, resulting in science-dependent, low-cost, high-profit, technical solutions produced in First World laboratories. Historically malaria was defined as a problem within the context of colonial administration and Western imperialism, because of its devastating effects on First World demands for resources and labour.

Both of the two most important early workers on malaria were military officers serving in colonial outposts. Ronald Ross worked for the Indian Medical Service attached to the British Army in India, and Alphonse Laveran for the French Army in Algeria. Similarly many of the major attempts at eradication occurred as a direct result of the impact of malaria on troops—in Cuba during the Spanish-American War, and in the tropics during and after the Second World War. Equally, international agencies like the Rockefeller Foundation have always voiced explicitly economic arguments:

> Because of its widespread geographic distribution, its extremely high prevalence in most tropical and sub-tropical regions where it's responsible for more death and illness than all other diseases combined and because of its obvious effects on direct financial losses, unequal economic efficiency and retardation of mental and physical development, malaria must be considered the manifestation of the most serious medical and hygienic problem we have to face.[24]

Disease research in general has always been associated with political interests, but the connection is especially strong in the case of tropical medicine and public health. Joseph Chamberlain, speaking in support of the establishment of the London and Liverpool Schools of Tropical Medicine in 1889 said, 'the study of tropical disease is a means of promoting Imperial policies'.[25] Similarly, the Dean of the Harvard School of Public Health claimed in 1950 that 'through health we can prove to ourselves and to the world the wholesomeness and rightness of democracy. Through health we can defeat the evil threat of communism'.[26] In 1957 Dr. Paul Russell of the Rockefeller Foundation, in a report to the U.S. International Development Advisory Board, reiterated the explicit interconnection of malaria research and political and economic policy, when he asserted that malaria eradication would benefit U.S. policy and finance.[27] Similar sentiments are still being expressed, for example at the World Summit on Malaria in Amsterdam in 1992, 'Malaria is not just a troublesome tropical disease, it is an impediment to world development. The disease affects tourism and trade, while badly planned development can unleash epidemics'.[28]

The spending of billions of dollars[29] on malaria research and control has to be seen against an economic background in which the simple dependency of Western capitalism on Third World labour and resources is undergoing a complex set of transitions, which include a demand for Third World markets for First World products, an increased exploitation of the Third World through aid and development, and the piracy of Third World intellectual and biological resources.[30] These processes intersect with transitions in science itself. Science is becoming bigger and more capital intensive, more commercialised and more directly connected to private capital.[31] This transition is particularly marked in biomedicine, which has always been an inherently applied and commercial science, resulting in corruption at one extreme and a shift in the nature and ownership of intellectual property at the other.[32]

Molecular Biology's Agenda and the Problems of Messiness

Since the early 1940s the advent of molecular biology has apparently provided the technical possibility of a malaria vaccine. Each type and stage of malaria is thought to be immunologically specific—that is, a vaccine has to produce antibodies that are uniquely tailored to the antigens involved. It is now possible to identify proteins on the surface of each stage of the parasite using monoclonal antibodies, gene cloning and all the other tools that together constitute a manipulable system, more familiarly known as genetic engineering. There are difficulties involved in this search since it is currently believed that many of these antigens act as decoys tricking the host into an ineffective immunological response. Nonetheless, molecular biology provides for the possibility of identifying the antigen involved in the merozoite stage penetrating the red blood cell, and developing an antibody to block it.[33]

The capacity of such systems to create order out of messy complexity has, however, more to do with 'technique' than 'truth'. A Melbourne botanist, Geoff McFadden, has recently shown that malaria parasites may carry a 'residual plastid'.[34] In lay terms this suggests that genetic engineers have been wrong to assume the parasite is an animal; it may also be a plant, or at least was once a plant in the distant past. This seemingly fundamental issue has not slowed the pace of their research at all. Indeed it seems to have been irrelevant. However, it does mean that alternative approaches to either destroying or nullifying the parasite by using herbicides have been overlooked. Nonetheless the current task set by the molecular biological agenda is to identify the significant antigens amongst the array of surface proteins.

The vaccine oriented agenda that the manipulable system of molecular biology so readily supports has also blinded researchers to another problem. All vaccines are dependent on the addition of an adjuvant. Adjuvants are immunology's 'dirty little secret', according to Charlie Janeway at Yale University.[35] No one is quite sure how they work, but they contain a complex range of ingredients like 'detergent, oil and water, aluminium hydroxide and dead bacteria that have nothing to do with the disease the vaccine protects against.'[36] The messiness of adjuvants is made more complex by recent evidence showing that different adjuvants cause different immune responses.[37] Nonetheless research proceeds, despite any clear understanding of how vaccines or the immune system work, or what the parasite is.

However, it is in its combination of specificity and variability that the messy heterogeneity of malaria really manifests itself. The parasite's antigens are specific to each stage and each strain, and are subject to constant variation—so-called antigenic diversity. A vaccine will either have to be strain specific, or be changed to meet the varieties of antigens in the same way that we have different 'flu shots each year for each new strain of 'flu. Alternatively, a vaccine has to be developed for an as yet undiscovered antigen that has an invariant function in the life cycle of the parasite. There is also genetic diversity in the human host population. In PNG, for example, the red blood cells of the coastal people cells are less easily invaded by the merozoites than those of the highlanders.[38] This genetic polymorphism means that the response to a vaccine may vary considerably. Some may gain a boost to their immune system, while others may not. Another category of problems associated with specificity and variability is the expression of the disease itself. Given that it is a complex set of interactions between the host, the vector and the parasite in a particular environment, eliminating it from a particular population is a very localised, site-specific problem requiring varying solutions according to changing circumstance.

A curious fact about malaria vaccine research is that none of the participants in the story have an unreservedly sanguine view of its likely outcome. Indeed if you add all their reservations together, the chances of a successful vaccine look rather thin. Despite the huge amount of money put into malaria vaccines and the constant hope that a breakthrough is just around the corner, no vaccine has yet proved successful. The great hope for a while, and the subject of much controversy about test conditions, was the vaccine developed by the Columbian scientist Manuel Patarrayo.[39] While it seems to offer some protection in South America it failed to offer any in the Gambia and Thailand.[40] This may well reflect the inherent problems of heterogeneity and discipline that are common to the control of all but the simplest of diseases. For example, the vaccine against TB which works so well in Britain does not work at all in Africa, apparently because of the presence of local mycobacteria.[41]

What then were thought to be the problems with a sporozoite vaccine—that is, a vaccine specific to the first stage and the one the Americans wanted to test in PNG? First and foremost, it was specific to only one stage of the parasite cycle. Further, that stage is only vulnerable to antibodies for about thirty minutes, one circulation of the blood, before it enters the liver cells and becomes inaccessible to the immune system.[42] In those few minutes all the sporozoites have to be destroyed. Just one entering the liver is thought to be sufficient to cause malaria, since once there it multiplies many thousand-fold. Antigenic diversity will mean that such a vaccine will have a finite efficacy, though how long it might last is a matter of speculation.

Amongst the immune population a vaccine may even have a negative effect. Inhabitants of areas where malaria is endemic tend to have a high degree of immunity acquired as the result of a lifetime's exposure. Curing these people of malaria will also render them non-immune, and hence highly vulnerable to a full-scale malaria attack once the vaccine wears off. A further drawback is that the vaccine specific to P. falciparum is not specific to P. vivax, which is also common in PNG.

Vaccines in the Third World are problematic in a more general way because of difficulties associated with delivery. In PNG it is difficult to achieve more than a 50% delivery rate, and frequently vaccines are hard to store in a viable condition, especially in the tropics. In Africa, for example, the measles vaccine has only a 5% delivery rate, in contrast to the small-pox vaccine which is stable in hot conditions. But the broadest problem with a parasite vaccine is that, despite our technical ability to produce a vaccine, little is known about the detailed functioning of the human immune system. The effects of immunising immune populations are waiting to be discovered through the trials now envisaged. Equally, there is much to be learned about the epidemiology of malaria. Varying considerably from region to region and over time, malaria has also been found to vary at the village level.[43] Thus what is now required is micro-epidemiological analysis. There are similar problems of antigenic variation with merozoite vaccines. A gametocyte vaccine would possibly be effective in breaking the transmission cycle but would not immunise the individual patient. Currently it is thought likely that an effective vaccine will have to be some sort of 'cocktail' like the Patarrayo vaccine.

A Vaccine for PNG

Despite the complications of the situation in PNG where all the parties involved in the trial have strong and conflicting interests; despite their awareness of the problems involved with a vaccine and knowledge of alternatives; and despite the disastrous consequences of trying to eliminate malaria using DDT, all their interests coalesced in favour of testing a sporozoite vaccine in PNG.

The major research groups relevant to PNG formed three main constellations, each combining funding agencies, research institutes and commercial connections. The first was the Nussenzwieg group, which initially led the field with a synthetic peptide sporozoite vaccine. This group was funded largely by USAID, and was based at the New York University Center for Vaccine Research, with Hoffman La Roche as commercial partners. Second, the Walter Reed Army Institute for Research was working on the recombinant DNA sporozoite vaccine, in collaboration with the National Institutes of Health with their commercial partners Smith, Kline and Beckman. The third was an Australian group, whose history was more complicated. WEHI, PNGIMR and their collaborators started a joint research project, funded by the Rockefeller Foundation and the National Health and Medical Research Council, looking for a merozoite vaccine. This spawned the Australian Malaria Joint Venture group bringing together WEHI and QIMR, the Commonwealth Serum Laboratories, Biotechnology Australia Pty, Ltd, and the Australian Industry Development Corporation, to operate under the name Saramane Pty. Ltd.[44] For these three competing research groups winning the race for a malaria vaccine was expected to bring prestige, especially the prestige of a Nobel Prize. So strongly did the participants equate getting the vaccine with getting the prize, that they frequently reflected on how seriously their competition interfered with their research, and wondered wistfully whether there were not some way to abolish the prize. There were also other groups of interests that must be taken into account.

At the highest level, these include the interests of the national governments of the USA, Australia, PNG and other countries with endemic malaria. These interests partly overlap with those of the funding bodies and the malaria control groups, such as USAID, The

Rockefeller Foundation, and WHO. Then there are the multi-national pharmaceutical companies, which as always stand to profit no matter what the outcome. At the next level down are those who represent rival approaches to malaria research and control, like chemotherapy, larviciding and biological controls. Finally, at the lowest levels, there is the most interested group of all—the malaria sufferers.

At the level of national governments, the prestige attached to the 'discovery' of the vaccine is important in so far as it forms part of the ability to control and utilise the vaccine. However, the USA's major interest in PNG at that time was based on its rivalry with the Russians in the Asia-Pacific region. The USSR had signed fishing agreements with various Pacific Island states and had made approaches to PNG. Indonesia looked less attractive as an ally in the light of events in the Philippines, and control of the passages between the Indian and Pacific Oceans is of great strategic importance. Equally, the Americans and Russians were vying for influence in the Third World, given its then new-found voice in the UN.

For the US, possibly the highest stake of all, was and is, military.[45] Malaria has always caused major losses of combat strength in endemic regions. A smaller, but nonetheless significant problem, is the growing incidence of malaria among tourists and the resulting recurrence of malaria in the First World.[46] Many of the problems associated with the sporozoite vaccine do not apply to non-immunes who are likely to be in an endemic region only for a brief period. The two major groups in this category are troops and tourists.

The Australian government has an interest in cooperating with its Southwest Pacific neighbours, and was then also committed to a technology-led industrial development plan that laid special emphasis on biotechnology. The fact that it injected A$9 million into the Australian Malaria Vaccine Joint Venture showed the importance it attached to such development.[47] The PNG government views malaria as a serious bar to economic development given that it is an endemic disease throughout much of PNG.

Commercially, vaccines in general are problematic and may or may not turn out to be big business. Hoffman La Roche, for example, argues that there is no market for a malaria vaccine. But it could be a high value-added, low export-cost item with a vast market. It is thought that there are 280 million people infected with malaria and 110 million develop the disease per year worldwide.[48] We are now experiencing a dramatic increase in malaria with 40% of the world affected; if the anticipated global warming occurs it could return to areas such as Britain, Europe and Australia.[49] The vaccine is presently targeted on the 10 million infants who get malaria per year. However, the military and tourist market alone may be sufficient to make it a commercially viable proposition. As one of the parties to the Joint Malaria venture commented, 'Biotech isn't interested in curing malaria, it just wants the troops and tourists'; whereas Biotech sees 'the troops and tourists as a means of financing a Third World vaccine'. Though the malaria vaccine will be the first for a human parasitic disease, it may well lead to breakthroughs in other parasitic diseases like schisto-somiasis, filariasis, and leishmaniasis.

Thus there is an international race to develop a malaria vaccine (there are other groups in the US, England, France and Sweden that I have not mentioned) in which the main stakes are political and econ-omic as well as scientific. This is strongly illustrated by two points. First, the US government decided to select PNG as a trial site prior to the visit of the site selection committee, and despite the fact that PNG might not be an ideal site for such a trial.[50] Second, the Australian gov-ernment invoked the 'national interest', requiring the approval of both houses of Federal Parliament, to persuade the Australian Industry Development Corporation (AIDC) to invest in the Australian Joint Malaria Venture.[51] This investment was made despite the commercially high risk in producing an effective vaccine, despite the other contenders in the race, and despite the fact that, at best, Australia will only provide a component of a successful vaccine. For the US and Australian governments, political and economic interests are at one with scientific and medical interests.

Are There Alternatives?

To assess the value of developing a malaria vaccine for an indigenous population one has to consider a number of related questions. What attempts have been made to control malaria in the past? What were their strengths and weaknesses? What alternative methods are being tried? What is the reality of malaria from the 'local's' point of view? What are the local solutions?

Of contemporary attempts to control malaria in PNG, the most common method is chemotherapy. The earliest drug treatment for malaria in PNG was quinine. Robert Koch studied its effects near Madang, and Klaus Schilling, the first German doctor in New Guinea, thought Koch's results showed that quinine, even in 'a hot-bed of malaria', was capable of 'making it disappear altogether.'[52] This hollow claim has been repeated with amnesiac regularity each time a new technological solution appears. Quinine is still used, but continuous heavy doses have deleterious side effects and resistance is now widespread in SE Asia with a real fear that it could spread to Africa. We now appear to be running short of chemotherapeutic alternatives, resistance has developed to all the major drugs, and mefloquine is now thought to have very serious side effects.[53] The only hope is artemisinin which, like quinine, is derived from a local herbal treatment. Quinine was a South American remedy using the bark of the chinchona tree. Artemisinin is derived from the Chinese herbal medicine Qinghaosu or sweet wormwood.[54]

After quinine, DDT was thought to be the answer, and WHO started a world-wide program to eradicate malaria using DDT as an insecticide spray. In PNG, apart from a few limited areas in the Highlands and islands, DDT spraying was stopped after twenty years because it did not work. In fact, during the period of large-scale spraying, the incidence of malaria increased as migrant workers helped to spread it into non-endemic areas. Three major problems were encountered: the high cost and large bureaucratic structures required to sustain quality control in the program; the change in behaviour of the vector from resting indoors, where it is vulnerable to spraying, to outdoors where it is invulnerable; and a lack of compliance by PNG villagers. In other words a discipline problem, the government officials, the villagers and the mosquitos all proved too hard to keep in line.

Elsewhere in the world the ultimate reason for the failure of DDT was another discipline problem—the development of resistance. Interestingly however, DDT resistance did not occur in PNG. This lack of resistance indicates that no effective pressure was applied to the mosquito vector. It also shows that malaria, like all diseases, is as much a social problem as a technical one. The villagers' behaviour, and their perceptions and beliefs about the significance of malaria and the efficacy of its treatment, are all important. They baulked at the attempt to impose a spraying regime for a variety of reasons. Primarily it ran counter to their views about social ordering since it required strangers to enter their houses, always something fraught with anxiety in a culture that focuses so strongly on rivalry, enemies and 'payback'. Some believed that the spray could be used to poison people, and that it killed their domestic animals. By an odd twist of fate, DDT is effective in killing the parasites of a moth that eats roof thatch, resulting in an increased moth population and consequently thatched roofs suddenly needed replacing.[55]

Although it was successful in the regions where malaria had a less tenacious foothold, DDT spraying did not just prove a failure in New Guinea.[56] It ultimately proved disastrous throughout the tropics. Following the decline in the efficacy of DDT, the incidence of malaria increased to pre-spraying levels or worse. Explanations for the failure of the campaign to eradicate malaria using DDT is a matter of debate, but one of the reasons was the failure to recognise that the campaign's success was crucially dependent on discipline. Once eradication seemed in sight the discipline of constant inspection and spraying was relaxed and immediately all the bodies that had been held in line returned to their old undisciplined ways. Moreover the restrictive consequences of the campaign are clear. It led to a concentration on just one definition of malaria at the expense of alternative definitions, resulting among other things in the winding down of research and training in malaria generally. There was a massive resurgence of malaria, because other approaches and the specific and local character of malaria were ignored. Ultimately, world-wide vulnerability to malaria was increased.[57] DDT provides an important historical example of the devastating consequences of the way in which First World interests conduce to the introduction of a simple, universal, technological fix. A fix for which there was no absolute necessity, and which was known from the start to have serious resistance and toxicity problems.[58] Insecticides may still provide an answer, especially those that have low environmental impact and do not generate resistance such as those derived from Chrysanthemums and Marigolds.[59] However, they are only likely to be successful if utilised in a low discipline regime like the integrated pest management system in Indonesia that creates the local experts mentioned in Chapter 1.

There are, however, a variety of alternative approaches to dealing with malaria in PNG that have some hope of success. These include: mosquito coils; elevated living platforms; environmental and dietary modifications; health education; biological control of vectors; and the reduction of vector-person contact.[60] The last two illustrate the socio-political reality of malaria in PNG.

One form of biological control lies in the introduction to streams and lakes of mosquito larvae-eating fish, such as Gambusiae. These fish were first introduced in New Ireland in 1933 and the practice continues. The PNG Department of Health is optimistic for their success while the researchers from PNGIMR at Yagaum near Madang are rather dismissive of such solutions. A more recent biological control is a bacillus (*Bacillus thuringiensis*) BT14.[61] BT14 destroys the mosquito larvae that consume the bacillus after it has been spread on pools and lakes. It is completely non-toxic to all other life forms and is extremely effective. In Africa it has been supplied to villagers in a form that the villagers themselves can brew up and spread cheaply and easily on water in the area as it becomes necessary. This is an effective way of putting control at low cost, using low technology, into the hands of the locals, albeit control based on First World biomedical engineering. However, it all depends on the specifics of local implementation. In PNG it looked set to play out rather differently. An Australian company was in the process of signing a deal with the PNG Department of Health to supply BT14 in its fully prepared form, and with the recommendation that it be sprayed by specialist teams. This deal, according to one of my informants, seemed likely to go through without proper evaluation or reference to the African experience and would almost certainly have been completely inappropriate; only time will tell.

Another way of tackling malaria is to reduce vector human contact. An example of 'appropriate' research at Yagaum is a simple cost effective solution—Permethrin impregnated bed nets. The major carriers of gametocytes are infants. If babies can be kept from infecting mosquitos by sleeping in bed nets, one of the more enthusiastic supporters of the scheme claims that the transmission cycle can be broken in three months.[62] The low tech, low cost, local solution of using bed nets is proving very successful in the Gambia, another hyperendemic region where they expect to reduce death rates by a massive 70%.[63] It is, of course, a mistake to think that bed nets will provide a universal solution, especially given the discipline required. In some areas the people are not accustomed to using bed nets and in others the mosquitos are not accustomed to resting indoors. In PNG an effective and customary way to reduce transmission rates is to have a companion dog or pig to sleep beside, whom the mosquitos are accustomed to biting as a matter of preference.[64]

Within the knowledge space of Western science, indigenous beliefs about malaria are 'folk' beliefs and should be set against the 'reality' of malaria in PNG. But within the knowledge spaces of the New Guineans the reality of malaria is constructed by their perceptions, and perceptions of the disease vary from group to group. The lowlanders, having spent their lives in a hyperendemic region, have a high degree of parasitaemia (up to 40% in the wet season), and suffer mostly from

P. falciparum, though they have *P. vivax* and *P. malariae* as well.[65] Consequently lowlanders are continuously reinfected and develop a high level of 'natural immunity' as well as some genetic advantages. Their perception of malaria is one of a permanent, unshakeable condition that it is hard to imagine life without. They expect to get 'hot skin' (i.e., fever) several times a year and seem to think of it much as we do a heavy cold or flu. Since they do not regard malaria as a serious disease like filariasis, they are likely to be less willing to comply with a vaccination program, especially if the results are ambivalent.

The highlanders have no natural immunity or genetic advantage. Many of them go down to the lowlands to work on the plantations, become infected, and on their trips home are responsible for bringing malaria into a region where it did not previously exist. They suffer quite severely from malaria and it can be fatal in their children. Highlanders are consequently more likely to be in favour of a vaccination program. On the other hand, the supposedly real incidence of malaria in PNG is hidden in the inadequacy of the data base. According to one of the doctors involved:

> In the hospital at Port Moresby you might as well toss a coin as rely on malaria blood slides for case detection. There is no effective quality control and no blind controls. They are understaffed by people in need of retraining and support. The cause of death is often attributed to malaria just because of parasitaemia. In Port Moresby and Rabaul they have to read 100 slides per day. Verification work is supposedly done in the provinces. But basically, since the quality is unknown, the data is fundamentally unreliable.[66]

In PNG, the economic, political, technical and disciplinary conditions were set for the possibility of a vaccine and its trial. Such a trial was seen as desirable by all parties, despite their differing interests, and their knowledge of the possible dangers and difficulties. This constellation of forces conduced to a push for a vaccine because the scientists, funding agencies, national governments and pharmaceutical companies all operate within a mutually reinforcing economic system.

Western biomedical research is both very expensive and technique driven. Its need for large amounts of research funding necessitates a particular set of relationships with governments and commercial enterprises. Equally, the research itself derives from a set of practices that are particular to the laboratory. Both factors mitigate against a vaccine's ready transmission into the field situation unless the knowledge space is extended to incorporate it and the attendant discipline imposed. These factors lead to a preference for an unstable technological fix over a relatively stable local solution. Technologically sophisticated solutions are incompatible with local solutions reflecting contingent circumstances and individual conditions, precisely because their efficacy depends on a transcendence of the local. Bio-medical research scientists working in laboratories, though individually altruistic, have acquired through their disciplinary training and experience a set of skills and practices, like gene-splicing and cloning antibodies, which enable them to produce candidate vaccines. Such entities are capable of being the stuff of commercial enterprise and international diplomacy, whereas site-specific simple solutions are not.

Controlling malaria is a multi-faceted problem which requires the simultaneous treatment of a range of interacting elements, given the diversity and local specificity of the disease, host and vector. Since major epidemiological and immunological problems still remain, vaccination can only succeed as part of a balanced approach in which all existing and potential methods are integrated in a program allowing a high degree of local responsibility and autonomy.[67] It is possible that the alternative definitions of malaria may be kept open and that a vaccine may actually be of long-term benefit in the endemic regions. But unless the vaccine is integrated into the local health services and local practices, political and economic issues will override the medical and social ones; unless there is a dialectical interaction between the needs of the particular people in particular places and the technical requirements of vaccines, chemotherapy, or insecticides, the program will fail, as did the DDT program, because externally imposed discipline cannot be sustained in the long run[68] That is, it will fail to cure the millions who get malaria each year, but may well succeed in promoting the interests of First World research and entrepreneurs.

What the malaria case suggests is that the kinds of epistemological, moral and ontological disciplining of people, practices and places that characterise the ways in which the knowledge space of Western laboratory science is extended are inappropriate in the disordered, complex world of tropical disease. As with Pacific navigation we need to encourage the growth of indigenous knowledge and the creation of spaces in which the contrasting knowledge traditions can work together allowing alternatives to proliferate.

Notes

1   Max Charlesworth, Lyndsay Farrall, Terry Stokes and David Turnbull, *Life Among The Scientists: An Anthropological Study of an Australian Scientific Community*, (Melbourne: Oxford University Press, 1989).

2   H. Cleaver, 'Malaria and the Political Economy of Public Health', *International Journal of Health Services*, Vol. 7, (1977), pp. 557–579; S. Franco-Agudelo, 'The Rockefeller Foundation's Antimalarial Program in Latin America: Donating or Dominating?', *International Journal of Health Services*, Vol. 13, (1983), pp. 51–67. On the failure of malaria eradication, see L. Bruce-Chwatt, 'Malaria: From Eradication To Control', *New Scientist*, Vol. 19 April, (1984), pp. 17–20 and M. A. Farid, 'The Malaria Programme—From Euphoria To Anarchy', *World Health Forum*, Vol. 1, (1980), pp. 8–33.

3   Western efforts to eliminate schistosomiasis have focused heavily on developing chemotherapy, snail control and mathematical models on the supposition that the key is snail population density. Only in China where snail eradication and sanitation programs are integrated and implemented at the local level have any significant inroads been made. F. R. Sandbach, 'Preventing Schistosomiasis: A Critical Assessment of Present Policy', *Social Science and Medicine*, Vol. 9, (1975), pp. 517–527.

4   Michael Day, '"Poor" Vaccine Ruled out in TB Puzzle', *New Scientist*, Vol. 151, July 13, (1996), pp. 14.

5   According to the theoretical biologist Sunetra Gupta, see Phyllida Brown, 'How the Parasite Learnt to Kill', *New Scientist*, Vol. 152, 16th Nov, (1996), pp. 32–6, p. 35.

6   Or as Mol and Law found with anaemia, different kinds of spaces are performed with different understandings of the disease, see Annemarie Mol and John Law, 'Regions, Network, and Fluids: Anaemia and Social Topology', *Social Studies of Science*, Vol. 24, (1994), pp. 641–71.

7   I. A. Clark and G. A. Butcher, 'Cell-mediated Aspects of Malaria', *Papua New Guinea Medical Journal*, Vol. 29, (1986), pp. 59–62.

8   W. Peters, 'New Answers Through Chemotherapy', *Experientia*, Vol. 40, (1984), pp. 1311–1317.

9   See G. N. Godson, 'Molecular Approaches to Malaria Vaccines', *Scientific American*, Vol. 252, (1985), pp. 32–39; J. V. Ravetch, J. Young, et al., 'Molecular Genetic Strategies for the Development of Anti-malarial Vaccines', *Biotechnology*, Vol. 3, (1985), pp. 729–40.

10 G. F. Mitchell, 'Short Odds for Malaria Vaccines', *BioEssays*, Vol. 13, (1986), pp. 126–7.

11 E. H. Ackernecht, *Malaria in the Upper Mississippi Valley 1760–1900*, (Baltimore: Johns Hopkins University Press, 1945), p. 130.

12 J. D. Charlwood, 'Which Way Now for Malaria Control?', *Papua New Guinea Medical Journal*, Vol. 27, (1984), pp. 159–162.

[13] S. D. Onabamiro, University College, Ibadan, quoted in P. F. Russell, *Man's Mastery of Malaria*, (Oxford: Oxford University Press, 1955), p. 244.

[14] J. P. Kreier, ed., *Malaria: Vol.1; Epidemiology, Chemotherapy, Morphology, and Metabolism*, (New York: Academic Press, 1982), p. 9; W. H. McNeill, *Plagues and People*, (New York: Anchor Press, 1966); Franco-Agudelo, 'The Rockefeller Foundation's Antimalarial Program in Latin America', p. 18.

[15] E. Gruenbaum, 'Struggling with the Mosquito: Malaria Policy and Agricultural Development in Sudan', *Medical Anthropology*, Vol. 7, (1983), pp. 51–61.

[16] 'The presence of urban malaria is an administrative crime' Farid, 'The Malaria Programme—From Euphoria to Anarchy', p. 9.

[17] General William Gorgas defined malaria as a 'military problem' and eradicated it in Panama, as did Dr Fred Soper in Italy, Franco-Agudelo, 'The Rockefeller Foundation's Antimalarial Program in Latin America', p. 54. Similarly yellow fever was eradicated because it was defined as a military problem. See Nancy Stepan, 'The Interplay Between Socio-economic Factors and Medical Science: Yellow Fever Research, Cuba, and the United States', *Social Studies of Science*, Vol. 8, (1978), pp. 397–423.

[18] Farid, 'The Malaria Programme—From Euphoria to Anarchy', p. 12; G. Chapin and R. Wasserton, 'Pesticides Use and Malaria Resurgence in Central America and India', *Social Sciences and Medicine*, Vol. 17, (1983), pp. 273–90.

[19] V. P. Sharma cited in Laurie Garrett, *The Coming Plague: Newly Emerging Diseases in a World out of Balance*, (London: Virago Press, 1994), p. 454.

[20] F. L. Hoffman, *The Malaria Problem in Peace and War*, (London: Prudential Press, 1918), p. 7.

[21] Garrett, *The Coming Plague*, p. 444.

[22] Garrett, *The Coming Plague*, p. 449.

[23] H. T. Engelhardt, 'The Concept of Health and Disease', in H. T. Engelhardt and S. F. Spicker, eds., *Evaluation and Exploration in the Biomedical Sciences*, (Dordrecht: Reidel, 1975), p. 127.

[24] *Rockefeller Foundation Report 1915*, cited by S. Franco-Agudelo, 'The Rockefeller Foundation's Antimalarial Program in Latin America: Donating or Dominating?', p. 54.

[25] *The Times*, (10 May, 1899) cited in L. Doyal and I. Pennell, *The Political Economy of Health*, (London: Pluto Press, 1983), p. 241.

[26] Cleaver, 'Malaria and the Political Economy of Public Health', p. 569.

[27] Reported in the summary minutes of the U.S. International Development Advisory Board cited in Doyal, L. and I. Pennell, *The Political Economy of Health*, p. 275.

[28] David Nabarro head of British delegation quoted by Phyllida Brown, 'Malaria Summit Demands Plans Before Cash', *New Scientist*, Vol. 136, 7th Nov, (1992), p. 4.

29 World-wide between 1957 and 1977 the total was US$2.65 billion. Bruce-Chwatt, cited in G. V. Brown and G. J. V. Nossal, 'World Endemic Disease: Costs and Potential Fiscal Benefits of Medical Research', in H. H. Fudenberg, ed., *Biomedical Institutions, Biomedical Funding and Public Policy*, (New York: Plenum Press, 1983), p. 122.

30 Anil Agarwal and Sunita Narain, 'Pirates in the Garden of India', *New Scientist*, Vol. 152, 26th Oct, (1996), pp. 14–15.

31 See David Dickson, *The New Politics of Science*, (Chicago: University of Chicago Press, 1984).

32 See E. Yoxen, 'Life as a Productive Force: Capitalising the Science and Technology of Molecular Biology', in L. Levidow and B. Young, eds., *Science Technology and the Labour Process*, vol 1, (London: Free Association Books, 1981), pp. 66–122. On corruption in malaria vaccine research see R. Desowitz, *The Malaria Capers: Tales of Parasites and People*, (New York: W. W. Norton, 1991).

33 J. V. Ravetch, J. Young, 'Molecular Genetic Strategies for the Development of Anti-malarial Vaccines'.

34 Geoffrey McFadden, Michael Reith, et al., 'Plastid in Human Parasites', *Nature*, Vol. 381, 6th June, (1996), p. 482.

35 Phyllida Brown, 'Dirty Secrets', *New Scientist*, Vol. 152, 2nd Nov, (1996), pp. 26–9, p. 27.

36 Ibid, p. 26.

37 Ibid, p. 27.

38 J. Cattani, H. Vrbova, et al., 'Inter-cluster Variation in Malariometric Rates in a Coastal Area of Papua New Guinea', in J. Bryan and P. M. Moodie, eds., *Malaria: Proceedings of a Conference to Honour Robert H. Black, Sydney 1983*, (Canberra: Australian Government Publishing Service, 1984), pp. 112–118.

39 Phyllida Brown, 'Trials and Tribulations of a Malaria Vaccine', *New Scientist*, Vol. 129, 16th March, (1991), pp. 14; Phyllida Brown, 'Columbia's Malaria Vaccine Approved for Trials', *New Scientist*, Vol. 135, 26th Sept, (1992), p. 6; Phyllida Brown, 'Malaria Vaccine Trials Stopped by Anonymous Experts', *New Scientist*, Vol. 133, 22nd Feb, (1992), p. 6.

40 Michael Day, 'Malaria Vaccine Fails to Deliver', *New Scientist*, Vol. 151, 21st Sept, (1996), p. 8.

41 Michael Day, '"Poor" Vaccine Ruled out in TB Puzzle', *New Scientist*, Vol. 151, July 13, (1996), p. 14.

42 Charlwood, 'Which Way Now For Malaria Control?', p. 160.

43 J. Cattani, H. Vrbova, et al., 'Inter-cluster Variation in Malariometric Rates in a Coastal Area of Paua New Guinea'.

44 The only commercial partner still involved in 1998 is CSL.

45 D. MacKenzie, 'Drug Firms Turn Down Malaria Breakthrough', *New Scientist*, Vol. 26 April, (1984), p. 4.

[46] L. J. Bruce-Chwatt, 'Imported Malaria; An Uninvited Guest', *British Medical Bulletin*, Vol. 38, (1982), pp. 179–85.

[47] Anon, 'Malaria Vaccine Strikes Problems', *Scitech*, September, (1984), pp. 13.

[48] Phyllida Brown, 'Who Cares About Malaria', *New Scientist*, Vol. 136, 31st Oct, (1992), pp. 37–41, p. 37.

[49] Fred Pearce, 'A Plague on Global Warming', *New Scientist*, Vol. 136, 19/26th Dec, (1992), pp. 12–13.

[50] Desowitz, *The Malaria Capers*, pp. 257ff.

[51] B. Birnbauer, 'As Malaria Rampages Out of Control, Australian Scientists Race To Stop It', *Age*, (Melbourne: 1986), p. 3.

[52] R. H. Black, 'Malaria', in *Encyclopedia of Papua New Guinea*, (Melbourne: Melbourne University Press, 1972), p. 679.

[53] Clare Thompson, 'Malaria Pill Stands Accused', *New Scientist*, Vol. 150, April 27, (1996), pp. 14–15.

[54] First described by Ge Hang in 340 AD in *The Handbook for Emergency Treatments* cited in Desowitz, *The Malaria Capers*, p. 207.

[55] J. Moir and P. Garner, 'Malaria Control Through Health Services', *Papua New Guinea Medical Journal*, Vol. 29, (1986), pp. 27–33.

[56] A. W. A. Brown, J. Haworth, et al., 'Malaria Eradication and Control From a Global Standpoint', *Journal of Medical Entomology*, Vol. 13, (1976), pp. 1–25.

[57] Farid, 'The Malaria Programme—From Euphoria to Anarchy', p. 8.

[58] T. F. West and G. A. Campbell, *DDT: The Synthetic Insecticide*, (London: Chapman and Hall, 1946), pp. 134 and 178.

[59] Paul Simons, 'Could Marigolds Slay Killer Mosquitos?', *New Scientist*, Vol. 139, 17th July, (1993), p. 18.

[60] J. Moir and P. Garner 'Malaria Control Through Health Services', p. 31.

[61] Bruce-Chwatt, 'Malaria: From Eradication To Control', p. 19.

[62] J. Moir and P. Garner 'Malaria Control Through Health Services', p. 31.

[63] Brown, 'Who Cares About Malaria', p. 41.

[64] J. D. Charlwood, H. Dagoro, et al., 'Blood-feeding and Resting Behaviour in the *Anopheles Punctulatus* Complex (Diptera: Culicidae) from Papua New Guinea', *Bulletin of Entomological Research*, Vol. 75, (1985), pp. 463–475.

[65] J. Moir and P. Garner 'Malaria Control Through Health Services', p. 28.

[66] This, like all the other direct quotations from participants has been kept anonymous. The full text and sources are available in my field notes.

[67] J. Cattani, 'Malaria in the South-west Pacific; a Prototype Defined Population for Vaccine Trials', unpublished paper given at the Asia-Pacific Conference on Malaria, (Honolulu: 1985).

[68] Many of those at the Hall are acutely aware of these issues. See G. V. Brown and G. J. V. Nossal, 'World Endemic Disease' especially pp. 126–28.

6 MESSINESS AND ORDER IN TURBULENCE RESEARCH

Disorder, Order, Collective Work and Assemblages

This chapter, like the previous one, is focused on contemporary Western technoscientists in action. In this case it is based on an extended visit I made to a group of turbulence researchers at The Fluid Dynamics Laboratory in the Department of Mechanical and Aerospace Engineering, Princeton University in 1989, and subsequent visits in 1990 and 1994.

In the malaria example I was concerned with ways in which attempts to extend a knowledge space often serve to eliminate local complexities. In this case I am concerned with the ways in which the actors deal with the situation through the imposition of order. Scientists obviously impose order on nature, but they do so in part by the imposition of order on the disciplinary field.[1] This second-level social ordering is often made manifest only as a consequence of a third-level ordering, that of the social analyst. Sociologists of scientific knowledge attempt to gain analytic leverage and rhetorical authority by revealing the ways in which scientists 'naturalise the arbitrary'.[2] Sociologists themselves naturalise the arbitrary when they claim to reveal what scientists are 'really' doing. There is, however, an extra twist to all this. Just as sociologists of science have opened up new areas of exploration through the opportunities offered by 'interpretive flexibility', and just as the 'deconstructive turn' has transformed much of social and cultural inquiry, so too have the natural sciences themselves been transformed by their own recognition of the consequences of non-linear complexity and Gödel's theorem. Nature can no longer be conceived as having one true order. Instead all is chaos; order and disorder go hand in hand; the future is unpredictable even though chaos itself has a kind of order as a consequence of our modes of interpretation.[3] Hence the analysts' categories and the actors' categories are not truly independent, rather their notions of order are at least indirectly related.

One way of escaping the seeming contradictions generated by our past bondage to mimetic representation lies in accepting that neither society nor nature has a determinate order knowable as laws or specifiable as structures. From this perspective nature and society are known to us only through our own orderings; and though these may impose limitations, both material and social, on the range of possible orderings, there is no one ordering of nature or society that structures our understanding. Our orderings of nature and society can then be treated as consequences of the collective social work that constitute our endeavours to understand ourselves and our environment. The task of the sociologist and of the scientist is to explain society and nature, both of which are complex and open systems having a diversity of heterogeneous and asynchronous inputs. On this view our understandings or orderings, that is our theories, have neither a determinate set of relations to nature nor are they fixed social entities about which everyone must agree.

Scientific knowledge cannot simply be equated with a system of abstract statements or universal truths. It cannot be equated with an emergent fallible consensus, nor is it separable from the techniques, practices, instrumentations and technologies through which it is manifested. Rather, technoscientific knowledge is, at root, local, situated knowledge as we have already seen in cartography, cathedrals and malaria. It is produced at specific organised sites by people in face-to-face circumstances and results from contingent chains of negotiated judgements and concrete practices. It is the product of systems that have a wide variety of mixed, incompatible and disconnected components that come from an equally diverse set of times, places and circumstances. This aggregated localness is a source of science's robustness.[4]

The essential localness of scientific knowledge, as has been discussed in the Introduction and Chapter 1, was first captured by Kuhn in his distinction between paradigms as concrete exemplars and paradigms as global matrices. While the second type of paradigm underpinned his theory of scientific revolutions and has become part of the received view of science, the philosophically and sociologically more profound usage is that of the concrete exemplar.[5] Kuhn points out that scientists construct their understandings of the physical world through the imposition of learned similarity relations. They take a known solution to a known problem and learn to see other unsolved problems as being sufficiently similar to allow the solution to be transposed: 'Paradigms are not primarily agreed upon theoretical commitments but exemplary ways of conceptualising and intervening in particular empirical contexts.'[6]

The exemplars, analytical techniques, instruments, data and materials that are the standard components of technoscientific knowledge production, precisely because of their local, situated and heterogeneous character, do not assemble themselves. As Kuhn points out, 'Scientists can agree in their identification of a paradigm without agreeing on or even attempting to produce, a full interpretation or rationalisation of it. Lack of a standard interpretation or of an agreed reduction to rules will not prevent a paradigm from guiding research'.[7] The question then arises, how are the universality and connectedness that typify technoscientific knowledge spaces achieved? Given all these discrete knowledge/practices, imbued with their concrete specificity, how can they be assembled into fields or disciplines? The answers considered in this chapter once again lie in a variety of social strategies and technical devices that treat instances of knowledge/practice as similar or equivalent and make connections through ordering; that is, in the contingent assemblage of people, practices and places in a knowledge space.

Research fields or bodies of technoscientific knowledge/practice are assemblages whose otherwise disparate elements are rendered equivalent, general and cohesive through processes of 'heterogeneous engineering'.[8] Among the many social strategies that enable the possibility of equivalence are processes of standardisation and collective work to produce agreements about what counts as an appropriate form of ordering. Technical devices that provide for connections and mobility are also essential. Such devices may be material or conceptual and may include maps, calendars, theories, books, lists, and systems of recursion, but their common function is to enable otherwise incommensurable and isolated knowledges to move in space and time from the local site and moment of their production to other places and times.

This chapter examines a particular example of scientists' work in ordering a knowledge space, and at the same time reflexively recognises the work of the analyst/jester in revealing that ordering. The sociology of science, covering as it does such a wide range of subjects and approaches, has as little or as much cohesion as sociology itself; but the sub-field, the sociology of scientific knowledge, has serious problems of unity and coherence. There have been few attempts to establish equivalences or connections between analyses and hence it is hard to gain any sense of a growing understanding of the subject area. Until recently coherence was largely a product of the defence of constructivism against its anti-relativist critics and the reference to a large body of empirical research. However, in 'laboratory studies', for example, one finds a plethora of approaches, theoretical schemes, methods and foci of research; but the only cohesion derives from an unexamined assumption that the kinds of ordering imposed in one laboratory, both that of the actors and that of the analysts, can somehow be generalised to other laboratories. Recently the pretence of coherence in the sociology of scientific knowledge has been dropped and dissension has broken out amongst some of its major proponents.[9] This struggle for theoretical supremacy and authority betrays a certain lack of reflexive insight and a failure to recognise that the demand for theoretical dominance parodies the very activities that the antagonists have analysed: the negotiations and struggles in the collective work to display order in the social world of the scientist. There is no simple or unique way out of this dilemma, but one possible course is that proposed in this book—to consider the differing ways in which actors create and work with assemblages by establishing equivalences between different empirical findings and connections between different situations in both Western technoscience and in other knowledge traditions. In diversity lies strength. The rest of this chapter examines contrasting instances of assemblage work in turbulence research.

Complexity in Turbulence

My local entrée into turbulence research, the work being done by Alexander Smits and his group at the Princeton Fluid Dynamics Laboratory, was chosen as an example of engineering research to provide a contrast with the biomedical research of the previous chapter and with a bias in laboratory studies generally towards biomedicine and high energy physics. The phenomenon that is of central concern to fluid mechanics is turbulent flow in gases and liquids. From the fluid mechanical point of view, turbulent phenomena are ubiquitous: in the words of one of the senior researchers of the field, 'Most of nature is turbulent flow, if you do not understand turbulence you don't understand anything.'[10] A less hegemonic claim by one of the researchers at Princeton is that 'turbulence is the last unsolved Newtonian mechanics problem.'[11] Though chaos theory has a part in this story it has relatively little to do with the actual research or theorising at Princeton, which is in large part a Newtonian tale. Hence turbulence research is an especially interesting case for the sociology of technoscientific knowledge. So 'normal' and Newtonian has this research become that, like a great deal of physics, it now has the deceptive appearance of being routinised and much of it is conducted under the aegis of engineering. It is firmly ensconced in physics and engineering schools world wide and has been, in many cases, for over half a century. There are specialised chairs, professorships, journals, funding agencies and the whole social infrastructure that typifies research in the physical sciences. This situation makes turbulence research something of a test case. One might expect that such research would be predominantly theory-driven with relatively little controversy. That turbulence research does not fit the unified view of science that Kuhn's paradigm as global matrix suggests, results in part from the messiness involved in rendering the phenomena tractable and manipulable. As the story unfolds, it will also become apparent that the example of turbulence research tells against the notion of an agreed theoretical paradigm that underpins the received view of Kuhn's generalisations and instead indicates that research can, for much of the time, be local, complex, multiple and messy, guided only by specific practices.

Until recently it was commonly supposed that, though science may be able to sketch out some broad descriptions and classifications, it will never be able to produce precise mathematical models of complex irregular natural phenomena, like waterfalls, cloud formations, or smoke plumes from an erupting volcano. They are simply too disordered, too chaotic, too 'natural'. And indeed,

> Thirty years ago the accepted picture of turbulence was as a 'random jiggling' without structure and therefore unanalysable by statistical means that [typically] ignored turbulence production.[12]

This lack of order manifests itself to the investigator as complexity:

> I don't know if this is a widely held view but the people in turbulence think of turbulence as being the most complex phenomena outside quantum mechanics. It is one of the most complex phenomena that can still be described using Newtonian mechanics.[13]

Though the 'Navier-Stokes' equations have been developed to describe all fluid flow, they can only be solved for turbulent flow in very limited conditions:

> The Navier-Stokes equations are one of those cases where you always have at least one more variable than you have equations. So people are always trying to find a way to close the system; the closure problem.[14]

Such equations are non-linear and describe all the random phenomena which have previously been ignored as too complex for laboratory manipulation, or written off as 'noise' or experimental artifacts. The essentially non-regular character of most natural processes, and science's tendency to bracket them all together, is neatly captured in Stanislaw Ulam's remark, 'to call the study of chaos "non-linear science" is like calling zoology "the study of non-elephant animals."'[15]

Not only does the field of turbulence research have closure as a central problem, which is close to the heart of the sociology of scientific knowledge, but it also turns out to be a field which cannot be characterised by agreement on the fundamental questions. As will become clear in this chapter, there is no consensus on what turbulence is or what constitutes the real task of turbulence research; is it the classification of structures or is it the articulation of a physical/mathematical model?

> We don't even have a definition for turbulence, although it is generally agreed that it has the following properties. It is unsteady; three dimensional; apparently random; dissipative; and has motions which are spread over a range with nonlinear interactions among the scales.[16]

There is no consensus on ontology, about whether structures exist in turbulent flows, and if they do what sort of things they are and how they relate to each other. (see Fig. 33) There is no consensus on what is the best approach, on what is the best method, or on what counts as good science or who is a good scientist.

A recent example of this kind of disagreement in turbulence is the controversy over whether one of the fundamental equations—the so-called 'law of the wall' is wrong. The Berkeley turbulence researcher Alexander Chorin, and an English mathematician Gregory Greenblatt claim that the logarithmic law should be replaced with an exponential one.[17] Some have claimed the law as a well known 'fudge factor', others a 'rule of thumb' to cover the messiness and local variation in wind tunnels. However, Smits, a major player in this controversy, claims that Chorin and Greenblatt are simply wrong. Their equation does not fit the empirical data but his does.

There are of course individual and local evaluations of these issues, but no unified agreement across the field or clear criteria for making such judgements. Something of the flavour of the situation is captured in the slightly hyberbolic description of the field that was handed out in a flyer for a conference at Cornell University in 1989 entitled 'Turbulence at the Crossroads, or Whither Turbulence':

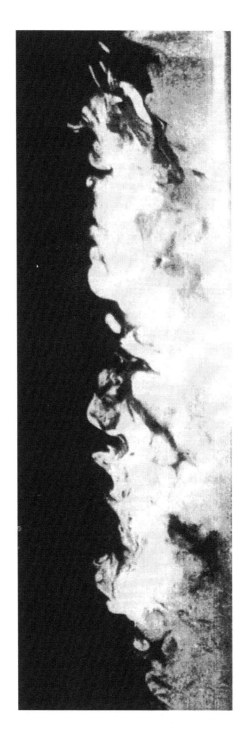

Figure 33   Characteristic turbulent flow near a boundary. With permission of the American Institute of Physics.

Turbulence is rent by factionalism. Traditional approaches in the field are under attack and one hears intemperate statements against long term averaging, Reynolds decomposition, and so forth. Some of these are reminiscent of the Einstein-Heisenberg controversies over quantum mechanics, and smack of a mistrust of any statistical approach. Coherent structure people sound like the *Emperor's New Clothes* when they say that *all* turbulent flows consist primarily of coherent structures in the face of visual evidence to the contrary. Dynamical systems theorists are sure that turbulence is chaos. Simulators have convinced many that we will be able to compute *anything* within a decade. Modelling is thus attacked as unnecessary or irrelevant because it starts with Reynolds averaging or ignores coherent structures. The card carrying physicists dismiss everything that has been done on turbulence from Osborne Reynolds till the last decade. Cellular Automata were hailed on their appearance as the answer to a maiden's prayer, so far as turbulence was concerned. It is no wonder that funding agencies are confused.[18]

Yet despite this lack of consensus there is sufficient coherence for the practitioners to act as if there is a field of turbulence research. Coherence in this case does not derive from a unifying paradigm or the adoption of an agreed set of instruments or methods. It derives from a very loose recognition that the phenomenon at issue is turbulence, even though its nature cannot be specified and even though it occurs in a very diverse set of flow situations from blood vessels to aircraft wings to the earth's atmosphere. But equally important, coherence results from the work of the researchers in the field trying to establish equivalences and connections in problem solving while also struggling for authority.[19]

External Coherence and the Ordering of Turbulence

That the ordering of turbulence is not determined by the ordering of nature itself nor by an internal scientific logic, but is the product of social negotiations which produce differing assemblages in differing circumstances, is further revealed in the collective work of a large cross-section of the international turbulence research community who attended a conference 'New Approaches to Experimental Turbulence Research' held at Princeton in September 1990. This was a somewhat unusual conference in that the scientists were explicitly forbidden to report on their own research results, while the participants included industrial as well as academic scientist/engineers and both public and private funding monitors. All participants were required to devote themselves to considering the directions, goals and difficulties of turbulence research in the future. The initial reaction of many of the conferees was one of anger, frustration and rejection, especially in discussions that very quickly became centred on the difficulties being experienced as a consequence of severe funding cutbacks. One widespread reaction at the end of the first day was 'We should simply get on with the job. My research projects are producing good results. I will simply have to get some more money from somewhere'. This frustrated response reflects the absence of the researchers' normal mode of achieving equivalence and connection through the collective presentation of research. As the conference progressed a variety of solutions to the funding cutback problem were proposed: a national research facility with a gigantic 5 kilometre wind tunnel to which all could have access and where all could do experiments from a distance; an international data bank; a concentration on computer simulation; a concentration on ultra-small experiments with pipette-sized wind tunnels. These proposals reflected a fundamental problem that all researchers recognised; their data and research practices were very hard to integrate and synthesise. They had all experienced great difficulty in trying to transport their results from one research site to another and in standardising experiments. Hence they were forced to consider the problems of establishing equivalences and making connections in order to create an assemblage.

The problem that quickly emerged as central was how to advocate the spending of the research funds the community felt it needed (approximately US$20 million initially and US$10 million per annum thereafter). It was apparent that the kinds of order and coherence that were sufficient for research were not adequate to the task of external representation of the field. It is difficult to persuade the central funding bodies to support a research area that cannot define itself adequately, cannot point to a significant accumulation of established facts despite huge amounts of data and cannot specify what understandings it has achieved. The initial approach the conference took was to draw up a list of the varieties of turbulence research; not surprisingly there were almost as many items as there were participants. However, as an awareness gradually spread among researchers that they all had a common problem, it became accepted that ordering the field of turbulence research had to be achieved by reconciling pure research and application and hence by drawing up a list of the 'most important problems' of turbulence and of 'important examples' of turbulence.[20]

Thus the participants at the conference, with some difficulty and unwillingness, brought themselves to recognise the necessity of imposing a social ordering on their field of research. The kind of external coherence and the work required in ordering it in these circumstances is rather different from the strategies employed in achieving internal coherence in the field.

Internal Coherence and the Ordering of Turbulence

It is the complexity of the phenomena and the diversity of their occurrence that provide the grounds for the disagreement and controversy that characterises the field. One of the social strategies used by the actors in their struggle for both order and authority is their discursive mode of controversy management.[21] These strategies can be observed in the views of three of the actors representing some of the disagreements and interests that are prevalent in the field. An elder statesman of the field, Steve Kline, depicts the discipline as in disarray and needing consensus about what constitute the basic phenomena in the field. Lex Smits, a relatively young researcher, claims there is broad consensus, but a new theory is needed to tidy up the conflicting details. Such controversy management strategies reflect the particular way in which these actors attempt to impose order and achieve authority. Kline's interest is in getting the community to accept that there is no general theory to explain the phenomena of turbulence and that his phenomenological typology must be taken as the basis of all research, thereby ensuring a fundamental role for his life's work which has been principally to produce such a typology. Smits, on the other hand, wants to promulgate a new general model, but as a younger member of the field wants to minimise confrontation with the patriarchs. The strategy for him, then, is to portray the field as unified, thereby down-playing any disagreement and muting any antagonism to his own model, which he depicts as merely tidying up a few loose ends. Yet another strategy is that of Steve Robinson, once a student of Kline's, who wants to transform the field through the introduction of a radical new mode of analysis. His approach to the controversy is to embrace and transcend it through the use of computer simulation to generate massive data sets detailing turbulent flows.

Much of the essence of the controversies and the strategies can be seen in three papers of the three actors and in their reactions to each other's work.[22] At one level the disagreements are about theory, method, technique, mode of analysis and the basic phenomena, but at base the principal issue at stake is what constitutes understanding, or in the terms of this account, what constitutes an appropriate mode of ordering.

The opening moves of these three actors in their coherence management strategies are to establish their view of how the field is constituted. Primarily this is done by displaying the field as incoherent or incomplete, and secondarily by dissolving that incoherence through their view of what is to count as understanding. This parallels my own strategy as analyst: I first of all display the field as in a state of controversy, then, after simplifying the phenomena, I go on to establish a higher order which I claim to discover through research and which is thus 'natural' in the sense of being really out there waiting to be found.

Kline depicts the field as lacking coherence in his claim that:

> The present state of knowledge concerning the quasi-coherent motions in the turbulent boundary layer is still in a highly mixed state...when it comes to understanding how the classes of structures relate to and/or interact with each other we are still very much in the dark.

He concludes that 'we have about as many views of the complete structural model as there are active research groups studying the problem'. He perceives this condition of incoherence as a major difficulty and his proposed solution involves two different kinds of collective work. Firstly he suggests a community-wide evaluation of accumulated knowledge to 'distinguish what we know from matters still in doubt'. This can be achieved by the adoption of four criteria 'that are needed to improve the practices in the field', essentially by separating the 'reliable' data from the 'unreliable'.[23] He then proposes that the apparent disorder of the phenomena can be resolved by a synthetic review of the research. Such a review reveals just eight basic structures and permits the adoption of a 'classification of the known quasi-coherent boundary layer structures.'[24]

In interview Kline commented that:

> In '68 and '81 we did community evaluations of the state of the art because the process of closure wasn't working. The turbulence community is turbulent. The inherent complexity of the problems means that the problems never get sorted out, at meetings nobody clearly understands each other ... the field is both paradigmatic with the Navier-Stokes equations and non-paradigmatic. There are common goals, but no common methodology or strategy, there is basic agreement on data but none on inferences. Each

individual has their own interpretation because the datafile they each possess is not good enough to permit adequate inferences.[25]

One of the most fundamental issues of all is, what are the basic phenomena and what characterises them? Robinson and Kline argue that:

> A consistent and accepted definition of 'structure' (in the turbulence) sense has not yet surfaced. Thus it may be viewed as a hopeless task to categorise the many flavours of turbulent structure to be found in the literature. However a taxonomy, even though some what arbitrary can help focus thinking and inject organisation into the somewhat tangled information on the subject.

In interview Kline put it rather more forcefully: 'There are eight structures that are common to the data and there is no disagreement that these structures cause and dissipate turbulence.'[26]

Kline's account of the condition of the field, and the kind of collective work required to give it coherence, suggests that we should reject the requirement of a paradigm in the form of an overarching theory or global matrix sufficiently powerful to unify the field. There is no community agreement on any of the fundamentals. Turbulence appears to be pre-paradigmatic and not a mature field capable of problem solving. How then has it proved possible to pursue a productive research program without a paradigm of the global matrix variety? The answer appears to be that the practitioners achieve equivalences and connections by establishing the similarity relations that are symptomatic of Kuhn's characterisation of paradigm as shared problem solution or exemplar.

Smits agrees that there is no clear understanding of what a structure is: 'Structure, event, process, are all close to being the same. Because we are so fuzzy about what is a coherent structure, we allow a wide range of things in that category and that's where a lot of the problems come from.' But he does suggest a basic definition:

> A structure is a correlation with a velocity field, say, which being maintained over some distance and time, gives coherence. But I think the essential question is whether something is a cause or an effect. For example, the streaks are well observed phenomena, well documented, we have measured the hell out of them. But is that the structure in itself or is it just an indication that another structure is present? Structures do things, they are not just effects in my book.[27]

In contrast to Kline, Smits seeks to establish equivalences in a common physical model and doubts the need or the value of the proposal for a community-wide evaluation of the known, arguing that:

If the survey is accurate it will give you ten views. I think, as do many others, that rather than there being eight structures as Kline believes, the diversity of structures 'near-wall' will probably be explicable in terms of a single motion. Some idealisation will be needed but a mechanical model will do. I think that there is widespread consensus and there has been for about ten years.[28]

Contrary to Kline's plea for a classification of structures, Smits argues that understanding is achieved through the construction of simplified models:

It is this development of working models that represents the fundamental aim of turbulence research, to reduce the complexity of the actual flow field dynamics to a simple set of flow phenomena, without sacrificing any important physical mechanisms.[29]

While Smits agrees that understanding is incomplete in the sense that applied turbulence problems can only be resolved empirically, he argues that 'understanding means taking the complicated flow field and abstracting the variability, so that you can construct a lower order system that accurately reflects the real flow.'[30]

This contention is not, however, without its problems. Katepalli Sreenivasan at Yale, whom Smits cites as supporting the existence of consensus, in reviewing the state of play in Turbulent Boundary Layer research claims that:

Few explanations in currency are quantitative and self consistent—that is almost no existing explanation satisfactorily accounts for each aspect of the boundary layer in relation to every other aspect.[31]

Moreover there is no consensus on how to characterise the structures in turbulent flow, on what they are, or on how they are to be measured. As Sreenivasan notes in discussing the question of the relationship between the inner and the outer layer of the flow:

A study of the details of measurements, not merely of the final results reported in publications, suggests that an equally likely explanation for the conflicting measurements is that different authors were in fact measuring facets of the same event, or even different events altogether.[32]

Robinson, taking a third position, concurs with Kline that things are in a bad way.

In spite of decades of experimental research the structure of turbulent boundary layers and the dynamical processes by which turbulence is created and maintained, turbulent boundary layers are only partially understood. The incomplete nature of our understanding has prevented the results of turbulent structure research from making any significant contribution to either predictive modelling schemes or to turbulent control methodologies.[33]

He also advocates 'a community wide re-evaluation of the knowledge' but sees the essential difficulty as neither the complexity of the phenomena nor the lack of a coherent theory, but rather as one of finding a technique capable of generating enough detailed information about the diversity of aspects of a given turbulent flow. Since he holds experimentation to be inherently problematic, the way of the future in Robinson's view is computer simulation.

Simulation versus Experimentation

One of the most important transformations of turbulence research has been brought about by the introduction of computer modelling. In external relations it is seen by Smits and other experimentalists as a major threat in the distribution of funding. Internally, computer simulation has the power to order both the phenomena and the field. Once again something of the struggle can be seen by looking at the management strategies, in a situation where, as in this case, the parties involved wish to cooperate. Robinson, one of the leading proponents of computer simulation, argues that experimentation has inherent limitations, but rather than risk confrontation by claiming that simulation should replace experimentation altogether, he suggests they complement each other. For Smits, a proponent of the established but nonetheless threatened, experimental approach, the situation is different. He wants to display experiment as fundamental, and simulation as inherently limited and at best complementary to experiment.

Robinson is able to make some very cogent criticisms of experimentation in turbulent flow.

> The limitations of experimental methods for unravelling the problems of turbulence physics are well understood but are, to a large degree inherent. Fixed probes at a small number of points in space can be weak tools for determining the characteristics of three dimensional structures with large variations in time and space. Although many groups agree that the simultaneous use of flow visualisation and probe arrays are optimum, it remains

difficult to resolve Eulerian probe based quantitative data with visual information from markers in a three dimensional unsteady flow-field.[34]

So surprising is it that anything has been learnt about turbulent flow according to this characterisation of experimental procedure, that Robinson is led to make the superficially complimentary but basically rather threatening and patronising remark, 'It is to the credit of the researchers in the field that so much has been learned about the structure of turbulence through experimentation'.[35]

Smits concedes that 'the sentiment is accurate given the limitations of what we have in the way of experimental tools', but counters by pointing out that experimentalists 'know more about flow than the people doing the computer simulations'.[36] Again he claims it is a question of understanding:

An experimentalist will always begin by trying to make things simple. Because he's only got a few probes in the flow he tries to infer from that what hypothetical motions produced the signal. He uses flow visualisation which is a very powerful tool that gives some quantitative measurements and tries to fit this into some kind of very simple picture of the mechanics of the motions. The people who do numerical simulations, because they are using the latest techniques and latest computers and latest in algorithms, tend not to know very much about fluid mechanics. They know a lot about computers, they run them and get all these numbers out but then what do they do with them? Getting the numbers doesn't tell you anything. You are still stuck with trying to interpret the data. Because you are interested in it as a physical phenomena, you are trying to understand the real world in some way, you have to put this data in some kind of model in your mind and also because the data is coming from flows that are not realistic and you are trying to use that information to understand realistic flows. All Robinson has done is take a vast database and make it intelligible but the process of interpretation has yet to begin.[37]

Facing what looks like an impasse in which neither side can win, Robinson proposes fairly modestly that, 'to complement the large volume of experimental results in the field ... advantage should be taken of the direct Navier-Stokes turbulence simulation data bases at NASA Ames'.[38] And indeed at that level Smits is actively interested in such complementarity. However, he perceives it as problematic. Firstly, computer simulation appears to be a very powerful and impressive technique, so impressive and powerful that it could displace experimentation altogether. Secondly, he regards that power as largely impression rather than reality, so that its displacement of experiment would be a disadvantage to all research and not just to him as a turbulence experimentalist.

What is the 'direct Navier-Stokes turbulence simulation database'? In essence it is the numerical modelling of turbulent flow. This is done by conceiving of the flow as passing through a very large but finite number of little boxes, each of which consists of a fluid element whose state is described by a set of numbers derived from an approximate form of the Navier-Stokes equations with boundary and initial conditions set for a particular flow. The section of the flow under consideration has a million boxes, each with four numbers in it; and in order to simulate the flow in time there has to be a minimum of a 100 time steps or repetitions of the whole process. The complete simulation procedure is at least four orders removed from 'reality': an equation is formulated for a simplified type of flow; the boundary conditions are set for a specific section of the flow; the boxes, while being taken as points, are actually set at a given size; and finally a limited set of data points is selected and time stepped to make the flow visible. The result is a moving, coloured, three-dimensional image on a computer screen which shows evolving and dissipating structures that give a very seductive impression of being the 'real thing'.

The technique is 'direct' in the sense that it tries to capture all scales without modelling, in contrast to large eddy simulations or Reynolds averaged Navier-Stokes equations. The use of the term database is symptomatic of the problem that worries Smits. It gives the impression that what the computer is dealing with is data derived empirically from real flows, whereas in fact they are derived from hypothetical models and are data only in the sense that they are numbers in a computer. Indeed, in a very interesting co-option of experimental discourse, there is talk of 'doing experiments' and of having a 'numerical wind tunnel' when what is actually being done is to run a computer simulation. There is a sense in which this seems perfectly sound. Gigi Martinelli, who along with Antony Jameson at Princeton has developed computer simulations to show the flow over a wing or a whole airplane, can quite reasonably say, 'I'm doing an experiment to test my display of computational results by using graphic probes', or 'Here I'm doing an experiment by injecting the flow with a trace. Now you can interrogate the flow just like you can in the lab.'[39]

While it is true that they are not running a 'real' flow field and are only solving equations, it is nonetheless possible to get empirical results that are beyond the capacity of the experimentalists, for example, 'many things we can observe in the shock wave are impossible in a real flow using probes'.[40] Kline and Martinelli both cite the example of Boeing using computer simulation to analyse the interference between the engine and the wing and thereby calculating the optimal length of the support required to carry the engine below the wing, a calculation that is otherwise impossible to perform except by testing in full-scale trials.

Using such techniques, which are a combination of the visual and the computational, it is possible to 'see' relationships, physical phenomena and flow field patterns that can not be derived from the equations in any other way. If it is possible to obtain empirical results which are not simply inherent in the equations or the coding for graphical display, then it is feasible to claim that 'experiments' can be done with a computer. This move opens up a whole new realm for experiment. In addition computer simulation could potentially displace hands-on experimental research in much the same way that computers have taken over drafting and design, resulting in the kind of deskilling that Mike Cooley, David Noble and others have discussed.[41] It could also introduce an even greater distance between theory and practice, and an even greater abstraction from reality than is already inherent in contemporary experimental research.

The problems of the wholesale displacement of experiment by computer simulation aside, there are some limitations and difficulties involved in simulating turbulent flow. So far, only Spalart's numerical simulation of a flat plate turbulent boundary layer has been computed. This is a very simple canonical flow with very low Reynolds numbers; to get to a realistic Reynolds number, which would be of the order of one hundred times greater, a billion-fold increase is required in computer time. The computational simulation of the Spalart case took 200 Cray hours. There are only 6000 Cray hours in a year if the computer is run 24 hours a day. According to Smits the Spalart trial would be enormously expensive if computer time were calculated on the same basis as wind tunnel time, although in fact most computing time is deemed to be of zero cost in much research budgeting. Kline acknowledges that:

> ... the ILLIAC computer at Ames was so awkward to use we were able to get to use it at night and got $250,000 worth of free computer time that we would never have got otherwise. They have developed a way of detecting numerical errors from experimental errors, so now we can put in randomised data and run the computer for three to six months till the results settle down, so now we are confident the simulations match experimental data very well. But that is a vast amount of free computer time.[42]

Though computer simulation is limited to simple low Reynolds number flows and has serious cost limitations, Smits does acknowledge it also has considerable strengths if used as an aid to experimental research, since it enables a very detailed examination of a given point of the flow.

> What Robinson can do is like me with these pictures; I have a picture of the density field at a given instant, if I take a line in that field and plot the intensity versus distance it looks much like a picture of turbulence. So, what he has is a box of data points, at each point in his box he has the velocity and pressure field. So he could simulate putting a hot wire of finite length in there and he could sweep it through his box and get a signal out. Then he could answer questions like what happens if you make the wire twice as long, what information would I lose? That would help us to know at what point is the probe so big that the information you get is useless. It's starting to prove useful.[43]

But the main issue for Smits and Robinson is authority. Robinson claims that his 'data *confirm* a number of published experimental findings as well as presenting new information on the structure of turbulent boundary layers'.[44] Smits on the other hand dismisses this claim:

> 'Confirm'—I tend to think it should come the other way round. Numerical simulation is confirmed by reference to experiments. For example one of the things the people over at NASA Ames make a big song and dance about, which I really don't think is worth it, is that hairpin loops are rare, that nice symmetrical structure is not often observed and they are saying that there are not only positive hairpin loops, there are negative hairpin loops. I think that's just a lot of smoke. (see Figs. 34 and 35) They are essentially people who are trying to justify their simulations, they are driven by a lot of pressures and they are driven to say that they are discovering some new physical phenomena from their simulations. I think they are carrying it a bit too far because, so what if hairpin loops are rare? What they are seeing is largely a question of what they want to look at. Robinson has a picture of the pressure field, what he gets instead of the fully formed loop, is the head and one leg. The trouble with that picture is that it may or may not be real. What he could have done is—he had to set the outline of that lump—he could have said I'm going to plot the contour where the pressure has a certain value. Therefore that contour is a volume in space, inside pressure is lower, outside it's higher. If I change that level I can make this leg disappear. Then they could say there are only heads out there and no legs. The only thing that is new is the negative hairpin vortex, even so it was first described experimentally. But it is a red herring; if you look at the motion between two hairpin vortices it will look like a negative hairpin, you don't need any new kinds of motions.[45]

Downstream light plane   Upstream light plane

Figure 34 'Typical' turbulence phenomina: eddies and loops. From: Head and Bandyopadhyay, *Journal of Fluid Mechanics*, Vol. 107 (1981), pp. 297–308. With permission of Cambridge University Press.

However, Robinson claims that the advantages of simulation are that structures can be run forward and backward in time, all structures can be made visible simultaneously, spatial relations between structures can be studied, and structures that are virtually unmeasurable can be displayed.[46]

In Smits' view, 'calculating the entire flow does not mean we understand it, any more than turning on the wind tunnel does, because you cannot extrapolate to other conditions.' But so problematic does Smits conceive the whole question of understanding and the role of computer

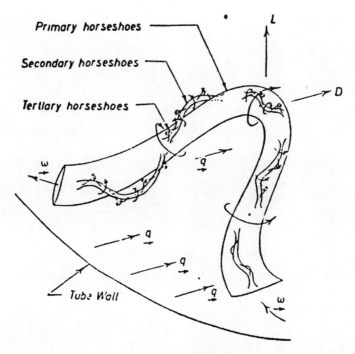

Figure 35 Horseshoe or hairpin loop: candidate for basic turbulence structure. With permission of Friedr Vieweg & Sohn, Braunschweig.

simulation to be, that he begins the introduction of a recent research proposal with a discussion of these issues—a rather unusual procedure, he agrees, in what is essentially a funding application.

> Computations like Spalart's are part of turbulence research in the same way that experiments are, it is important to recognise what their role is, because in some people's minds, not in my contract monitor's mind, but out there is a group in the community who think experiment is not important any more. All we have to do is get a bigger computer and we can crunch our way through all these problems. We won't ever have to deal with this turbulence modelling stuff. We'll just compute it all. I think it's very easy to show that's an unrealistic viewpoint.[47]

Thus he argues in the proposal that direct numerical simulation is valuable because it:

> ... provides us with such an enormous amount of information that our usual response is to look for relatively simple concepts, or models that

represent the database in a more organised and comprehensible fashion; exactly the process we follow in interpreting the far more limited data sets generated by experiment.[48]

Nevertheless he insists that simulation cannot be the sole or primary source of understanding; this can only be achieved through experimentally tested, simplified physical models:

> It is this development of working models that represents the fundamental aim of turbulence research, to reduce the complexity of the actual flow field dynamics to a simple set of flow phenomena, without sacrificing any important physical mechanisms ... observation and experiment play a crucial role in the unravelling the proper physics, especially in the study of high Reynolds number compressible turbulent flows.[49]

For Smits, the essential ordering derives from a simplified physical model and his principal objection to computer simulation lies in the way it creates large aggregations of data but does not provide a way of simplifying that complexity.

By contrast, for Robinson, an experimentalist himself, a very different awareness of the ways in which research can be aggregated came with his adoption of the new tool of computer simulation. Using a simulated flow he made a number of phenomenological 'discoveries' about turbulent flow, only to find that the vast majority of his results had already been published. However, these results though published and confirmed by his own experimental work, were not accepted by the turbulence community as established facts. They were isolated bits of local knowledge that required collective work to mould them into an assemblage.

Moving Local Knowledge Out of the Lab

By early 1994 Robinson had ceased being a major player. He had not implemented his strategy for moving his characterisation of turbulence out of his laboratory. Kline had retired from active research in turbulence and consequently the cataloguing of the apparent variety of structural forms now seems to be in abeyance.

Smits, however, has had considerable success in moving his local knowledge claims. He has enabled them to form part of an assemblage through the joint articulation of a technical device and a social strategy.

The technical device is a laser-based system for producing three dimensional images of turbulent flow.[50] The two-colour photographs that this technique produces have to be looked at through coloured spectacles with one green lens and one red lens, like the kind that were used for 3D movies in the fifties. They are an extremely effective device for the visualisation and hence transmission of the images of turbulence that Smits' model produces.

Smits' social strategy was to establish a collaborative research program with Jim Brasseur at Pennsylvania State University and Sreenivasen at Yale. Sreenivasen is both a theorist and an experimentalist who, while unconvinced that Smits' model is correct, is nonetheless, like Smits, fundamentally concerned with explanations of turbulence in terms of physical and structural models.

Brasseur has developed the computational modelling technique in such a way that it is possible to include experimental parameters. His model of turbulent boundary layers permits the interpretation of the computer-generated data as though they were experimentally produced, so for the first time computational and experimental data have been rendered commensurable.[51] An alliance has been formed between the rival approaches of simulation and experiment through a process of standardisation and equivalence. At the same time the vast, unwieldy and uninterpretable data-set that simulation produces can now be limited and interpreted in the physical terms that Smits and Sreenivasan deem necessary. This social strategy combined with a technical device for making the flow visible, has produced an assemblage that has succeeded in moving Smits' local knowledge out of the Engineering labs at Princeton. How much further it may move remains to be seen.

Technoscientific knowledge results from the imposition of order on nature through the collective work of practitioners in the area. The kinds of ordering that are achieved are contingent, depending on the ways in which the situated actors locally deploy a wide variety of elements in the assemblage, including theory, tools and funds. What has emerged in this imposition of order on the simplified phenomena is that technoscientific practice is messy and heterogeneous. Controversy and disagreement can occur at the most fundamental levels, and experimental practice and results can be very localised and discrete, but nonetheless an assemblage can be achieved. Such assemblages are sustained in part by the development of technical devices that can enable the transmission of a body of knowledge/practice from one local site of production to another. These devices can be simplified physical models, typologies, theories, computer simulations, or lists of problems and applications. It is through the local usage of such devices that otherwise disparate findings and practices can be treated as equivalent and connected in the collective work of creating assemblages. Equally, assemblages are constituted through social strategies for achieving order and authority. It is out of these collective practices of linking disparate sites, practices and people that knowledge spaces are created.

Each of the participants in this story—Kline, Robinson, Smits and other members of the wider turbulence community—characterised the field in different ways and used differing strategies to do so. What has been at issue for them has been the imposition of their own conceptions of order and understanding, which also plays a role in their attempts to transmit their site-specific knowledge claims to other sites.

Meanwhile, I, as a jester/sociologist, continue to attempt to impose order on the field by focusing on local knowledge/practices, struggles for authority, and social strategies and technical devices for moving technoscientific knowledge and creating knowledge spaces as coherent structures in the turbulent flow of the sociology of science. These reflexive difficulties will be addressed at greater length in the concluding chapter.

Notes

1. Susan Leigh Star, 'Simplification in Science Work', p. 205.
2. Woolgar has called this revelatory process 'ironicising' see Steve Woolgar, 'Irony in the Social Study of Science', in K. D. Knorr and M. Mulkay, eds., *Science Observed: Perspectives on the Social Study of Science*, (London: Sage, 1983), pp. 239–266; and on the naturalisation of the arbitrary see Bourdieu, *Outline of a Theory of Practice*.
3. See Katherine Hayles, *Chaos Bound: Orderly Disorder in Contemporary Literature and Science*, (Ithaca: Cornell University Press, 1990).
4. Susan Leigh Star, 'Simplification in Science Work: An Example from Neuroscience Research', *Social Studies of Science*, Vol. 13, (1983), pp. 205–28, p. 45. See also the discussion of theories as collective work in Star, *Regions of Mind*, pp. 15–37. She attributes the robustness of theories to plasticity and coherence which I take to be close analogues of equivalence and connectivity, see Chapter 1.
5. On the different readings of Kuhn see Rouse, *Knowledge and Power*.
6. Kuhn, *The Structure of Scientific Revolutions*, p. 30.
7. Ibid, p. 44.
8. Law, 'Technology and Heterogeneous Engineering'.

9   Michel Callon and Bruno Latour, 'Don't Throw the Baby Out with the Bath School!', in A. Pickering, ed., *Science As Practice and Culture* (Chicago: University of Chicago Press, 1992), pp. 343–368 and Harry Collins and Steven Yearly, 'Epistemological Chicken', ibid, pp. 301–326.

10 S. Kline, physicist at Stanford. All direct quotes like this one are taken from my field notes and tapes made at Princeton and Stanford in 1989 (available for examination if required), referred to hereafter as FN89.

11 Mike Smith, research scientist at Princeton. FN89.

12 S. Kline, *Quasi-coherent Structures in the Turbulent Boundary Layer: Part 1. Status Report on a Community-wide Summary of the Data.* Zoran P. Zaric Memorial International Seminar on Near-Wall Turbulence, (Dubrovnik: 1988), p. 2.

13 A. Smits FN89.

14 M. Smith FN89.

15 Quoted in James Gleick, *Chaos: Making a New Science*, (London: Viking Penguin, 1987), p. 68.

16 Tony Perry quoted in A. Smits, ed., *Proceedings of the Princeton Workshop on 'New Approaches to Experimental Turbulence Research'*, *MAE Report No. 1924*, (Princeton: Princeton University Department of Mechanical and Aerospace Engineering, 1991), p. 16.

17 Vincent Kiernan, 'Article of Faith Fails Aero Engineers', *New Scientist*, Vol. 150, 2029, 11 May, (1996), p. 5.

18 J. Lumley, 'Turbulence at the Crossroads, or Whither Turbulence', (Mathematical Sciences Institute, Cornell University, Workshop Poster, 1989).

19 Pierre Bourdieu, 'The Specificity of the Scientific Field and the Social Conditions of the Progress of Reason', *Social Science Information*, Vol. 14, (1975), pp. 19–47.

20 Problems: combustion and mixing; complex flows; two dimensional versus three dimensional; effects of chemical reaction; extra strain rates. Examples: control of turbulence; compressible turbulent flows; hypersonic boundary layers; hypersonic mixing layers; supersonic aerodynamics; geophysical fluid turbulence; turbulence modeling. Doyle Knight in Smits, *New Approaches to Experimental Turbulence Research*, p. 115.

21 G. N. Gilbert and M. Mulkay, *Opening Pandora's Box*, (Cambridge: Cambridge University Press, 1984).

22 S. Robinson, S. Kline, et al., *Quasi-Coherent Structures in the Turbulent Boundary Layer: Part 2. Verification and New Information from a Numerically Simulated Flat-Plate Layer.* (Dubrovnik: 1988); Kline, *Quasi-coherent Structures in the Turbulent Boundary Layer: Part 1*; A. Smits, *The Structure of Supersonic Turbulent Shear Layers. A Draft Proposal to the Air Force Office of Scientific Research*, (Fluid Dynamics Laboratory, Dept. of Mechanical and Aerospace Engineering, Princeton University, 1989).

23 These criteria should (1) distinguish between results which are reliable data, or are direct deductive consequences from reliable data, on the one hand, and 'inferences (or hypotheses, or suggestions, or hunches) that go beyond the data and its deductive consequences'; (2) distinguish between possible, actual and real events; (3) enable the inclusion of 'all the structures' and not argue that any one or two structures is sufficient for full understanding; and (4) consider all flows not just 'the canonical flat plate layer' and the 'canonical planar flow'. Kline, *Quasi-coherent Structures in the Turbulent Boundary Layer: Part 1*, pp. 2–5.

24 Ibid.

25 Kline FN89.

26 Kline FN89.

27 Smits FN89.

28 Smits FN89. Smits claims 'there exists a broad consensus on the overall features of turbulent motions found in incompressible flows' which is 'based on a simple model with two types of motions one scaling on inner layer variables the other on outer layer variables but admittedly with a poorly understood interaction about which there are competing views'. Smits, *The Structure of Supersonic Turbulent Shear Layers*, p. 20.

29 Ibid, p. 3.

30 Ibid.

31 K. R. Sreenivasan, *The Turbulent Boundary Layer*, (Mason Lab, Yale University, 1989).

32 Ibid, p. 17.

33 Robinson, *Quasi-Coherent Structures in the Turbulent Boundary Layer*, p. 2.

34 Ibid.

35 Ibid.

36 Smits FN89.

37 Ibid.

38 Robinson, *Quasi-Coherent Structures in the Turbulent Boundary Layer: Part 2*, p. 2.

39 Martinelli FN89.

40 Ibid.

41 Mike Cooley, *Architect or Bee: The Human Price of Technology*, (London: Chatto and Windus, 1987); David Noble, *America by Design: Science, Technology and the Rise of Corporate Capitalism*, (New York: Knopf, 1977); David Noble, *Forces of Production: A Social History of Industrial Automation*, (New York: Knopf, 1984).

42 Kline FN 89.

43 Smits FN 89.

44 Robinson, *Quasi-Coherent Structures in the Turbulent Boundary Layer: Part 2*, p. 10.

45 Smits FN89.

46 Robinson, *Quasi-Coherent Structures in the Turbulent Boundary Layer: Part 2*, p. 10.
47 Smits FN89.
48 Smits, *The Structure of Supersonic Turbulent Shear Layers*, p. 3.
49 Ibid p. 4.
50 C. Delo, J. Poggie, et al., *A System for Imaging and Displaying Three-Dimensional, Time Evolving Passive Scalar Concentration Fields in Fluid Flow*, (Princeton University, Department of Mechanical and Aerospace Engineering, 1994).
51 J. Brasseur, *The Structure of High Reynolds Number Turbulent Boundary Layers Part A*, (University Park: Pennsylvania State University, Department of Mechanical Engineering, 1993).

CONCLUSION
RATIONALITY, RELATIVISM AND THE POLITICS OF KNOWLEDGE

Public Knowledge and the Knowledge of the Public

Thirty years ago John Ziman made a modest proposal that went somewhat unremarked in the midst of the Kuhnian revolutionary uproar.[1] Science, he claimed, is basically social because it is as much driven by the need for consensus and convention as it is by logic and method. Science is first and foremost public knowledge.

Now some of the social constraints on Ziman's slightly normative perspective on science as public knowledge have been very nicely delineated in the work of Brian Wynne and others who have brought to light the problems experienced by members of the public in dealing with experts. They have found that science seamlessly interweaves memory, trust, uniformity, history and authority constructing the kind of knowledge space I have described earlier. But the universalised and standardised scientific expertise this produces connects very poorly to the lived experience of lay people and their local knowledge.[2]

The mismatch between 'public knowledge' and the 'knowledge of the public' is reflected in debates in other arenas about the lack of recognition of the role of 'social capital' and its associated decline and in debates about the supposed transition to reflexive modernity.[3] One way of conceiving of social capital is as local knowledge manifested in participation, trust and cooperation of informal groupings, for example, commercial fishermen, neighbourhood watch and the PTA. The concept of social capital gives recognition to the value of the forms of lay knowledge embedded in the intricate varieties of horizontal connectedness or informal Latourian networks not normally recognised by the more formal, vertically connected, standardised forms of knowledge production through which 'science gains its image of intellectual universality'.[4]

Robert Putnam developed the notion of social capital to explain the relative success of Northern Italy in developing democratic forms of government and economic progress. He has since gone on to find it in decline in the US, as Eva Cox has in Australia, a decline that reflects the failure not of the public to understand science, but of science to understand the public's knowledge.[5]

Similar problems concerning the disjuncture between scientific knowledge and local knowledge have been apparent in the cases examined earlier in the book. Cathedrals were built without plans or standardised measures, Pacific Islanders navigated without maps or compasses, maps became adopted by the state through a social process of linking local sites; turbulence research and malaria vaccine research, like all technoscience, is local and site-specific in the first instance. In every case disorganised local knowledge was assembled in contingent circumstances; yet scientific knowledge is publicly presented as universal and rational.

Rationality, Universality and SSK

The problems of universality and rationality are central to the real world political issues concerning the question of whose knowledge should be authoritative. They are also central to the more internal problems of the sociology of scientific knowledge. As we saw in the last chapter, the turbulence of turbulence research points to analogous forms of turbulence prevalent in the sociology of scientific knowledge in particular and in science studies generally.

From one point of view it might appear that the sociology of scientific knowledge is hamstrung by the reflexive dilemmas raised by its apparent lack of unity and coherence, and by the questionable validity of any given theoretical ordering. However, the quest for coherence and unity is as much a chimera in sociology as it is in science; all our understandings of the natural and the social are complex, multiple and messy. Equally, just as messiness proved no obstacle in engineering research, it need not be an obstacle in the sociology of scientific knowledge. Indeed, the revelation of messiness and its celebration can be seen as an essential strength in the sociology of scientific knowledge.

The sociology of scientific knowledge is also awash in claims that it has reached maturity, has proven sterile, is an attack on civilisation as we know it, has been of no use in policy making or liberating the Third World, is obsessed with the social, has moved beyond the social, like all forms of constructivism and relativism is self-contradictory and therefore just more postmodern claptrap, is at heart the old orthodoxy and should be replaced by cultural theory. SSK is under attack from without and within and has almost as many variants and theoretical orientations as there are proponents.

However, I would argue that this barrage of criticism does not necessarily mean the sociology of scientific knowledge is in a phase of terminal self destruction or that it is doomed to be a victim of the 'science wars'.[6] Rather, it can be seen as an indicator that the sociology of scientific knowledge has reached maturity and that a great deal is at stake. The considerable and vocal opposition shows both that it is having an impact and is being taken seriously, though it may also be simply an opportunity for alternative views to gain some purchase. But perhaps a more significant sign of maturity is that it has developed enough common ground between its diversity of approaches to have thrown up, in the manner of a Kuhnian paradigm, some basic problems which have to be solved.

Some of what I take to be its basic problems are coincident with the criticisms of its opponents, and some of its problems have been brought to light through the maturation of the program. Whatever their origin, they all, in effect, turn on the question of the relationship between local and universal knowledge and the basic aim of the enlightenment project, which must still have salience today—the improvement of the human condition through our own efforts. Or in sum, what forms of knowledge and reasoning are going to improve our lot? This is not just a dilemma for the sociology of scientific knowledge, it is *the* millennial problem. We appear to be stuck with irreconcilable and equally problematic alternatives. The forms of universal reason that are taken to stand behind science have been seen as the problem by constructivists, feminists and post-colonialists alike. On this scenario there is little or no correspondence between the universals of science and the reality of people's lives and cultures; the world ends in exploitation of people and resources with the attendant probability of a capitalist if not a nuclear winter. But on the opposing scenario, if local knowledges proliferate there is nothing to choose between them and we become enmired in Balkanised epistemes where criticism, enlightenment and progress are impossible and the world ends in a postmodern 'bonfire of the dualities'.

In this last chapter I want explore the reasons why this clash between the local and the universal is irresolvable unless we devise a strategy that will embrace the contradiction, celebrate the messiness, but also avoid the central weakness of postmodernism, which is that its critique of modernism and progress has led to the abandonment of the possibility of the improvement of the human condition. Such a strategy some have called 'transmodern'.[7] In order to get to the transmodern I want to explore the vital and thorny problems of rationality.

According to the more positivistic accounts now gaining renewed currency, the key to understanding the unparalleled success of science lies in its embodiment of the highest form of rationality and objectivity in the scientific method. This mythical underpinning of science also provides the rationale for the celebration of modernism and the current domination of the West. A view, unselfconsciously exemplified by the arch-rationalist Ernest Gellner who, in one of his more hard-nosed moods, claimed 'If a doctrine conflicts with the acceptance of the superiority of scientific-industrial societies over others, then it really is out.'[8]

But rationality is a deeply problematic concept. It is very profoundly embedded in the hidden assumptions of late twentieth-century occidentalism about what it is to be a knowing, moral, sane individual. Indeed, so embedded is it that to be anything other than rational is to be ignorant, immoral, insane or the member of an undifferentiated herd. Hence rationality cannot be treated as simply an epistemological concept about the conditions under which one can know something, it also carries ideological overtones, privileging certain ways of knowing over others. Rationality is a constitutive element in the moral economy.

Yet despite, or perhaps because of, this central role of rationality, there are no fully articulated rules or criteria for being rational in the acceptance of beliefs or in the pursuit of knowledge, nor is there a single type of rationality. This sense of incoherence in the concept reaches total intransigence in the recognition that ultimately there can be no rational justification for being rational. Nonetheless, critical rationalism as advocated by Karl Popper has a primal persuasiveness in contemporary Western society. Mario Bunge has captured some of that self-evidentiality and variability in his 'Seven Desiderata for Rationality':[9]

1. Conceptual: minimising fuzziness, vagueness, or imprecision.
2. Logical: striving for consistency, avoiding contradiction.
3. Methodological: questioning, doubting, criticising, demanding proof or evidence.
4. Epistemological: caring for empirical support and compatibility with bulk of accepted knowledge.
5. Ontological: adopting a view consistent with science and technology.
6. Valuational: striving for goals which are worthy and attainable.
7. Practical: adopting means likely to attain the goals in view.

Indeed, seeing them set out like this makes their denial seem irrational. But epistemologically speaking, even if the claim for rationality's governing role is weakened to talk of aims or desiderata as Bunge does, Wittegenstein's point prevails: no body of rules can contain the rules for their application. So even on its own terms the project of a transcendental rationality supervening all local variation seems problematic.

But from a constructivist's historically contingent perspective there are no universal criteria of rationality. What counts as rational has always been contested and cannot help but be the outcome of locally negotiated criteria in particular contexts of struggle.

The concept of the individual as a rational actor that is now so basic to Western ways of thought is not derived from first principles, but rather arose in conjunction with the development of modern science in the seventeenth century. This was a period which saw the debates over the appropriate forms of rationality between the Cartesian rationalists and the Baconian empiricists. Whether true knowledge was to be derived deductively from self-evident first principles or by observation and experiment, it had already been accepted that the acquisition of such knowledge was within the capacity of human individuals. The recognition that human reason and experience was not inherently limited, and could be a source of knowledge, re-emerged in the twelfth and thirteenth centuries in the West with the separation of the church from the state and with the development of secular law from the accompanying canon law.[10] The development of this conception of rationality was not universal, for example it was not paralleled in Islamic society where men were denied rational agency; they were held to lack the capacity to change nature or to understand it. Knowledge was instead to be derived from traditional authority. This is not to deny that there has been any Islamic science or any Islamic discussion of rationality. On the contrary, there have of course been major achievements in Islamic science, but in a radically different moral economy.

While the notion of the rational actor, unconstrained by circumstance or authority and moved only by logic and evidence, has become embedded in our legal, economic and scientific presuppositions, such an idealised conception is at variance with our lived reality both at the societal and the individual level. At the societal level modern Western capitalism has become a bureaucratic system which, as Weber pointed out, relies on a calculative rationality. The administration and perpetuation of this system is crucially dependent on a system of rules from which legal and administrative calculations can be derived by professional, objective experts. Hence modern science and capitalism are interdependent; they were co-produced on the basis of a calculability derived in part from rational structures of law and administration. In Weber's view it is the specific and peculiar rationalism of Western culture that makes science unique to the West.[11] Even if Weber was right, what needs further examination is how specific and peculiar calculative rationalism is. That form of rationality has a number of interwoven components, for example the acceptance of written documents as evidence as opposed to oral testimony. This transition also occurred in the twelfth and thirteenth centuries, but required the development of a 'literate mentality' before it became self-evident that records and archives were more belief worthy than the word of 'twelve good men and true'.[12] Some, like Goody, have further argued that the accumulation of knowledge and the possibility of criticism and hence rationality are only possible in a literate culture.[13] Similarly, vision also had to be rationalised to provide grammar or rules for the relationship between the representation of objects and their shapes as located in space.[14] Yet another component of the form of rationality we equate with science is the empiricist requirement that theory conform with the evidence. But this of course requires the prior acceptance of the validity of empirical and experimental evidence, which as we have already seen in Chapter 2, was not established until the mid-17th century.[15]

The historically contingent character of the outcome between competing forms of rationality is beautifully illustrated in Ken Alder's account of the struggles over appropriate forms of cannon manufacture in the French revolutionary period. The revolutionaries fought for standardised, deskilled interchangeability of artillery components, while the Bonapartists championed a moral economy in which entrepreneurs, skilled artisans and social harmony were to be celebrated. The kind of precision calibrated measurement that we now take as essential to both modern science and industrial production did not in the first instance become adopted, for the Bonapartists won. It was not until the American civil war that appropriate conditions prevailed and the kinds of measured calculative rationality based on conventionally agreed standards started to become commonplace and self-evident. Alder concludes that precision, uniformity, control and efficiency are not the innate commitments of engineers: 'rationality is not a set of timeless abstractions; it is a set of social practices which have emerged historically'.[16]

It is a mistake then to conceive of rationality as a form of mentality or as a particular human capacity either limited or universal. Rather, there are forms and compounds of rationality which at the societal level, as Foucault has shown, are dependent on particular social and historical institutions, constituted through the interwoven practices, techniques, strategies and modes of calculation that traverse them.[17] Moreover, at the individual level we do not behave like the ends/means optimization calculators that economic rationalism would have us believe we are. We are at least as interested in meaning, significance and personal values as we are in economic concerns. Nor are we quite the rational agents basing our knowledge simply on direct experience that some legal and philosophical theorists claim. A considerable proportion of our knowledge derives from books, television, newspapers, journals, teachers, experts and our community traditions. In other words our knowledge is a blend of the testimony of others, and of our own experience of public and local knowledge. Thus our individual lived rationality is based in a range of social practices, traditions and moralities, that are suppressed and concealed in the portrayal of rationality as an ahistorical universalistic form of reasoning exemplified by science.

Much the same can be said of objectivity. Objective knowledge is held to be the product of science that has established methods to ensure individual, institutional and cultural biases are eliminated. On closer examination objectivity is not a special characteristic of one kind of knowledge-science, rather it is the result of whatever institutionalised practices serve in a particular culture to create self-evident validity. Objective knowledge, in modern terms, is held to contrast with subjective knowledge. It is knowledge that is not local, that is not contingent on the circumstance, authority or the perspective of the individual knower. However, the concept of objectivity, like that of rationality, is not immutable. It is an historic compound. In the seventeenth century objectivity meant 'the thing insofar as it is known'. The concept of aperspectival objectivity emerged in the moral and aesthetic philosophy of the late eighteenth century, and spread to the natural sciences only in the mid-nineteenth century as a result of the institutionalisation of scientific life as a communal rather than an individual activity.[18]

This characterisation of objectivity as the 'view from nowhere' represents one of the essential contradictions of scientific knowledge production.[19] Knowledge is necessarily a social product; it is the messy, contingent, and situated outcome of group activity. Yet in order to achieve credibility and authority in a culture that prefers the abstract over the concrete and separates facts from values, knowledge has to be presented as unbiased and undistorted, without a place or a knower.

Objectivity, like rationality and democracy, is at best a worthy goal but one that is never capable of achievement. Since knowledge is the product of social processes it can never completely transcend the social. Objective knowledge cannot, for example, simply be knowledge which is unaffected by non-rational psychological forces, since scientists always have motivations even if they pursue knowledge for its own sake.[20] Nor can objectivity be restricted to the avoidance of dogmatic commitment, because there have been scientists like Kepler whose obsession with regular solids and cosmic harmony led to his derivation of the laws of planetary motion. While it may be possible to avoid personal idiosyncrasy, this can only be achieved through the establishment of communal or public knowledge, as Ziman suggests. If knowledge is a communal product, then the question arises how should the scientific community be constituted? Should it be an essentially Western institution? Should it be constituted of scientific experts? These questions bring us back to the starting point of this chapter: can we conceive a new form of communal space for knowledge which embraces non-experts and other traditions?

Relativism and Reflexivity

There remains, however, a core set of problems for the sociology of scientific knowledge that have to be dealt with before we can reach such a transmodern space. These core problems concern the inherent relativism and reflexivity of SSK and the temptation to abandon these qualities, which seems an attractive option to some sociologists of science, given the virulence of the attacks on the supposed irrationality of relativism and the apparent neutrality and plausibility of more atheoretical empiricist approaches.

The issue was brought into focus in the provocative challenge thrown down at the end of the first decade of the sociology of scientific knowledge by the historian of medicine Roy Porter,

> The science of science is not reflexive, self-critical, it is self-protective, a believer not an agnostic. The subject cordons off the object. When Joseph Ben-David, a leading scientific sociologist wrote, in 1971 that 'the possibilities for either an interactional or institutional sociology of the conceptual and theoretical contents of science are extremely limited', his jargon proclaimed the immunity of scientific knowledge. It must be taken on its own terms, read at face value. The science of science is science's flunkey![21]

Porter's very damning remark clearly asserts that the possibility of the critique of science is dependent on a reflexive sociology of science and, I would argue, the concomitant necessity of a robust form of relativism. But it is also necessary to be clear on what a critique of science can and should consist of. Critique in the Marxist sense means seeing both how technoscience came to be as it is and how it could be other. Critique is therefore crucially dependent on the possibility of change, on technoscience not being autonomous or above the constellation of social, economic, political and cultural processes that somehow bring about our sociocultural world. Critics of the sociology of scientific knowledge are often confused on this essential issue. They take anything that does not preserve the autonomy of science as being anti-science. This shows the very point which such critics wish to deny, that there is a nexus between knowledge and power. If science was either autonomous or separate from power, then SSK would be of no concern to scientists.[22] Clearly what characterises the kind of SSK that I wish to advocate is the capacity to provide for a critique of technoscientific knowledge and its relationship to power. But such a critique is in no sense anti-science, quite the opposite. As Popper argued, science like democracy depends on the growth of criticism, or as Feyerabend put it, following Chairman Mao, it depends on letting a thousand blossoms bloom.[23] The capacity for the sociology of science to provide such a critique is dependent in large part on the position taken on the joint problems of relativism and reflexivity.

To advocate relativism has always been to invite a critical and nega-tive reaction; consequently the problem of relativism was a major concern in the 1970s when SSK was trying to establish itself in the face of critical opposition from people like Ben-David. Relativism has reemerged as a central issue in the study of science for a complex set of reasons. There has been a renewed emphasis on the nexus between anthropology, sociology, psychology, cultural studies, feminism, post-colonialism, political science, economics, philosophy and the history of science; but there has also been a movement within the sociology of science to abandon anything that smells of relativism because there has been a renewed political critique of relativistic and constructivist doctrines.[24]

The general form of relativism underpinning the sociology of sci-entific knowledge derives from the recognition that we do not have a set of fixed and universal criteria for truth, logic, or rationality that are sufficient either to choose between competing knowledge claims within a knowledge tradition, or to bridge differing knowledge traditions. It is always necessary to have an additional set of pragmatic criteria of simplicity, plausibility, coherence, fit with the evidence and so on, as well as assumptions about space, time, agency and causality. Such criteria are seldom fully articulated; they are often tacit and usually the constantly evolving outcome of negotiations amongst a group who share systems of trust and a classificatory network which is largely conventional. The acceptance of a given belief or set of beliefs cannot be accounted for on purely epistemological grounds but can only be understood with respect to the time, place and circumstance of the generation and acceptance of the belief in question.[25]

There are sub-varieties of relativism within this general form. Mandelbaum, for example, has distingushed between subjective, objective and conceptual relativism, which vary according to which aspects of the background situation are selected for locating the knowledge claim: whether it be the individual's beliefs and attitudes, the total context, or more specifically the intellectual and conceptual background of the individual.[26] In turn these positions reflect the kind of social theory with which a particular relativist is operating. As yet insufficient attention has been paid to the nature of the implicit social theory that underlies any given position within the sociology of scientific knowledge. Equally significant is the fact that relatively few sociologists of science seem to have paid substantial attention to any of the contemporary debates in sociology and anthropology about whether a value free sociology is possible, or the extent to which the attempt by one group of human beings to study another is an interpretive dialogue in which understanding is achieved through an interactional process of constructed meanings.[27] These problems have become particularly acute since the advent of empirical investigations of scientific practice. The works of Karin Knorr-Cetina, Bruno Latour, Steve Woolgar, and Harry Collins in the first generation and Sharon Traweek, Joan Fujimura and others in the second, are all avowedly anthropological in that they are based on direct observation of scientists in their institutional settings.[28] This move from historical case studies and textual analyses into the examination of the 'taken for granted' practices, rituals and rites of the scientific tribe, highlights the necessity of considering the resolution of the problems endemic to anthropology and sociology in particular, and the social sciences generally.

An aphorism that is often offered us by statisticians, economists and politicians in solace for life's vicissitudes, is 'It will be all right in the long run'. As a hidden assumption behind the orthodox history, philosophy and sociology of science it serves to nullify the critical stance on science and technology. The 'long run' argument is also one of the most telling criticisms of the sociology of knowledge.[29] The essence of the argument is that 'knowledge' or 'truth' will emerge in the long run, because any social contaminants or determinants will be eradicated by the demands of common sense practice, fit with the evidence, consistency with other theories and so on. On this account a sociological analysis of science is highly restricted in scope and any relativistic tendencies it might encourage will be negated by the autonomy of emergent truth. Unwillingness to fully embrace relativism within the sociology of knowledge first manifested itself in the work of Karl Mannheim, one of the founding fathers of the discipline. Although a thorough relativist in other respects, Mannheim avoided what he perceived as its unacceptable consequences by making a special case of scientific knowledge.[30] This immunising stratagem has also been adopted by the more orthodox sociology of science which considers the social factors affecting the rate and direction of scientific development rather than those affecting the form and content of scientific ideas.[31] Thomas Kuhn, along with Stephen Toulmin, N. R. Hanson and Paul Feyerabend, was largely responsible for establishing the current relativistic and sociological orientation of the history and philosophy of science. But he too is well known to have repudiated the more fundamentally relativistic consequences of his position by adopting some supposedly universal criteria for choosing between otherwise incommensurable paradigms.[32] The explicit inclusion of the form and content of scientific knowledge in a sociological analysis, the assertion that all beliefs—true or false, rational or irrational, successful or unsuccessful—require similar causal explanation, is the principle of symmetry that lay at the core of the so called 'strong program' initiated by Bloor and Barnes.[33]

Relativism has, of course, a history going back to the Greeks. The most famous early formulation was Protagoras' dictum, 'Man is the measure of all things', which brought its earliest rebuttal by Plato in the *Theaetetus* (171a): 'Let us suppose that whatever seems true to any person, is true for the person to whom it seems so. If this is the doctrine of Protagoras then Protagoras will hold that those who hold that Protagoras' theory is false are holding the truth'.[34] Plato's argument seems to be an extremely powerful one and has appeared in a variety of guises ever since.[35] But all arguments to the effect that relativism is self-refuting, contradictory or paradoxical are dependent on a central presupposition that there is some Archimedean point, some set of absolute, fixed and universal criteria for what is to count as knowledge and truth, which are beyond any existential determination.[36] A general form of the argument from self-refutation is given by Mary Hesse: 'Let P be the proposition "All criteria of truth are relative to a local culture"; hence nothing can be known to be true except in senses of "knowledge" and "truth" that are relative to that culture. Now if P is asserted as true, it must itself be true only in the sense of "true" relative to a local culture ... hence there are no grounds for asserting P'.[37]

This argument depends on the assumption of absolute criteria for knowledge and truth, while the proposition P explicitly denies the assumption of such criteria. If the proposition is judged by its own criteria then it is not self-refuting or contradictory. Thus the simple knock-down argument against relativism that it is self-refuting can be dismissed; but it does focus our attention on the essential equivocation of the terms 'knowledge', 'truth' and 'grounds'. Knowledge for the relativist is not true belief but accepted belief; knowledge is what is collectively accepted as such in a belief system.[38]

This then is the core of the sociology of knowledge which is concerned with why and how propositions, statements, theories and beliefs come to be accepted. If it is claimed that there are some absolute universal criteria for assessing knowledge claims, knowledge of which is not open to sociological analysis, or that scientific knowledge is objective and hence not open to sociological analysis either, then the sociology of knowledge is reduced to the 'weak program' of explaining how and why false beliefs are accepted. To deny both of these exceptions and demand that the sociology of knowledge embrace all accepted beliefs necessitates acknowledging that the sociology of knowledge in general as well as SSK in particular is inherently and thoroughly relativistic. While many of the leading proponents of the strong program—Bloor, Barnes and Collins for example—all at one time acknowledged the relativistic nature of their enterprise, none of them seems willing to grasp the consequences of this acknowledgment. It appears to have little or no effect on their epistemology or methodology. Bloor holds that the strong programmer should 'only proceed as other scientists and all will be well', and Collins that it is sensible for sociologists of scientific knowledge to assume that what they find about scientific knowledge is 'objective'.[39] Yehuda Elkana has argued that one can only be a relativist between frameworks, that of necessity one must be a realist within a framework.[40] On this account the position of Bloor and the strong program could be acceptable but it seems to me to seriously weaken their whole position, leaving their relativism and hence their sociology to do no real work.

However, if one accepts that relativism is not self-refuting, one must also accept that there are no *conclusive* arguments or proofs for adopting the sociology of knowledge. Does this mean that there are no grounds at all for adopting it? This question in turn raises a set of prior issues: relativism seems to deny the possibility of choice, judgement or assessment on rational grounds; it is a recipe for anarchy or 'anything goes'. Seen ultimately in the context of the political critique of science, this criticism takes the form of the question as to whether a relativist sociology of science is quietist, in that it precludes making moral judgements or advocating change. So, is relativism quietist? The problem here is the one John Krige so neatly summed up in the aphorism much admired by Alan Chalmers: *'anything goes ... means ... everything stays'*[41] This criticism is dependent on showing that 'epistemic relativism which asserts that knowledge is rooted in a particular time and culture ...   and does not just mimic nature' leads inevitably to judgemental relativism which 'claims that all forms of knowledge are equally valid and that we cannot compare different forms of knowledge and discriminate among them'.[42] To deny that there are any fixed or universal criteria of truth or rationality does not necessitate the abandonment of any criteria at all. On the contrary, the relativist can and does make choices, judgements and assessments about what to do and what to believe, but on the basis of criteria that are flexible and negotiable. Instead of accepting that there are self-evident or necessary criteria for rationality, or that science itself should be taken as the exemplar of rationality, the sociology of knowledge must take as a question of research the ways in which particular criteria are articulated in particular circumstances. The plausibility of a relativistic position gains strength and support from a number of problems which have become central in contemporary history and philosophy of science and which have already been canvassed in the opening chapter: the Quinian thesis on the underdetermination of theory by data, and the theory-ladenness of observations. Another key issue for relativism is the character of our classification of the natural world. All propositions or observation statements contain descriptive predicates which imply a classification or categorisation of the world based on postulated essences or natural kinds. On standard empiricist accounts our knowledge of essences or natural kinds is supplied by theories which in turn are derived from observations. This leaves us with a problem of circularity unless it is acknowledged that classifications are at least in part conventional and hence not universal and fixed.[43]

Thus I would argue that the relativist in making judgements, theory choices and so on, is in the same position as many contemporary philosophers of science who are endeavouring to cope with the problems of empiricism without lapsing into metaphysical realism. All such choices require some presuppositions which are not directly knowable or analytically true. Consequently such presuppositions will be judged appropriate or applicable in particular circumstances on grounds that derive from elements in the total belief system which are other than purely epistemological or cognitive. As such they are likely to fall within the ambit of the sociology of knowledge.

Let us return to the question of the grounds on which the adoption of relativism can be advocated. If, as has been argued, relativism is not self-refuting, and if all judgements or theory choices depend on conventional elements that require analysis that goes beyond simple comparison of the theory with the evidence and conformity with logical prescriptions, what can be said in favour of adopting the position? Underlying this question is the profound sense of unease that many people find in contemplating relativism. It has been variously described as an 'incubus', a 'seductive temptation', a 'spectre in need of exorcism', 'the ideology of hopeless surrender'. Krausz and Meiland have identified the source of this rejection of relativism as the implication that 'there is no point to intellectual work'.[44] This is an important insight because it helps to explain both the rejection of relativism and also the various moves that relativists themselves have made to mitigate the consequences of relativism. As we shall see, many of these moves can be seen as attempts of sociologists to legitimate their own disciplinary practice rather than embrace the full consequences of relativism.

To put the matter briefly, the grounds for accepting relativism can only be located in the theoretical practice of relativism. To unpack this claim we must consider two issues: the inherently pragmatic character of knowledge claims and the necessity of reflexivity. By the pragmatic character of knowledge claims I mean quite simply that they are performative, they are the result of human actions. We cannot know nature directly, we have to work on it to gain knowledge of it. This conception of knowledge or belief as performative, as being the result of human bodies and minds working collectively, is central to the sociology of knowledge and to knowledge spaces as contingent assemblages. That we do not merely passively mirror or reproduce reality, but purposively appropriate and transform it, has been extensively argued by writers from Bacon to Marx as well as Bob Young, Karin Knorr-Cetina, Richard Rorty and, more recently, Joan Fujimura and Andy Pickering. I have already discussed this issue in the introduction and I will not reiterate the arguments here. Instead I want to allude briefly to the consequences of accepting this view. It means that the inspection of the logical content of ideas, or of the relations between abstractly conceived beliefs, will provide at best a very limited insight into their use and significance. It is only by attending to the deployment of beliefs in specified contexts, by considering their function in purposive activity that we can reach a fuller understanding of how and why they came to be accepted. This does not, of course, make the analytical task any easier, but it does mean that we cannot ignore the role of human intentions, purposes, goals and values in assessing knowledge claims or beliefs.

If we accept that all knowledge claims or beliefs are value-laden, then the sociology of knowledge itself is an inherently value-laden and consequently an evaluative program. At the same time it must embrace the full consequences of relativism and recognise the necessity of reflexivity, of providing explanations and evaluations of itself. Thus the very grounds for adopting relativism and the sociology of knowledge must also be permeated with values, and hence the reasons for rejecting or accepting relativism are at least partly moral and political in character. As the sociology of scientific knowledge takes its subject matter to be an inherently evaluative activity, one guided by political, moral and social objectives as well as technical and practical ones, so in order to provide grounds for its own theoretical practice it can only have recourse to similar objectives and can therefore only be accepted or rejected on a combination of political, moral, social, technical and practical grounds. A major focus of concern must therefore be: what kind of understanding of our relations to nature and to each other are desirable or good, rather than simply 'true' or 'probable'? Of course there are no fixed and universal criteria for moral and political judgements, but the grounds for adopting relativism are that human purposes and values should be considered explicitly instead of being transformed and absorbed into relations between objects. It should, furthermore, go without saying that all this again shows that relativism, when viewed in an appropriate reflexive mode, far from being quietist, requires that we recognise that the 'pattern of all inquiry, scientific as well as moral, is deliberation concerning the relative attractions of various concrete alternatives',[45] and further, that it is the old rationalist orthodoxy which attempts to preclude the possibility of 'science being other than it is' and hence of change.

The foregoing argument raises the concern of the political effectiveness of the form of relativism and reflexivity that is advocated. On the one hand it is reasonable to reject those forms that are quietist or for which anything goes, but on the other hand relativistic arguments are too weak to advocate positions in contexts like courts of law, commissions of inquiry and so on. In these contexts their strengths lie in the capacity for deconstruction rather than the articulation of policy or alternative solutions. It would appear that revelation and articulation of relativism and reflexivity are matters of strategy in the struggle over whose knowledge counts.

This strategic element and the attendant problems are revealed in positions taken by some of the proponents of SSK. Barry Barnes for example appears to suppress the evaluative demands of the relativism and reflexivity of SSK by claiming that the sociology of knowledge must examine knowledge 'without any concern for the implications of its findings if it is to maintain its own integrity'.[46] Likewise Harry Collins, who has gone further than most in embracing relativism, disavows reflexivity: 'Just as it is no part of the natural scientist's job to consider the social construction of scientific knowledge it is not part of the social scientist's job to consider the construction of social scientific knowledge'.[47] These strategic remarks appear to vitiate their authors' position by seeking to legitimate their own disciplinary practice in terms of the criteria of the disciplines they set out to criticise. This of course reflects the central problem for all endeavours to criticise or understand human understanding. How do you rebuild the raft while at sea? How do you achieve a standpoint, which itself is uncriticisable, from which to criticise? This is Mannheim's problem and that of his followers: and it is also the issue which fuels the criticism of the sociology of knowledge from both the right and the left.[48] The temptation to resolve the self-referential paradox involved in thinking about thinking, by opting for one privileged standpoint, must be resisted.[49] As we shall see, if this temptation is not resisted, several dire consequences would seem to follow: the analysis which has led to a denial of the great divide and the fact/value, knowledge/power, science/ideology distinctions will ultimately be rendered ineffective; science or some other knowledge tradition will (again) become autonomous and the sole source of authority. The sociology of knowledge will become science's flunkey; and the possibility of a meaningful critique of science and technology will be foreclosed. But is such a resistance possible or is relativism doomed to vitiation? Can a complex multiplicity of viewpoints be sustained? Is it not the case that I have used claims about 'the facts', logical argument forms and so on, in presenting my case here? Moreover, in arguing that the sociology of knowledge is essentially evaluative, is it not the case that competing claims of how the world ought to be, and how to bring such a world about, can only be evaluated in terms of criteria like empirical success, fit with the data and so on? Thus it would seem that despite my relativistic assertions I am unable to interpret, criticise or communicate without rational criteria for argument evaluation and theory choice that are independent of a belief system.

That relativism and the sociology of knowledge is vitiated or cannot do any useful work by virtue of the fact that there is only one rational form of human reasoning, or that certain logical laws are preconditions for communication and understanding, is an argument that has in part been answered earlier in the book. Even if it is granted that despite its 'problems' we have no alternative to a form of reasoning such as induction for generating empirical knowledge claims or for assessing our beliefs,[50] this is insufficient to account for how and why particular beliefs come to be adopted in particular circumstances. Logical laws and rational criteria are not by themselves sufficient, for the reasons I have already mentioned. They can tell us nothing about the content of our ideas or about why we have organised and classified the natural world in the way that we have. They leave unanswered questions about meaning, significance, purpose or value. Such laws and criteria do not of themselves provide the conditions of their application; they cannot do any substantial work in the generation of knowledge claims without additional assumptions which are subject to variation and negotiation (the *ceteris paribus* clause, for example). The underlying reason for this is that all our representations of reality (be they images, theories, paintings or movies) are contingent assemblages actively constructed from a variety of elements, conventions, prior beliefs, cultural resources of all kinds—including criteria of rationality, concepts of method, good experimental technique, repeatability, etc.

Thus it would seem that there is only one solution to the dilemma: to embrace it, to acknowledge that all knowledge claims, including this one, are active constructions and that in criticising them there is no possibility of stepping aside from the process of the continuous interaction of our ideas and the world.

There remains however the 'long-run' argument. The 'long run' argument gains its strength by allowing the possibility that all is indeed process and action, and that all the claims I have made about the social construction of knowledge are true, but holds that they are nonetheless trivial because in the long run the social circumstances and contaminants of knowledge production will be winnowed away. In the end, despite the vested interests, cultural background, or political ideology of a particular scientist or group of scientists, what comes to be accepted as knowledge will be that which has the greatest predictive success, fit with the data, conformity with other theories and so on. Shapin, for example, once one of the leading strong programmers, argues that the very process of justifying your own knowledge claims and of criticising those of your rivals has the effect of decontaminating, of rendering objective those knowledge claims.[51]

Another form of the argument appeals to the progress of science. We know more about the world than we used to; the evidence of this is our manifestly enhanced ability to predict and control nature. Science works; therefore we need turn no further than to its own methods to understand its success.[52] The assumption behind the 'long run' argument and its variant, the argument from progress, is that what we end up with is objective knowledge, or true belief; knowledge that is independent of the will and consciousness of human beings. There are two counter arguments to this: firstly, that although we may accumulate a host of such claims, we never know that they are true. Either, as has been argued, there is no Archimedean point from which to assess such claims, or if there is, we can have no knowledge of it. Secondly, the argument from the instrumentally progressive character of science does not on the one hand demonstrate that there is any theoretical or ontological progress, or that there is a way we can show that we have greater knowledge of 'the hidden workings of reality'. On the other hand, the increased ability to control and predict nature can only be assessed as successful or progressive in terms of what counts as success or progress, or from the point of view of human interests and purposes. That, of course, is a political and moral matter, and it brings us back to the question—will it be all right in the long run? My answer to that question is, no—if, that is, we merely attempt to understand the world. The ultimate reason for embracing relativism and reflexivity is that they make clear the necessity for criticising and changing our understanding of the world by recognising the messy and complex diversity of the multiple ways of knowing. What I have tried to show in this book is that all knowledge traditions, in assembling the heterogeneous components of people, practices and places, create knowledge spaces. All such knowledge spaces have transparent elements, concerning ontological assumptions about whom to trust, what counts as evidence and so on. It is in the revelation of these hidden messy and actively constructed components that the possibility lies of working together with people in other spaces. Herein lies the real work of putting on the motley. If we do not actively celebrate the messiness of all our knowledge making we will in the long run condemn ourselves to an inevitable death brought on by the inflexibility and sterility of a monoculture. In the long run, social and cultural complexity cannot be winnowed away; it's all there is.

Approaching the Transmodern: The Possibility of a Third Space

The final question then is, how do we go about putting on the motley? How do we pursue the liberatory enlightenment project without a universal rationality? How do we sustain our social capital and allow the flourishing of local knowledge both within our own culture and world wide? To do so means giving full recognition to other people's knowledge spaces, but this is no easy matter. First and foremost it is extremely difficult to move outside your own knowledge space in the same way that it is extremely difficult to become as fluent in another language as a native speaker. It is not just a question of learning to speak idiomatically, but of absorbing the values and embodying the practices of the culture. As Harry Collins has remarked, 'We both create our world and are in some sense products of it but to somehow capture this dialectic without freezing it remains the most difficult of human endeavours'.[53] But, there is I think, an extra difficulty for those of us who were enculturated in the Western scientific tradition. Not only is it hard for us, as it is for all cultures, to avoid taking our own tradition of rationality as frozen and immutable, it is also the case that our tradition has been both violent and contradictory in its emancipatory hegemony and denial of alternative traditions. From the perspective of the South American historian Enrique Dussel, modernity had its originary moment as a European phenomenon in 1492, when Europe defined itself as the centre of world history in its encounter with the non-European other—an altereity it has since erased.

> ... if 1492 is the moment of the birth of modernity as a concept, the moment of origin of a very particular myth of sacrificial violence, it also marks the origin of a process of concealment or misrecognition of the non-European.[54]

Dussel goes on to argue that we need to move beyond the modern to the 'transmodern' in which modernity and its negated altereity co-realise themselves in a process of mutual creative fertilisation.[55]

The kind of fertilisation between differing knowledge traditions that Dussel envisions in his concept of the transmodern requires the establishment of a third space. A third space would be an interstitial space, a space that is created through negotiation between spaces, where contrasting rationalities can work together but without the notion of a single transcendent rationality.[56] In such a space the question of trust and especially distrust needs to be negotiated, in order that we can avoid the kind of violent misrecognition that Dussel sees as definitional of our first encounter with the other. To revert to the figure of trickster/jester, we need to acknowledge the duplicity that is attendant on truth telling. A third space is then a space in which the hidden power assumptions about the kinds of selves, objects and their relations that is presumed in the moral order, have to be allowed to become visible. This, I suggest, is not feasible at the purely representational level. For differing knowledge traditions to coexist in a common third space they need to simultaneously agree to build such a space and to perform together.

Notes

[1] John Ziman, *Public Knowledge: The Social Dimension of Science*, (Cambridge: Cambridge University Press, 1968).

[2] Alan Irwin and Brian Wynne, eds., *Misunderstanding Science? The Public Reconstruction of Science and Technology*, (Cambridge: Cambridge University Press, 1996). See also Sheia Jasanoff, 'Public Knowledge, Private Fears: Review of Irwin & Wynne [eds], *Misunderstanding Science?*', *Social Studies of Science*, Vol. 27, 2, (1997), pp. 350–55.

[3] A very good overview of the social capital debate and its relevance in achieving citizen participation in policy formation and planning for the particular case of the Sydney Olympics is given in Albany Consulting Group, *Social Capital in the Olympic City*, (Sydney: Green Games Watch 2000 Inc, 1997). Ulrich Beck develops the thesis that what characterises the present stage of modernity is the decline of trust in science by the lay public and hence the need for a more reflexive form of expert knowledge; see Ulrich Beck, *Risk Society: Towards a New Modernity*, (London: Sage Publications, 1992). Brian Wynne cogently argues that the forms of trust in modern scientific knowledge that Beck presupposes have never prevailed; see Brian Wynne, 'May the Sheep Safely Graze?', in S. Lash, B. Szerszynski and B. Wynne, eds., *Risk, Environment and Modernity: Towards a New Ecology*, (London: Sage, 1996), pp. 44–83.

[4] Wynne, 'May the Sheep Safely Graze?', p. 71.

5 Robert Putnam, *Making Democracy Work: Civic Traditions in Modern Italy*, (Princeton: Princeton University Press, 1993); Robert Putnam, 'Bowling Alone: America's Declining Social Capital', *Journal of Democracy*, Vol. 6, (1995), pp. 65–78. See also Eva Cox, 'Beyond Economics: The Building of Social Capital', *Refractory Girl*, Vol. 50, Autumn, (1996), pp. 52–3.

6 Andrew Ross, ed., *Science Wars*, (Durham: Duke University Press, 1996).

7 Enrique Dussel, 'Eurocentrism and Modernity', *boundary*, Vol. 2, 20/3, (1993), pp. 65–76.

8 Gellner 1973 cited in Anne Salmond, 'Maori Epistemologies', in J. Overing, ed., *Reason and Morality*, (London: Tavistock Pbls., 1985), pp. 240–63, p. 259.

9 Mario Bunge, 'Seven Desiderata for Rationality', in J. Agassi and I. C. Jarvie, eds., *Rationality: The Critical View*, (Dordrecht: Martinus Nijhoff Publishers, 1987), pp. 5–15.

10 Toby Huff, *The Rise of Early Modern Science; Islam, China and the West*, (Cambridge: Cambridge University Press, 1993).

11 Max Weber, 'Law, Rationalism and Capitalism', in C. M. Campbell and P. Wiles, eds., *Law and Society*, (Oxford: Martin Robertson, 1979), pp. 51–89, p. 53.

12 Street, *Literacy in Theory and Practice*.

13 Goody, *The Domestication of the Savage Mind*. Jack Goody, *The Logic of Writing and the Organisation of Society*, (Cambridge: Cambridge University Press, 1986). See also Ruth Finnegan, *Literacy and Orality: Studies in the Technology of Communication*, (Oxford: Basil Blackwell, 1988).

14 William M. Ivins, *On the Rationalisation of Sight: With an Examination of Three Renaissance Texts on Perspective*, (New York: Da Capo Press, 1973).

15 Shapin and Schaffer, *Leviathan and the Air Pump*.

16 Ken Alder, *Engineering the Revolution: Arms and the Enlightenment in France 1763–1815*, (Princeton: Princeton University Press, 1997), p. 130.

17 Mitchell Dean, *Critical and Effective History: Foucault's Methods and Historical Sociology*, (London: Routledge, 1994).

18 Lorraine Daston, 'Objectivity and the Escape from Perspective', *Social Studies of Science*, Vol. 22, (1992), pp. 597–618; Peter Dear, 'From Truth to Disinterestedness in the Seventeenth Century', *Social Studies of Science*, Vol. 22, (1992), pp. 619–31. Theodore Porter, *Trust in Numbers: The Pursuit of Objectivity in Science and Public Life*, (Princeton: Princeton University Press, 1995).

19 T. Nagel, *The View From Nowhere*, (Oxford: Oxford University Press, 1986).

20 Randall Albury, *The Politics of Objectivity*, (Geelong: Deakin University Press, 1983).

21 Roy Porter, 'White Coats in Vogue', *Times Higher Educational Supplement*, Vol. Nov 5, (1982), pp. 12–13.

22 One of the first anti SSK articles in what became the 'science wars' is T. Theocharis and M. Psimopoulos, 'Where Science Has Gone Wrong', *Nature*, Vol. 329, 15th Oct, (1987), pp. 595–98 which explicitly links Popper, Kuhn and Feyerabend to a decline in science funding.

23 Feyerabend, *Against Method;* Karl Popper, *The Open Society and its Enemies*, (Princeton: Princeton University Press, 1950).

24 Much of this can be seen in the 'science wars', see the special issue of *Social Text*, Vol 46–7, 1996; *Times Higher Educational Supplement* section on Science's Social Standing, Sept 30, 1994. The internal criticisms can be seen in the special issue of *Studies of Science* on The Politics of SSK, Vol. 26, 1996. The external critics include Paul Gross and Norman Levitt, *Higher Superstition: The Academic Left and its Quarrels with Science*, (Baltimore: Johns Hopkins University Press, 1994); Steven Weinberg, *The Search for the Fundamental Laws of Nature*, (New York: Pantheon, 1992); Lewis Wolpert, *The Unnatural Nature of Science: Why Science Does Not Make (Common) Sense*, (London: Faber & Faber, 1992); Paul Gross, Norman Levitt, et al., eds., *The Flight From Science and Reason*, (New York: New York Academy of Sciences, 1997).

25 Mary Hesse, *Revolutions and Reconstructions in the Philosophy of Science*, (Sussex: Harvester Press, 1980), Introduction and chapter 2, passim. See also Alasdair MacIntyre, *Whose Justice? Which Rationality?*, (London: Duckworth, 1988).

26 Maurice Mandelbaum, 'Subjective, Objective and Conceptual Relativism', in M. Krausz and J. Meiland, eds., *Relativism: Cognitive and Moral*, (South Bend: University of Notre Dame Press, 1982).

27 See Alvin Gouldner, *The Coming Crisis of Western Sociology*, (London: Heinemann, 1971); Stephen Webster, 'Dialogue and Fiction in Ethnography', *Dialectical Anthropology*, Vol. 7, (1982), pp. 91–114; Paul Rabinow, *Reflections on Field Work in Morocco*, (Berkeley: University of California Press, 1977). This is reflected in the thematic issue on the 'Politics of SSK' in *Social Studies of Science*, 26, May 1996, which is largely concerned with the neutrality question but does not acknowledge anything beyond the confines of SSK.

28 K. D. Knorr-Cetina and M. Mulkay, eds., *Science Observed: Reflections on the Social Study of Science*, (London: Sage, 1982), gives a sample of the first generation, Sheila Jasanoff, Gerald Markle, et al., eds., *Handbook of Science and Technology Studies*, (Thousand Oaks: Sage Publications, 1995) of the second generation.

29 I owe the descriptive term 'long run argument' to Dr Henry Krips, Department of HPS, University of Melbourne. Cf Gilbert, G. N. and M. Mulkay, *Opening Pandora's Box*, chapter 5.

30 See, for example, Karl Mannheim, *Ideology and Utopia*, (London: Kegan Paul, 1936), p. 239.

31 For example, Robert K. Merton, *The Sociology of Science*, (Chicago: University of Chicago Press, 1973).

32 Kuhn, *The Structure of Scientific Revolutions*. For his anti-relativism, see Thomas S. Kuhn, 'Reflections on My Critics', in I. Lakatos and A. Musgrave, eds., *Criticism and the Growth of Knowledge*, (London: Cambridge University Press, 1970), pp. 231–78, pp. 259ff.

33 David Bloor, *Knowledge and Social Imagery*, (London: Routledge & Kegan Paul, 1976); Barry Barnes, *Scientific Knowledge and Sociological Theory*, (London: Routledge & Kegan Paul, 1974).

34 G. B. Kerferd, 'Protagoras of Abdera', in P. Edwards, ed., *The Encyclopedia of Philosophy*, (New York: Collier Macmillan, 1967), p. 506.

35 Jack W. Meiland deals with several of these varieties in Jack W. Meiland, 'On the Paradox of Cognitive Relativism', *Metaphilosophy*, Vol. 11, (1982), pp. 115–126. See also Jack W. Meiland, 'Concepts of Relative Truth', *The Monist*, Vol. 60, (1977), pp. 568–582. Michael Krausz, ed., *Relativism: Interpretation and Confrontation*, (Notre Dame: University of Notre Dame, 1989); Diederick Raven, Lieteke Tijssen, et al., eds., *Cognitive Relativism and Social Science*, (New Brunswick: Transaction Pbl., 1992).

36 Bloor, *Knowledge and Social Imagery*, p. 14, cites an example of this argument.

37 Hesse, *Revolutions and Reconstructions in the Philosophy of Science*, p. 42.

38 See, ibid; Barnes, *Scientific Knowledge and Sociological Theory*, chapter 1; and Bloor, *Knowledge and Social Imagery*, p. 2.

39 For their relativism see Bloor, *Knowledge and Social Imagery*, p. 42; Barnes, *Scientific Knowledge and Sociological Theory*, p. 179; and Barry Barnes and David Bloor, 'Relativism, Rationalism and the Sociology of Knowledge', in M. Hollis and S. Lukes, eds., *Rationality and Relativism*, (Oxford: Blackwell, 1982); H. M. Collins and G. Cox, 'Recovering Relativity: Did Prophecy Fail?'. For their disavowal, see Bloor, ibid, p. 141, and H.M. Collins, 'What is TRASP'.

40 Yehuda Elkana, 'Two-Tier Thinking: Philosophical Realism and Historical Relativism', *Social Studies of Science*, Vol. 8, (1978), pp. 309–326.

41 Alan F. Chalmers, *What is This Thing Called Science*, 2nd edn, (Brisbane: University of Queensland Press, 1983), p. 144.

42 Knorr-Cetina in K. D. Knorr-Cetina and M. Mulkay, eds., *Science Observed: Reflections on the Social Study of Science*, (London: Sage, 1982), p. 5.

43 Hesse, p. viiiff. See also Barry Barnes, 'On the Conventional Character of Knowledge and Cognition', *Philosophy of the Social Sciences*, Vol. 11, (1981), pp. 303–333.

44 M. Krausz and J. Meiland, eds., *Relativism: Cognitive and Moral*, (South Bend: University of Notre Dame Press, 1982), p. 5.

45 Richard Rorty, *The Consequences of Pragmatism*, (Brighton: Harvester, 1982).

46 Barry Barnes, *T.S. Kuhn and Social Science*, (London: Macmillan, 1982), p. xi. A position he and Bloor both now maintain see Barry Barnes, David Bloor, et al., *Scientific Knowledge: A Sociological Analysis*, (London: Athlone, 1996), p.viii.

47 H. Collins, 'Special Relativism: The Natural Attitude', *Social Studies of Science*, Vol. 12, (1982), p. 140.

48 A. P. Simonds, *Karl Mannheim's Sociology of Knowledge*, (Oxford: Clarendon Press, 1978). For a right-wing criticism, see Popper, *The Open Society and its Enemies*, and for a left-wing criticism, see H. Rose and S. Rose, 'Radical Science and its Enemies', *The Socialist Register*, Vol. 16, (1979), pp. 317–335.

49 Many feminists who have done so much to augment the scope of SSK have found standpoint epistemologies irresistible. See for example Sandra Harding, *Whose Science? Whose Knowledge?: Thinking from Women's Lives*, (Ithaca: Cornell University Press, 1991).

50 As claimed for example by John Clendinnen, 'Epistemic Choice and Sociology', *Metascience*, Vol. 1/2, (1984), pp. 61–9.

51 S. Shapin, 'The Politics of Observation'. Bourdieu's argument in Bourdieu, 'The Specificity of the Scientific Field' is an interesting variant in which you can have struggle for authority and your emergent truth as well.

52 That science works is the argument which all the critics of SSK rely on. See for example Peter Atkins, 'Science's Social Standing: Against', *Times Higher Educational Supplement*, (1994), p. 19.

53 Collins, H. M. and G. Cox 'Recovering Relativity: Did Prophecy Fail?', pp. 424–425.

54 Enrique Dussel, 'Eurocentrism and Modernity', *boundary*, Vol. 2, 20/3, (1993), pp. 65–76.

55 Ibid, p. 76.

56 This conception of a third space is Tambiah's; see Stanley Jeyaraja Tambiah, *Magic, Science, Religion, and the Scope of Rationality*, (Cambridge University Press: Cambridge, 1990), p. 122. On interstitial spaces see Homi K. Bhabha, *The Location of Culture*, (New York: Routledge, 1994), p. 312. See also Jacobs, 'Shake 'Im This Country', p. 104. Edward Soja, *Thirdspace: Journeys to Los Angeles and Other Real-and-Imagined Places*, (Cambridge, Mass: Blackwell, 1996).

BIBLIOGRAPHY

J. Ackerman, '"Ars Sine Scientia Nihil Est": Gothic Theory of Architecture at the Cathedral of Milan', *Art Bulletin*, Vol. xxxii, (1949), pp. 84–111.

E. H. Ackernecht, *Malaria in the Upper Mississippi Valley 1760–1900*, (Baltimore: Johns Hopkins University Press, 1945).

Ian Adam and Helen Tiffin, eds., *Past The Last Post; Theorising Post-Colonialism and Post-Modernism*, (New York: Harvester Wheatsheaf, 1991).

Henry Adams, *The Education of Henry Adams*, (New York: New York Modern Library, 1931).

Anil Agarwal and Sunita Narain, 'Pirates in the Garden of India', *New Scientist*, Vol. 152, 26th Oct, (1996), pp. 14–15.

Arun Agrawal, 'Dismantling the Divide Between Indigenous and Scientific Knowledge', *Development and Change*, Vol. 26, 3, (1995), pp. 413–439.

Kjell Åkerblom, *Astronomy and Navigation in Polynesia and Micronesia: A Survey*, (Stockholm: Ethnographical Museum, 1968).

Albany Consulting Group, *Social Capital in the Olympic City*, (Sydney: Green Games Watch 2000 Inc, 1997).

Randall Albury, 'The Politics of Truth: A Social Interpretation of Scientific Knowledge, with an Appplication to the Case of Sociobiology', in M. Ruse, ed., *Nature Animated*, (Dordrecht: Reidel, 1982).

Randall Albury, *The Politics of Objectivity*, (Geelong: Deakin University Press, 1983).

Ken Alder, 'A Revolution to Measure: The Political Economy of the Metric System in France', in N. Wise, ed., *The Values of Precision*, (Princeton: Princeton University Press, 1995), pp. 39–71.

Ken Alder, *Engineering the Revolution: Arms and the Enlightenment in France 1763–1815*, (Princeton: Princeton University Press, 1997).

W. H. Alkire, 'Systems of Measurement on Woleai Atoll, Caroline Islands', *Anthropos*, Vol. 65, (1970), pp. 1–73.

P. Allport, 'Still Searching for the Holy Grail', *New Scientist*, 132, Oct 5th, (1991), pp. 51–2.

Atholl Anderson and Bruce McFadgen, 'Prehistoric Two-way Voyaging', *Archaeology in Oceania*, Vol. 25, April, (1990), pp. 37–42.

Francis B. Andrews, *The Mediaeval Builder and his Methods*, (Wakefield and Ottowa: EP Pbl and Rowman and Littlefield, 1925 reprinted 1976).

Anon, 'Malaria Vaccine Strikes Problems', *Scitech*, September, (1984), p. 13.

Maria Ascher and Robert Ascher, *Code of the Quipu: A Study in Media, Mathematics and Culture*, (Ann Arbor: University of Michigan Press, 1981).

M. Ascher, *Ethnomathematics: A Multicultural View of Mathematical Ideas*, (Pacific Grove: Brooks Cole, 1991).

Malcom Ashmore and Evelleen Richards, eds., 'Special Issue on 'The Politics of SSK: Neutrality, Commitment and Beyond' *Social Studies of Science*, Vol. 6 n2, (London: Sage, 1996).

Peter Atkins, 'Science's Social Standing: Against', *Times Higher Educational Supplement*, (1994), p. 19.

Gaston Bachelard, *The New Scientific Spirit*, (Boston: Beacon Press, 1985).

Greg Banford, 'Popper and his Commentators on the Discovery of Neptune: A Close Shave for the Law of Gravitation?', *BJHS (British Journal for the History of Science)*, Vol. 27, 2, (1996), pp. 207–233.

Peter Barber, 'England 1: Pageantry, Defense, and Government: Maps at Court to 1550', in D. Buisseret, ed., *Monarchs, Ministers and Maps: The Emergence of Cartography as a Tool of Government in Early Modern Europe*, (Chicago: University of Chicago Press, 1992), pp. 26–56.

Barry Barnes, *Scientific Knowledge and Sociological Theory*, (London: Routledge & Kegan Paul, 1974).

Barry Barnes, 'On the Conventional Character of Knowledge and Cognition', *Philosophy of the Social Sciences*, Vol. 11, (1981), pp. 303–333.

Barry Barnes, *T. S. Kuhn and Social Science*, (London: Macmillan, 1982).

Barry Barnes and David Bloor, 'Relativism, Rationalism and the Sociology of Knowledge', in M. Hollis and S. Lukes, eds., *Rationality and Relativism*, (Oxford: Blackwell, 1982).

Barry Barnes and David Edge, eds., *Science in Context*, (Milton Keynes: Open University Press, 1983).

Barry Barnes, David Bloor, and John Henry, *Scientific Knowledge: A Sociological Analysis*, (London: Athlone, 1996).

Andrew Barry, 'The History of Measurement and the Engineers of Space', *BJHS*, Vol. 26, (1993), pp. 459–68.

Gregory Bateson, *Mind and Nature: A Necessary Unity*, (New York: Dutton, 1979).

J. C. Beaglehole, ed., *The Voyage of the Resolution and Discovery 1776–1780 Part One*, (Cambridge: Cambridge University Press, 1967).

Ulrich Beck, *Risk Society: Towards a New Modernity*, (London: Sage Publications, 1992).

Barbara Belyea, 'Amerindian Maps: The Explorer as Translator', *Journal of Historical Geography*, Vol. 18, (1992), pp. 267–77.

Barbara Belyea, 'Images of Power: Derrida/Foucault/Harley', *Cartographica*, Vol. 29, (1992), pp. 1–9.

Barbara Belyea, 'Review Article of Denis Wood's *The Power of Maps*, and the Author's Reply', *Cartographica*, Vol. 29, 3 & 4, (1992), pp. 94–99.

Barbara Belyea, 'Inland Journeys, Native Maps', *Cartographica*, Vol. 33, 2, (1996), pp. 1–16.

Joseph Ben-David, *The Scientist's Role in Society: A Comparative Study*, (Englewood Cliffs: Prentice Hall, 1971).

J. D. Bernal, *Science in History*, Vol. 1, (Harmondsworth: Penguin, 1965).

Homi K. Bhabha, *The Location of Culture*, (New York: Routledge, 1994).

Wiebe Bijker, Thomas Hughes, and Trevor Pinch, eds., *The Social Construction of Technological Systems; New Directions in the Sociology and History of Technology*, (Cambridge: MIT Press, 1987).

Wiebe Bijker and John Law, eds., *Shaping Technology/Building Society: Studies in Sociotechnical Change*, (Cambridge: MIT Press, 1992).

David Billington, *The Tower and the Bridge: The New Art of Structural Engineering*, (Princeton: Princeton University Press, 1985).

David P. Billington, 'History and Esthetics in Suspension Bridges', *Journal of the Structural Division, Proceedings of the American Society of Engineers*, Vol. 130, (1977), pp. 1655–72.

David P. Billington and Robert Mark, 'The Cathedral and the Bridge: Structure and Symbol', *Technology and Culture*, Vol. 25, (1984), pp. 37–52.

David P. Billington and Robert Mark, 'In Response to "Another View of the Cathedral and the Bridge"', *Technology and Culture*, Vol. 25, (1984), pp. 595–601.

B. Birnbauer, 'As Malaria Rampages Out of Control, Australian Scientists Race To Stop It', *Age*, (1986), p. 3.

R. H. Black, 'Malaria', in *Encyclopedia of Papua New Guinea*, (Melbourne: Melbourne University Press, 1972), p. 679.

Reginald Blomfield, *Architectural Drawing and Draughtsmen*, (London: Cassell and Co., 1912).

David Bloor, *Knowledge and Social Imagery*, (London: Routledge & Kegan Paul, 1976).

Jean Bony, 'The Genesis of Gothic: Accident or Necessity?', *Australian Journal of Art*, Vol. ii, (1980), pp. 17–31.

Pierre Bourdieu, 'The Specificity of the Scientific Field and the Social Conditions of the Progress of Reason', *Social Science Information*, Vol. 14, (1975), pp. 19–47.

Pierre Bourdieu, *Outline of a Theory of Practice*, (Cambridge: Cambridge University Press, 1977).

Robert Branner, 'Villard de Honnecourt, Reims and the Origin of Gothic Architectural Drawing', *Gazette des Beaux-Arts*, Vol. 61, (1963), pp. 129–46.

Robert Branner, *Gothic Architecture*, (New York: George Braziller, 1965).

Augustine Brannigan, *The Social Basis of Scientific Discoveries*, (Cambridge: Cambridge University Press, 1981).

J. Brasseur, *The Structure of High Reynolds Number Turbulent Boundary Layers Part A*, (University Park: Pennsylvania State University, Department of Mechanical Engineering, 1993).

A. W. A. Brown, J. Haworth, et al., 'Malaria Eradication and Control From a Global Standpoint', *Journal of Medical Entomology*, Vol. 13, (1976), pp. 1–25.

G. V. Brown and G. J. V. Nossal, 'World Endemic Disease. Costs and Potential Fiscal Benefits of Medical Research', in H. H. Fudenberg, ed., *Biomedical Institutions, Biomedical Funding and Public Policy*, (New York: Plenum Press, 1983).

Lloyd A. Brown, *The Story of Maps*, (Boston: Little Brown & Co. reprint Bonanza Books, 1949).

Phyllida Brown, 'Trials and Tribulations of a Malaria Vaccine', *New Scientist*, Vol. 129, 16th March, (1991), p. 14.

Phyllida Brown, 'Columbia's Malaria Vaccine Approved for Trials', *New Scientist*, Vol. 135, 26th Sept, (1992), p. 6.

Phyllida Brown, 'Malaria Vaccine Trials Stopped by Anonymous Experts', *New Scientist*, Vol. 133, 22nd Feb, (1992), p. 6.

Phyllida Brown, 'Malaria Summit Demands Plans Before Cash', *New Scientist*, Vol. 136, 7th Nov, (1992), p. 4.

Phyllida Brown, 'Who Cares About Malaria', *New Scientist*, Vol. 136, 31st Oct, (1992), pp. 37–41.

Phyllida Brown, 'Dirty Secrets', *New Scientist*, Vol. 152, 2nd Nov, (1996), pp. 26–9.

Phyllida Brown, 'How the Parasite Learnt to Kill', *New Scientist*, Vol. 152, 16th Nov, (1996), pp. 32–6.

L. Bruce-Chwatt, 'Malaria: From Eradication to Control', *New Scientist*, Vol. 19 April, (1984), pp. 17–20.

L. J. Bruce-Chwatt, 'Imported Malaria; An Uninvited Guest', *British Medical Bulletin*, Vol. 38, (1982), pp. 179–85.

F. Bucher, 'Design in Gothic Architecture: A Preliminary Assessment', *Journal of the Society of Architectural Historians*, Vol. 27, (1968), pp. 49–71.

F. Bucher, *Architector: The Lodgebooks and Sketchbooks of Medieval Architects*, Vol. 1, (New York: Abaris Books, 1979).

David Buisseret, ed., *Monarchs, Ministers and Maps: The Emergence of Cartography as a Tool of Government in Early Modern Europe*, (Chicago: University of Chicago Press, 1992).

David Buisseret, 'Monarchs, Ministers, and Maps in France before the Accession of Loius XIV', in D. Buisseret, ed., *Monarchs, Ministers and Maps: The Emergence of Cartography as a Tool of Government in Early Modern Europe*, (Chicago: University of Chicago Press, 1992), pp. 99–123.

Mario Bunge, 'Seven Desiderata for Rationality', in J. Agassi and I. C. Jarvie, eds., *Rationality: The Critical View*, (Dordrecht: Martinus Nijhoff Publishers, 1987), pp. 5–17.

James Burke, *The Day The Universe Changed*, (London: BBC, 1985).

Barry Butcher and David Turnbull, 'Aborigines, Europeans and the Environment', in V. Burgman and J. Lee, eds., *A Most Valuable Acquisition: A People's History of Australia Since 1788*, (Melbourne: Mcphee Gribble/ Penguin, 1988), pp. 13–28.

Michel Callon and Bruno Latour, 'Don't Throw the Baby Out with the Bath School!', in A. Pickering, ed., *Science As Practice and Culture*, (Chicago: University of Chicago Press, 1992), pp. 343–368.

Michel Callon, John Law, and Arie Rip, eds., *Mapping the Dynamics of Science and Technology; Sociology of Science in the Real World*, (London: MacMillan, 1986).

John Carlson, 'Romancing the Stone, or Moonshine on the Sun Dagger', in J. B. Carlson and W. J. Judge, eds., *Astronomy and Ceremony in the Prehistoric Southwest*, (Albuquerque: University Of New Mexico, 1983), pp. 71–87.

Nancy Cartwright, *How the Laws of Physics Lie*, (Oxford: Clarendon Press, 1983).

J. Cattani, Malaria in the South-west Pacific; a Prototype Defined Population for Vaccine Trials. Unpublished paper given at the Asia-Pacific Conference on Malaria, (Honolulu: 1985).

J. Cattani, H. Vrbova, et al., 'Inter-cluster Variation in Malariometric Rates in a Coastal Area of Papua New Guinea', in J. Bryan and P. M. Moodie, eds., *Malaria: Proceedings of a Conference to Honour Robert H. Black, Sydney 1983*, (Canberra: Australian Government Publishing Service, 1984), pp. 112–118.

Alan F. Chalmers, *What is this Thing Called Science*, 2nd edn, (Brisbane: University of Queensland Press, 1983).

David Wade Chambers, *Locality and Science: Myths of Center and Periphery*, in A. Lafuente et al. eds., *Mundilization dela Sciencia y Cultura National*, (Madrid: Dola Callos, 1993), pp. 605–17.

G. Chapin and R. Wasserton, 'Pesticides Use and Malaria Resurgence in Central America and India', *Social Sciences and Medicine*, Vol. 17, (1983), pp. 273–90.

Max Charlesworth, Lyndsay Farrall, Terry Stokes and David Turnbull, *Life Among The Scientists: An Anthropological Study of an Australian Scientific Community*, (Melbourne: Oxford University Press, 1989).

J. D. Charlwood, 'Which Way Now for Malaria Control?', *Papua New Guinea Medical Journal*, Vol. 27, (1984), pp. 159–162.

J. D. Charlwood, H. Dagoro, et al., 'Blood-feeding and Resting Behaviour in the *Anopheles punctulatus* Complex (Diptera: Culicidae) from Papua New Guinea', *Bulletin of Entomological Research*, Vol. 75, (1985), pp. 463–475.

R. J. Chorley and P. Haggett, *Models in Geography*, (London: Methuen, 1967).

I. A. Clark and G. A. Butcher, 'Cell-mediated Aspects of Malaria', *Papua New Guinea Medical Journal*, Vol. 29, (1986), pp. 59–62.

Adele E. Clarke and Joan H. Fujimura, 'What Tools? Which Jobs? Why Right?', in A. E. Clarke and J. H. Fujimura, eds., *The Right Tools For the Job: At Work in Twentieth-Century Life Sciences*, (Princeton: Princeton University Press, 1992), pp. 3–46.

H. Cleaver, 'Malaria and the Political Economy of Public Health', *International Journal of Health Services*, Vol. 7, (1977), pp. 557–579.

John Clendinnen, 'Epistemic Choice and Sociology', *Metascience*, Vol. 1/2, (1984), pp. 61–9.

James Clifford, *The Predicament of Culture: Twentieth-Century Ethnography, Literature and Art*, (Cambridge: Harvard University Press, 1988).

Harry Collins, 'Special Relativism: The Natural Attitude', *Social Studies of Science*, Vol. 12, (1982), p. 12.

Harry Collins, *Changing Order: Replication and Induction in Scientific Practice*, (London: Sage, 1985).

Harry Collins, 'What is TRASP? The Radical Programme as a Methodological Imperative', *Philosophy of the Social Sciences*, Vol. 11, (1981), pp. 215–224.

Harry Collins and G. Cox, 'Recovering Relativity: Did Prophecy Fail?', *Social Studies of Science*, Vol. 6, (1975), pp. 423–444.

Harry Collins and S. Yearly, 'Epistemological Chicken', in A. Pickering, ed., *Science as Practice and Culture*, (Chicago: University of Chicago Press, 1992), pp. 301–326.

Harry Collins and T. Pinch 1993, *The Golem at Large: What You Should Know About Technology*, Cambridge University Press, Cambridge.

Harry Collins and T. Pinch 1993, *The Golem: What You Should Know About Science*, Cambridge University Press, Cambridge.

Pam Colorado, 'Bridging Native and Western Science', *Convergence*, Vol. xxi, 2/3, (1988), pp. 49–72.

Carl Condit, *The Chicago School of Architecture: A History of Public Buildings in the Chicago Area 1875–1925*, (Chicago: University of Chicago Press, 1964).

Carl Condit, 'Another View of "The Cathedral and the Bridge"', *Technology and Culture*, Vol. 25, (1984), pp. 589–594.

Mike Cooley, *Architect or Bee: The Human Price of Technology*, (London: Chatto and Windus, 1987).

A.C. Crombie, *Medieval and Early Modern Science; Vol.1 Science in the Middle Ages V-X111 Centuries*, (New York: Doubleday, 1959).

Patricia L. Crown and W. James Judge, eds., *Chaco and Hohokam: Prehistoric Regional Systems in the American Southwest*, (Sante Fe: School of American Research Press, 1991).

Andrew Cunningham and Perry Williams, 'De-centring the "Big Picture": The Origins of Modern Science and the Modern Origins of Science', *British Journal for the History of Science (BJHS)*, Vol. 26, 4, (1993), pp. 407–432.

Lorraine Daston, 'Objectivity and the Escape from Perspective', *Social Studies of Science*, Vol. 22, (1992), pp. 597–618.

Alastair Davidson, 'Arbitrage', *Thesis Eleven*, Vol. 38, (1994), pp. 158–62.

S. L. Davis and J. R. V. Prescott, *Aboriginal Frontiers and Boundaries in Australia*, (Melbourne: Melbourne University Press, 1992).

Michael Day, '"Poor" Vaccine Ruled out in TB Puzzle', *New Scientist*, Vol. 151, July 13, (1996), pp. 14.

Michael Day, 'Malaria Vaccine Fails to Deliver', *New Scientist*, Vol. 151, 21st Sept, (1996), p. 8.

Michel de Certeau, *The Practice of Everyday Life*, (Berkeley: University of California Press, 1984).

Mitchell Dean, *Critical and Effective History: Foucault's Methods and Historical Sociology*, (London: Routledge, 1994).

Peter Dear, 'From Truth to Disinterestedness in the Seventeenth Century', *Social Studies of Science*, Vol. 22, (1992), pp. 619–31.

Giles Deleuze and Felix Guattari, *A Thousand Plateaus; Capitalism and Schizophrenia*, (Minneapolis: University of Minnesota Press, 1987).

C. Delo, J. Poggie, et al., *A System for Imaging and Displaying Three-Dimensional, Time Evolving Passive Scalar Concentration Fields in Fluid Flow*, (City: Princeton University, Department of Mechanical and Aerospace Engineering, 1994).

Robert Desowitz, *The Malaria Capers: Tales of Parasites and People*, (New York: W.W. Norton, 1991).

David Dickson, *The New Politics of Science*, (Chicago: University of Chicago Press, 1984).

Rosalyn Diprose and Robyn Ferrell, eds., *Cartographies: Poststructuralism and the Mapping of Bodies and Spaces*, (London: Allen and Unwin, 1991).

Arthur Donovan, Larry Laudan, et al., eds., *Scrutinizing Science: Empirical Studies of Scientific Change*, (Baltimore: Johns Hopkins University Press, 1992).

Edwin Doran, *Wangka: Austronesian Canoe Origins*, (College Station: Texas A&M University Press, 1981).

L. Doyal and I. Pennell, *The Political Economy of Health*, (London: Pluto Press, 1983).

Pierre Duhem, *The Aim and Structure of Physical Theory*, (Princeton: Princeton University Press, 1954).

Enrique Dussel, 'Eurocentrism and Modernity', *boundary*, Vol. 2, 20/3, (1993), pp. 65–76.

Matthew H. Edney, 'Cartography Without "Progress": Reinterpreting the Nature and Historical Development of Mapmaking', *Cartographica*, Vol. 30, 2&3, (1993), pp. 54–68.

Matthew Edney, 'Mathematical Cosmography and the Social Ideology of British Cartography 1780–1820', *Imago Mundi*, Vol. 46, (1994), pp. 101–116.

Matthew Edney, *Mapping an Empire: The Geographical Construction of British India*, (Chicago: University of Chicago Press, 1997).

Clinton R. Edwards, 'Mapping by Questionnaire: An Early Spanish Attempt to Determine New World Geographical Positions', *Imago Mundi*, Vol. 23, (1969), pp. 17–28.

Yehuda Elkana, 'Two-Tier Thinking Philosophical Realism and Historical Relativism', *Social Studies of Science*, Vol. 8, (1978), pp. 309–326.

H. T. Engelhardt, 'The Concept of Health and Disease', in H. T. Engelhardt and S. F. Spicker, eds., *Evaluation and Exploration in the Biomedical Sciences*, (Dordrecht: Reidel, 1975).

Alain Erlande-Brandenburg, *The Cathedral: The Social and Architectural Dynamics of Construction*, (Cambridge: Cambridge University Press, 1994).

M. A. Farid, 'The Malaria Programme—From Euphoria to Anarchy', *World Health Forum*, Vol. 1, (1980), pp. 8–33.

Lyndsay Farrall, 'Knowledge and its Preservation in Oral Cultures', in D. Denoon and R. Lacey, eds., *Oral Traditions in Melanesia*, (Port Moresby: Institute of Papua New Guinea Studies, 1981), pp. 71–86.

Mike Featherstone, 'In Pursuit of the Postmodern: An Introduction', *Theory, Culture and Society*, Vol. 5, Special Issue on Postmodernism, (1988).

Elizabeth Ferrier, 'Mapping Power: Cartography and Contemporary Cultural Theory', *antithesis*, Vol. 4, 1, (1990), pp. 35–52.

Paul Feyerabend, *Against Method: Outline of an Anarchist Theory of Knowledge*, (London: Verso, 1978).

Ruth Finnegan, *Literacy and Orality: Studies in the Technology of Communication*, (Oxford: Basil Blackwell, 1988).

Ben Finney, *Hokule'a: The Way to Tahiti*, (New York: Dodd, Mead and Co., 1979).

Ben Finney, *Voyage of Rediscovery: A Cultural Odyssey Through Polynesia*, (Berkeley: University of California Press, 1994).

Lawrence Fitzgerald, *Java La Grande: The Portuguese Discovery of Australia*, (Hobart: The Publishers Pty, 1984).

Eric G. Forbes, *Tobias Mayer (1723–62): Pioneer of Enlightened Science in Germany*, (Gottingen: 1980).

Michel Foucault, *Discipline and Punish: The Birth of the Prison*, (New York: Vintage Books, 1979).

Michel Foucault, *Power/Knowledge: Selected Interviews and Other Writings 1972–77*, (New York: Pantheon Books, 1980).

Charles O. Frake, 'Cognitive Maps of Time and Tide Among Medieval Seafarers', *Man*, Vol. 20, (1985), pp. 254–70.

S. Franco-Agudelo, 'The Rockefeller Foundation's Antimalarial Program in Latin America: Donating or Dominating?', *International Journal of Health Services*, Vol. 13, (1983), pp. 51–67.

P. Frankl, *The Gothic: Literary Sources and Interpretations Through 8 Centuries*, (New Jersey: Princeton University Press, 1960).

Kendrick Frazier, *People of Chaco; A Canyon and its Culture*, (New York: W.W. Norton & Co, 1986).

Steve Fuller, *Social Epistemology*, (Bloomington: Indiana University Press, 1988).

Kathryn Gabriel, *Roads to Center Place: A Cultural Atlas of Chaco Canyon and the Anasazi*, (Boulder: Johnson Books, 1991).

Laurie Garrett, *The Coming Plague: Newly Emerging Diseases in a World out of Balance*, (London: Virago Press, 1994).

Clifford Geertz, *The Interpretation of Cultures: Selected Essays*, (New York: Basic Books, 1973).

Clifford Geertz, *Local Knowledge: Further Essays in Interpretive Anthropology*, (New York: Basic Books, 1983).

Arthur T. Geoghegan, *The Attitude Towards Labour in Early Christianity and Ancient Culture*, (Washington D.C.: Catholic University of America Press, 1945).

G. N. Gilbert and M. Mulkay, *Opening Pandora's Box*, (Cambridge: Cambridge University Press, 1984).

Jean Gimpel, *The Cathedral Builders*, (New York: Grove Press, 1961).

Jean Gimpel, *The Medieval Machine: The Industrial Revolution of the Middle Ages*, (London: Victor Gollancz, 1977).

Thomas Gladwin, *East Is a Big Bird: Navigation and Logic on Puluwat*, (Cambridge, Mass: Harvard University Press, 1970).

James Gleick, *Chaos: Making a New Science*, (London: Viking Penguin, 1987).

Anne Godlewska, 'The Napoleonic Survey of Egypt: A Masterpiece of Cartographic Compilation and Early 19th Century Fieldwork', *Cartographica*, Vol. 25, 1&2, (1988).

Anne Godlewska, 'Napoleon's Geographers (1797–1815): Imperialists and Soldiers of Modernity', in A. Godlewska and N. Smith, eds., *Geography and Empire*, (Oxford: Blackwell Publishers, 1994), pp. 31–55.

G.N. Godson, 'Molecular Approaches to Malaria Vaccines', *Scientific American*, Vol. 252, (1985), pp. 32–39.

Iskender Gökalp, 'On the Dynamics of Controversies in a Borderland Scientific Domain: the Case of Turbulent Combustion', *Social Science Information*, Vol. 26, (1987), pp. 551–76.

Iskender Gökalp, 'Turbulent Reactions: Impact of New Instrumentation on a Borderland Scientific Domain', *Science, Technology and Human Values*, Vol. 15, (1990), pp. 284–304.

Ward Goodenough, 'Navigation in the Western Carolines', in L. Nader, ed., *Naked Science: Anthropological Inquiry into Boundaries, Power and Knowledge*, (New York: Routledge, 1996), pp. 29–42.

Ward Goodenough and S. D. Thomas, 'Traditional Navigation in The Western Pacific: A Search for Pattern', *Expedition* (Published as a pamphlet by the University of Pennsylvania Museum of Archaeology/Anthropology, Philadelphia PA., Vol. 30, (nd), pp. 4–7.

Ward Goodenough, *Native Astronomy in the Central Carolines*, (Philadelphia: University of Pennsylvania, 1953).

Jack Goody, *The Domestication of the Savage Mind*, (Cambridge: Cambridge University Press, 1977).

Jack Goody, *The Logic of Writing and the Organisation of Society*, (Cambridge: Cambridge University Press, 1986).

Paul Gross and Norman Levitt, *Higher Superstition: The Academic Left and its Quarrels with Science*, (Baltimore: Johns Hopkins University Press, 1994).

Paul Gross, Norman Levitt, et al., eds., *The Flight From Science and Reason*, (New York: New York Academy of Sciences, 1997).

E. Gruenbaum, 'Struggling with the Mosquito: Malaria Policy and Agricultural Development in Sudan', *Medical Anthropology*, Vol. 7, (1983), pp. 51–61.

Ian Hacking, *Representing and Intervening: Introductory Topics in the Philosophy of Natural Science*, (Cambridge: Cambridge University Press, 1983).

Ian Hacking, 'The Self-Vindication of the Laboratory Sciences', in A. Pickering, ed., *Science as Practice and Culture*, (Chicago: University of Chicago Press, 1992), pp. 29–64.

Evan Hadingham, *Early Man and the Cosmos*, (New York: Walker and Co, 1984).

Stephen S. Hall, *Mapping the Next Millennium: The Discovery of New Geographies*, (New York: Random House, 1992).

Norwood Russell Hanson, *Patterns of Discovery: An Inquiry into the Conceptual Foundations of Science*, (Cambridge: Cambridge University Press, 1958).

Donna Haraway, *Simians, Cyborgs and Women: The Reinvention of Nature*, (London: Free Association Books, 1991).

Mikael Hård, 'Technology as Practice: Local and Global Closure Processes in Diesel-Engine Design', *Social Studies of Science*, Vol. 24, (1994), pp. 549–85.

Sandra Harding, *Whose Science? Whose Knowledge?: Thinking from Women's Lives*, (Ithaca: Cornell University Press, 1991).

Sandra Harding, ed., *The 'Racial' Economy of Science: Toward a Democratic Future*, (Bloomington: Indiana University Press, 1993).

Sandra Harding, *Is Science Multicultural? Postcolonialisms, Feminisms and Epistemologies*, (Bloomington: Indiana University Press, 1998).

J. Brian Harley, 'Maps, Knowledge and Power', in D. Cosgrove and S. Daniels, eds., *The Iconography of Landscape*, (Cambridge: Cambridge University Press, 1988), pp. 277–312.

J. Brian Harley, 'Silences and Secrecy: The Hidden Agenda of Cartography in Early Modern Europe', *Imago Mundi*, Vol. 40, (1988), pp. 57–76.

J. Brian Harley, 'Deconstructing the Map', *Cartographica*, Vol. 26, (1989), pp. 1–20.

J. Brian Harley, 'Power and Legitimation in the English Geographical Atlases of the Eighteenth Century', in J. Wolter and R. Grim, eds., *Images of the World: The Atlas Through History*, (Washington: Library of Congress, 1997), pp. 161–204.

J. Brian Harley and David Woodward, eds., *The History of Cartography, Vol. 1 Cartography in Prehistoric, Ancient and Medieval Europe and the Mediterranean*, (Chicago: University of Chicago Press, 1987).

Henry Harrisse, *The Discovery of North America: A Critical Documentary, and Historic Investigation*. Rep. 1961, (Amsterdam: N. Israel, 1892).

John Harvey, *The Medieval Architect*, (London: Wayland Press, 1972).

John Harvey, *Cathedrals of England and Wales*, (London: B. T. Batsford, 1974).

John Harvey, *The Mediaeval Craftsmen*, (London: Wayland Press, 1975).

P. D. A. Harvey, *Maps in Tudor England*, (London: The Public Record Office and The British Library, 1993).

Katherine Hayles, *Chaos Bound: Orderly Disorder in Contemporary Literature and Science*, (Ithaca: Cornell University Press, 1990).

J. L. Heilbron, 'The Measure of Enlightenment', in T. Frängsmyr, J. L. Heilbron and R. E. Rider, eds., *The Quantifying Spirit in the 18th Century*, (Berkeley: University of California Press, 1990), pp. 207–242.

David J. Hess, *Science and Technology in a Multicultural World*, (New York: Columbia University Press, 1995).

Mary Hesse, *Revolutions and Reconstructions in the Philosophy of Science*, (Sussex: Harvester Press, 1980).

Jacques Heyman, 'The Stone Skeleton', *International Journal of Solids and Structures,* Vol. 2, (1966), pp. 249–79.

F. L. Hoffman, *The Malaria Problem in Peace and War*, (London: Prudential Press, 1918).

Gerald Holton, 'Do Scientists Need a Philosophy?', *Times Literary Supplement:*, Nov 2, (1984), pp. 1231–4.

Robin Horton, 'African Traditional Thought and Western Science', *Africa*, Vol. 37, (1967), pp. 50–71 &155–87.

Robin Horton, 'Tradition and Modernity Revisited', in M. Hollis and S. Lukes, eds., *Rationality and Relativism*, (Oxford: Blackwell, 1982), pp. 201–260.

Robin Horton and Ruth Finnegan, eds., *Modes of Thought: Essays on Thinking in Western and Non-Western Societies*, (London: Faber, 1973).

Michael Howes and Robert Chambers, 'Indigenous Technical Knowledge: Analysis, Implications and Issues', *Institute of Development Studies (IDS) Bulletin*, Vol. 10, Jan 2, (1979), pp. 5–11.

Toby Huff, *The Rise of Early Modern Science; Islam, China and the West*, (Cambridge: Cambridge University Press, 1993).

Graham Huggan, 'Decolonising the Map: Post-colonialism, Post-structuralism and the Cartographic Connection', in I. Adam and H. Tiffin, eds., *Past the*

Last Post: Theorising Post-Colonialism and Post-Modernism, (New York: Harvester Wheatsheaf, 1991), pp. 125–138.

Eugene Hunn, 'What is Traditional Ecological Knowledge?', in N. Williams and G. Baines, eds., *Traditional Ecological Knowledge: Wisdom for Sustainable Development*, (Canberra: Center for Resource and Environmental Studies, 1993).

P. Hunter, 'The National System of Scientific Measurement', *Science*, Vol. 210, (1980), pp. 869–74.

Edwin Hutchins, 'Understanding Micronesian Navigation', in D. Gentner and A. L. Stevens, eds., *Mental Models*, (New Jersey: Lawrence Erlbaum Associates, 1983), pp. 191–226.

Alan Irwin and Brian Wynne, eds., *Misunderstanding Science? The Public Reconstruction of Science and Technology*, (Cambridge: Cambridge University Press, 1996).

Geoffrey Irwin, 'Against, Across and Down the Wind: A Case for the Systematic Exploration of the Remote Pacific Islands', *Journal of the Polynesian Society*, Vol. 98, (1989), pp. 167–206.

Geoffrey Irwin, *The Prehistoric Exploration and Colonisation of the Pacific*, (Cambridge: Cambridge University Press, 1992).

William M. Ivins, *On the Rationalisation of Sight: With an Examination of Three Renaissance Texts on Perspective*, (New York: Da Capo Press, 1973).

Peter Jackson, *Maps of Meaning: An Introduction to Cultural Geography*, (London: Unwin Hyman, 1989).

Christian Jacob, *L'Empire des Cartes: Approche Théorique de la Cartographie à Travers l'Histoire*, (Paris: Albin Michel, 1992).

Jane Jacobs, 'Understanding the Limitations and Cultural Implications of Aboriginal Tribal Boundary Maps', *Globe*, Vol. 25, (1986), pp. 2–12.

Jane Jacobs, 'Shake 'im This Country': The Mapping of the Aboriginal Sacred in Australia—The Case of Coronation Hill', in P. Jackson and J. Penrose, eds., *Constructions of Race, Place and Nation*, (London: University College London, 1993), pp. 100–120.

John James, *The Contractors of Chartres 2 vols*, (Wyong: Mandorla Publications, 1979).

John James, *Chartres: The Masons Who Built a Legend*, (London: Routledge and Kegan Paul, 1982).

John James, 'An Investigation into the Uneven Distribution of Early Gothic Churches in the Paris Basin, 1140–1240', *The Art Bulletin*, March, (1984), pp. 15–46.

John James, *The Template-Makers of the Paris Basin*, (Leura: West Grinstead Nominees, 1989).

H. Jantzen, *High Gothic*, (London: Constable, 1962).

Sheila Jasanoff, Gerald Markle, Trevor Pinch and James Petersen, eds., *Handbook of Science and Technology Studies*, (Thousand Oaks: Sage Publications, 1995).

Sheia Jasanoff, 'Public Knowledge, Private Fears: Review of Irwin & Wynne [eds], *Misunderstanding Science?*', *Social Studies of Science*, Vol. 27, 2, (1997), pp. 350–55.

R.E. Johannes,*Words of the Lagoon: Fishing and Marine Lore in the Palau District of Micronesia*, (Berkeley: University of California Press, 1981).

Stephen A. Johnston, *Making Mathematical Practice: Gentlemen, Practitioners and Artisans in Elizabethan England*, (City: London, 1994).

Barry Jones, *Sleepers Wake! Technology and the Future of Work*, (Melbourne: Oxford University Press, 1982).

W. James Judge, 'Archaeology and Astronomy: A View From the Southwest', in J. B. Carlson and W. J. Judge, eds., *Astronomy and Ceremony in the Prehistoric Southwest*, (Albuquerque: University Of New Mexico, 1983), pp. 1–8.

W. James Judge, 'New Light on Chaco Canyon', in D. G. Noble, ed., *New Light on Chaco Canyon*, (Santa Fe: School of American Research Press, 1984), pp. 1–12.

Ian Keen, 'Metaphor and the Meta-Language: "Groups" in Northeast Arnhemland', *American Ethnologist*, Vol. 22 (1995), pp. 502–27.

Karl Kerényi, 'The Trickster in Relation to Greek Mythology', in P. Radin, ed., *The Trickster: A Study in American Indian Mythology*, (New York: Schocken Books, 1972).

G. B. Kerferd, 'Protagoras of Abdera', in P. Edwards, ed., *The Encyclopedia of Philosophy*, (New York: Collier Macmillan, 1967), p. 506.

Vincent Kiernan, 'Article of Faith Fails Aero Engineers', *New Scientist*, Vol. 150, 11 May, (1996), p. 5.

M. D. King, 'Reason, Tradition, and the Progressiveness of Science', in G. Gutting, ed., *Paradigms and Revolutions: Applications and Appraisals of Thomas Kuhn's Philosophy of Science*, Notre Dame: University of Notre Dame Press, 1980), pp. 97–116.

S. Kline, *Quasi-coherent Structures in the Turbulent Boundary Layer: Part 1. Status Report on a Community-wide Summary of the Data*. Zoran P. Zaric Memorial International Seminar on Near-Wall Turbulence, (Dubrovnik: 1988).

D. Knoop and G. Jones, *The Medieaval Mason*, (Manchester: Manchester University Press, 1967).

Karen Knorr-Cetina, 'Tinkering Toward Success: Prelude to a Theory of Scientific Practice', *Theory and Society*, Vol. 8, (1979), pp. 347–76.

Karin Knorr-Cetina, *The Manufacture of Knowledge: An Essay on the Constructivist and Contextual Nature of Science*, (Oxford: Pergamon Press, 1981).

Karin Knorr-Cetina, 'The Couch, the Cathedral, and the Laboratory: On the Relationship Between Experiment and Laboratory in Science', in A. Pickering, ed., *Science as Practice and Culture*, (Chicago: University of Chicago Press, 1992), pp. 113–38.

K. D. Knorr-Cetina and M. Mulkay, eds., *Science Observed: Reflections on the Social Study of Science*, (London: Sage, 1982).

Spiro Kostof, *The Architect: Chapters in the History of the Profession*, (New York: Oxford University Press, 1977).

Spiro Kostof, *A History of Architecture: Settings and Rituals*, (New York: Oxford University Press, 1985).

Michael Krausz, ed., *Relativism: Interpretation and Confrontation*, (Notre Dame: University of Notre Dame, 1989).

M. Krausz and J. Meiland, eds., *Relativism: Cognitive and Moral*, (South Bend.: University of Notre Dame Press, 1982).

J. P. Kreier, ed., *Malaria: Vol.1; Epidemiology, Chemotherapy, Morphology, and Metabolism*, (New York: Academic Press, 1982).

Henry Krips, 'Epistemological Holism Duhem or Quine?', *Studies in History and Philosophy of Science*, Vol. 13, (1982), pp. 251–264.

Thomas Kuhn, *The Structure of Scientific Revolutions*, (Chicago: University of Chicago Press, 1970).

Thomas Kuhn, *The Essential Tension*, (Chicago: University of Chicago Press, 1977).

Thomas S. Kuhn, 'Reflections on My Critics', in I. Lakatos and A. Musgrave, eds., *Criticism and the Growth of Knowledge*, (London: Cambridge University Press, 1970), pp. 231–78.

Witold Kula, *Measures and Men*, (Princeton: Princeton University Press, 1986).

Ursula Lamb, 'Science by Litigation: A Cosmographic Feud', *Terrae Incognitae*, Vol. 1, (1969), pp. 40–57.

Ursula Lamb, 'The Spanish Cosmographic Juntas of the Sixteenth Century', *Terrae Incognitae*, Vol. 6, (1974), pp. 51–64.

Bruno Latour, 'Give Me a Laboratory and I Will Raise the World', in K. D. Knorr-Cetina and M. Mulkay, eds., *Science Observed: Reflections on the Social Study of Science*, (London: Sage, 1982), pp. 141–170.

Bruno Latour, 'The Powers of Association', in J. Law, ed., *Power, Action and Belief: A New Sociology of Knowledge?*, (London: Routledge & Kegan Paul, 1986).

Bruno Latour, 'Visualisation and Cognition: Thinking With Eyes and Hands', *Knowledge and Society*, Vol. 6, (1986), pp. 1–40.

Bruno Latour, *Science in Action*, (Milton Keynes: Open University Press, 1987).

Bruno Latour, *The Pasteurization of France*, (Cambridge: Harvard University Press, 1988).

John Law, ed., *Power, Action and Belief: A New Sociology of Knowledge?*, (London: Routledge & Kegan Paul, 1986).

John Law, 'On the Methods of Long Distance Control: Vessels, Navigation and the Portuguese Route to India', in Law, *Power, Action and Belief*, pp. 234–63.

John Law, 'On the Social Explanation of Technical Change: The Case of the Portuguese Maritime Expansion', *Technology and Culture*, Vol. 28, (1987), pp. 27–253.

John Law, 'Technology and Heterogeneous Engineering: The Case of Portugese Expansion', in W. Bijker, T. Hughes and T. Pinch, eds., *The Social Construction of Technological Systems; New Directions in the Sociology and History of Technology*, (Cambridge: MIT Press, 1987), pp. 111–34.

John Law, ed., *A Sociology of Monsters: Essays on Power, Technology and Domination*, Sociological Review Monograph 38, (London: Routledge, 1991).

John Law, 'Power, Discretion and Strategy', in Law, ed., *A Sociology of Monsters*, pp. 165–191.

J. Law, 1994, *Organizing Modernity*, (Oxford: Blackwell, 1994).

John Law and Wiebe Bijker, 'Postscript: Technology, Stability, and Social Theory', in W. Bijker and J. Law, eds., *Shaping Technology/Building Society: Studies in Sociotechnical Change*, (Cambridge: MIT Press, 1992), pp. 201–224.

Edmund Leach, *Culture and Communication: The Logic by Which Symbols Are Connected*, (Cambridge: Cambridge University Press, 1976).

Henri Lefebvre, *The Production of Space*, (Oxford: Blackwell, 1991).

Dana Leibsohn, 'Mapping Metaphors: Figuring the Ground of Sixteenth Century New Spain', *Journal of Medieval and Early Modern Studies*, Vol. 26, 3, (1996), pp. 497–523.

Stephen Lekson, Thomas C. Windes, et al., 'The Chaco Canyon Community', *Scientific American*, Vol. 259, July, (1988), pp. 100–9.

Timothy Lenoir, 'Practice, Reason, Context: The Dialogue Between Theory and Experiment', *Science in Context*, Vol. 2, 1, (1988), pp. 3–22.

Les Levidow and Bob Young, *Science, Technology and the Labour Process*, (London: Free Association Books, 1985).

David Lewis, *We The Navigators: The Ancient Art of Landfinding in the Pacific*, (Honolulu: University of Hawaii Press, 1994).

David Lewis, 'Voyaging Stars: Aspects of Polynesian and Micronesian Astronomy', in F. F. Hodson, ed., *The Place of Astronomy in the Ancient World*, (London: Oxford University Press, 1974), pp. 133–48.

Malcom Lewis, 'The Origins of Cartography', in J. B. Harley and D. Woodward, eds., *The History of Cartography, Vol. 1 Cartography in Prehistoric, Ancient and Medieval Europe and the Mediterranean*, (Chicago: University of Chicago Press, 1987).

K. Lincoln and A. Slagle, *The Good Red Road; Passages into North America*, (San Francisco: Harper and Row, 1983).

Pamela O. Long, 'The Contribution of Architectural Writers to a "Scientific" Outlook in the Fifteenth and Sixteenth Centuries', *Journal of Medieval and Renaissance Studies*, Vol. 15, (1985), pp. 265–98.

Helen Longino, 'Hard, Soft, or Satisfying', *Social Epistemology*, Vol. 6, (1992), pp. 281–7.

Alasdair MacIntyre, *Whose Justice? Which Rationality?*, (London: Duckworth, 1988).

Maurice Mandelbaum, 'Subjective, Objective and Conceptual Relativism', in M. Krausz and J. Meiland, eds., *Relativism: Cognitive and Moral*, (South Bend: University of Notre Dame Press, 1982).

Karl Mannheim, *Ideology and Utopia*, (London: Kegan Paul, 1936).

G.E. Marcus and M. M. J Fischer, *Anthropology as Cultural Critique: An Experimental Moment in the Human Sciences*, (Chicago: University of Chicago Press, 1986).

Joseph Margolis, 'The Technological Self', in E. F. Byrne and J. C. Pitt, eds., *Technological Transformation: Contextual and Conceptual Implications*, (Dordrecht: Kluwer Academic Publications, 1989), pp. 1–16.

Robert Mark, 'The Structural Analysis of Gothic Cathedrals', *Scientific American*, Vol. 227, Nov, (1972), pp. 90–99.

Robert Mark, *Experiments in Gothic Structure*, (Cambridge: MIT Press, 1982).

Robert Mark and David P. Billington, 'Structural Imperative and the New Form', *Technology and Culture*, Vol. 30, (1989), pp. 300–329.

Robert Mark and W. W. Clark, 'Gothic Structural Experimentation', *Scientific American*, Vol. 25, (1984), pp. 144–153.

Alexander Marshack, 'North American Indian Calendar Sticks: The Evidence for a Widely Distributed Tradition', in A. F. Aveni, ed., *World Archaeoastronomy: Selected Papers from the 2nd Oxford International Conference on Archaeoastronomy Held at Merida, Yucatan, Mexico, 1986*, (Cambridge: Cambridge University Press, 1989), pp. 308–324.

Stephen McCluskey, 'Historical Archaeoastronomy: The Hopi Example', in A. F. Aveni, ed., *Archaeoastronomy in the New World: Proceedings of an International Conference at Oxford 1981*, (Cambridge: Cambridge University Press, 1982), pp. 31–59.

Stephen McCluskey, 'Science, Society, Objectivity, and the Southwest', in J. B. Carlson and W. J. Judge, eds., *Astronomy and Ceremony in the Prehistoric Southwest*, (Albuquerque: University Of New Mexico, 1983), pp. 205–217.

Geoffrey McFadden, Michael Reith, et al., 'Plastid in Human Parasites', *Nature*, Vol. 381, 6th June, (1996), p. 482.

Kenneth McIntyre, *The Secret Discovery of Australia: Portuguese Ventures 200 Years Before Captain Cook*, (Menindie: Souvenier Press, 1977).

Marshall McLuhan, *Understanding Media: The Extensions of Man*, (New York: McGraw-Hill, 1964).

Daniel McNeill and Paul Freiberger, *Fuzzy Logic*, (Melbourne: Bookman Press, 1993).

W. H. McNeill, *Plagues and People*, (New York: Anchor Press, 1966).

Jack W. Meiland, 'Concepts of Relative Truth', *The Monist*, Vol. 60, (1977), pp. 568–582.

Jack W. Meiland, 'On the Paradox of Cognitive Relativism', *Metaphilosophy*, Vol. 11, (1982), pp. 115–126.

Robert K. Merton, *The Sociology of Science*, (Chicago: University of Chicago Press, 1973).

G. F. Mitchell, 'Short Odds for Malaria Vaccines', *BioEssays*, Vol. 13, (1986), pp. 126–7.

J. Moir and P. Garner, 'Malaria Control Through Health Services', *Papua New Guinea Medical Journal*, Vol. 29, (1986), pp. 27–33.

Annemarie Mol and John Law, 'Regions, Network, and Fluids: Anaemia and Social Topology', *Social Studies of Science*, Vol. 24, (1994), pp. 641–71.

Michel Mollat du Jourdin and Monique de La Roncière, *Sea Charts of the Early Explorers: 13th to 17th Century*, (London: Thames and Hudson, 1984).

Mark Monmonier, *How to Lie With Maps*, (Chicago: University of Chicago Press, 1991).

Sally Falk Moore, *Power and Property in Inca Peru*, (Connecticut: Greenwood Press, 1985).

E. E. Morison, *From Know-How to Nowhere: The Development of American Technology*, (Oxford: Blackwell, 1974).

Howard Morphy, *Ancestral Connections: Art and an Aboriginal System of Knowledge*, (Chicago: University of Chicago Press, 1991).

Barbara Mundy, *The Mapping of New Spain: Indigenous Cartography and the Maps of the Relación Geográficas*, (Chicago: University of Chicago Press, 1996).

S. Murray, 'Contractors of Chartres, [review]', *Art Bulletin*, Vol. 63, (1981), pp. 149–52.

S. Murray, *Building Troyes Cathedral: The Late Gothic Campaign*, (Bloomington: Indiana University Press, 1987).

Fred R. Myers, *Pintupi Country, Pintupi Self: Sentiment, Place and Politics among Western Desert Aborigines*, (Washington, London, Canberra: Smithsonian Institution Press and Australian Institute of Aboriginal Studies, 1986).

T. Nagel, *The View From Nowhere*, (Oxford: Oxford University Press, 1986).

David Noble, *America by Design: Science, Technology and the Rise of Corporate Capitalism*, (New York: Knopf, 1977).

David Noble, *Forces of Production: A Social History of Industrial Automation*, (New York: Knopf, 1984).

Bill O'Neill, 'Bridge Design Stretched to the Limits', *New Scientist*, Vol. 132, Oct 26, (1991), pp. 28–35.

David Olson, *The World on Paper: The Conceptual and Cognitive Implications of Writing and Reading*, (Cambridge: Cambridge University Press, 1994).

Walter Ong, *Orality and Literacy: The Technologizing of the Word*, (London: Methuen, 1982).

Adi Ophir and Steven Shapin, 'The Place of Knowledge: A Methodological Survey', *Science in Context*, Vol. 4, (1991), pp. 3–21.

Arnold Pacey, *The Maze of Ingenuity: Ideas and Idealism in the Development of Technology*, (London: Allen Lane, 1974).

Kingsley Palmer, 'Knowledge as a Commodity in Aboriginal Australia', in D. Turnbull, ed., *Knowledge, Land and Australian Aboriginal Experience*, (Geelong: Deakin University Press, 1991), pp. 6–10.

Fred Pearce, 'A Plague on Global Warming', *New Scientist*, Vol. 136, 19/26th Dec, (1992), pp. 12–13.

Monique Pelletier, *La Carte de Cassini: L'Extraordinaire Aventure de la Carte de France*, (Paris: Presses de l'École Nationale des Ponts et Chaussées, 1990).

W. Peters, 'New Answers Through Chemotherapy', *Experientia*, Vol. 40, (1984), pp. 1311–1317.

Andy Pickering, 'Objectivity and the Mangle of Practice', *Annals of Scholarship*, Vol. 8, (1991), pp. 409–425.

Andrew Pickering, ed., *Science as Practice and Culture*, (Chicago: University of Chicago Press, 1992).

Andrew Pickering, *The Mangle of Practice: Time, Agency, and Science*, (Chicago: University of Chicago Press, 1995).

Jan Douwe van der Ploege, 'Potatoes and Knowledge', in M. Hobart, ed., *An Anthropological Critique of Development*, (London: Routledge, 1993), pp. 209–27.

M. Polanyi, *Personal Knowledge: Towards a Post-critical Philosophy*, (London: Routledge and Kegan Paul, 1958).

Karl Popper, *The Open Society and its Enemies*, (Princeton: Princeton University Press, 1950).

Karl Popper, *Conjectures and Refutations: The Growth of Scientific Knowledge*, (London: Routledge Kegan Paul, 1963).

Roy Porter, 'White Coats in Vogue', *Times Higher Educational Supplement*, Vol. Nov 5, (1982), pp. 12–13.

Roy Porter, 'The History of Science and the History of Society', in R. C. Olby, G. N. Cantor, J. R. R. Christie and M. J. S. Hodge, eds., *Companion to the History of Modern Science*, (London: Routledge, 1990), pp. 32–46.

Theodore Porter, *Trust in Numbers: The Pursuit of Objectivity in Science and Public Life*, (Princeton: Princeton University Press, 1995).

Alain Pottage, 'The Measure of Land', *Modern Law Review*, Vol. 57, (1994), pp. 361–84.

Mary Louise Pratt, *Imperial Eyes: Travel Writing and Transculturation*, (London: Routledge, 1992).

A. W. Pugin, *The True Principles of Pointed or Christian Architecture*, (London: 1841).

Robert Putnam, *Making Democracy Work: Civic Traditions in Modern Italy*, (Princeton: Princeton University Press, 1993).

Robert Putnam, 'Bowling Alone: America's Declining Social Capital', *Journal of Democracy*, Vol. 6, (1995), pp. 65–78.

W. V. O. Quine, *Word and Object*, (Cambridge, Mass: MIT Press, 1960).

Jose Rabasa, 'Allegories of the *ATLAS*', in F. Barker, ed., *Europe and Its Others*, (Colchester: University of Essex, 1985), pp. 1–16.

Paul Rabinow, *Reflections on Field Work in Morocco*, (Berkeley: University of California Press, 1977).

Charles Radding and William Clark, *Medieval Architecture, Medieval Learning: Builders and Masters in the Age of the Romanesque and Gothic*, (New Haven: Yale University Press, 1992).

Diederick Raven, Lieteke Tijssen, et al., eds., *Cognitive Relativism and Social Science*, (New Brunswick: Transaction Pbl., 1992).

J. V. Ravetch, J. Young, et al., 'Molecular Genetic Strategies for the Development of Anti-malarial Vaccines', *Biotechnology*, Vol. 3, (1985), pp. 729–40.

Sal Restivo, 'Modern Science as a Social Problem', *Social Problems*, Vol. 33, (1988), pp. 206–25.

J. Revel, 'Knowledge of the Territory', *Science in Context*, Vol. 4, (1991), pp. 133–161.

Jonathon E. Reyman, 'Priests, Power and Politics: Some Implications of Socio-ceremonial Control', in J. B. Carlson and W. J. Judge, eds., *Astronomy and Ceremony in the Prehistoric Southwest*, (Albuquerque: University of New Mexico, 1983), pp. 121–42.

W. A. R. Richardson, 'Is Java-La-Grande Australia? The Linguistic Evidence Concerning the West Coast', *Globe* (Journal of the Australian Map Circle), Vol. 19, (1983), pp. 9–46.

A. H. Robinson and B. B. Petchenik, *The Nature of Maps: Essays Towards Understanding Maps and Mapping*, (Chicago: University of Chicago Press, 1976).

S. Robinson, S. Kline, et al., *Quasi-Coherent Structures in the Turbulent Boundary Layer: Part 2. Verification and New Information from a Numerically Simulated Flat-Plate Layer.* (Dubrovnik: 1988).

Richard Rorty, *Philosophy and the Mirror of Nature*, (Princeton: Princeton University Press, 1979).

Richard Rorty, *The Consequences of Pragmatism*, (Brighton: Harvester, 1982).

H. Rose and S. Rose, 'Radical Science and its Enemies', *The Socialist Register*, Vol. 16, (1979), pp. 317–335.

Gerhard Rosenberg, 'The Functional Aspect of the Gothic Style', *Journal of the Royal Institute of British Architects*, Vol. 43, (1936), pp. 273–90 and 364–71.

Andrew Ross, ed., *Science Wars*, (Durham: Duke University Press, 1996).

Joseph Rouse, *Knowledge and Power: Towards a Political Philosophy of Science*, (Ithaca: Cornell University Press, 1987).

José Pulido Rubio, *El Piloto Mayor de la Casa de Contratacion de Seville*, (Seville: Escuela de Estudios Hispano-Americanos, 1950).

Robert A. Rundstrom, 'A Cultural Interpretation of Inuit Map Accuracy', *Geographical Review*, Vol. 80, (1990), pp. 155–68.

Robert A. Rundstrom, 'Mapping, Postmodernism, Indigenous People and the Changing Direction of North American Cartography', *Cartographica*, Vol. 28, (1991), pp. 1–12.

P. F. Russell, *Man's Mastery of Malaria*, (Oxford: Oxford University Press, 1955).

Edward Said, *Orientalism: Western Conceptions of the Orient*, (New York: Pantheon Books, 1978).

Anne Salmond, 'Maori Epistemologies', in J. Overing, ed., *Reason and Morality*, (London: Tavistock Pbls., 1985), pp. 240–63.

Anne Salmond, *Two Worlds: First Meetings Between Maori and Europeans 1642–1772*, (Auckland: Penguin Books, 1991).

Sergio Luis Sanabria, 'From Gothic to Renaissance Stereotomy: The Design Methods of Philibert de l'Orme and Alonso de Vandelvira', *Technology and Culture*, Vol. 31, (1989), pp. 266–299.

F. R. Sandbach, 'Preventing Schistosomiasis: A Critical Assessment of Present Policy', *Social Science and Medicine*, Vol. 9, (1975), pp. 517–527.

B. De S. Santos, 'Law: A Map of Misreading. Toward a Postmodern Conception of Law', *Journal of Law and Society*, Vol. 14, 3, (1987), pp. 279–302.

Zia Sardar, ed., *The Revenge of Athena: Science, Exploitation and the Third World*, (London: Mansell, 1988).

Omar Sattaur, 'Native is Beautiful', *New Scientist*, Vol. June 2, (1988), pp. 54–7.

R. W. Scheller, *A Survey of Medieval Model Books*, (Haarlem: De Erven F. Bohn, 1963).

J. A. Schuster and R. Yeo, ed., *The Politics and Rhetoric of Scientific Method*, (Dordrecht: Reidel, 1986).

W. A. Seymour, ed., *A History of the Ordnance Survey*, (Folkstone: Dawson, 1980).

Steven Shapin, 'The Politics of Observation: Cerebral Anatomy and Social Interests in the Edinburgh Phrenology Disputes', in R. Wallis, ed., *On the Margins of Science*, (Keele: University of Keele, 1979), pp. 139–178.

Steven Shapin, 'Pump and Circumstance: Robert Boyle's Literary Technology', *Social Studies of Science*, Vol. 14, (1984), pp. 481–520.

Steven Shapin, *A Social History of Truth: Civility and Science in 17th Century England*, (Chicago: University of Chicago Press, 1994).

Steven Shapin and Simon Schaffer, *Leviathan and the Air Pump: Hobbes, Boyle and the Experimental Life*, (Princeton: Princeton University Press, 1985).

Andrew Sharp, *Ancient Voyagers in Polynesia*, (Sydney: Angus and Robertson, 1963).

Lon R. Shelby, 'Medieval Masons' Tools. 11. Compass and Square', *Technology and Culture*, Vol. 6, (1965), pp. 236–248.

Lon R. Shelby, 'The Education of Medieval English Master Masons', *Medieval Studies*, Vol. 32, (1970), pp. 1–26.

Lon R. Shelby, 'The "Secret" of the Medieval Masons', in B. Hall and D. West, eds., *On Pre-Modern Technology and Science*, (Malibu: Undena Publications, 1976), pp. 201–222.

Lon R. Shelby, *Gothic Design Techniques: The Fifteenth Century Design Booklets of Mathes Roriczer and Hans Schmuttermayer*, (Carbondale: Southern Illinois University Press, 1977).

Lon R. Shelby, 'The Contractors of Chartres, [review]', *GESTA*, Vol. XX, (1981), pp. 173–8.

Rodney Shirley, 'Epicthonius Cosmopolites: Who Was He?', *Map Collector*, Vol. 18 (March), (1982), pp. 39–40.

A. P. Simonds, *Karl Mannheim's Sociology of Knowledge*, (Oxford: Clarendon Press, 1978).

Paul Simons, 'Could Marigolds Slay Killer Mosquitos?', *New Scientist*, Vol. 139, 17th July, (1993), p. 18.

Otto Von Simson, *The Gothic Cathedral*, (New York: Pantheon Books, 1956).

R. Skelton, *Explorer's Maps: Chapters in the Cartographical Record of Geographical Discovery*, (London: Routledge & Kegan Paul, 1958).

R. A. Skelton and P. D. A. Harvey, *Local Maps and Plans from Medieval England*, (Oxford: Clarendon Press, 1986).

Catherine Delano Smith, 'The First English Maps', in C. D. Smith and R. Kain, eds., *La Cartografia Anglesa*, (Barcelona: Institut Cartografic de Catalunya, 1997), pp. 39–54.

A. Smits, *The Structure of Supersonic Turbulent Shear Layers. A Draft Proposal to the Air Force Office of Scientific Research*, (Fluid Dynamics Laboratory, Dept. of Mechanical and Aerospace Engineering, Princeton University, 1989).

A. Smits, ed., *Proceedings of the Princeton Workshop on 'New Approaches to Experimental Turbulence Research', MAE Report No. 1924*, (Princeton: Princeton University Department of Mechanical and Aerospace Engineering, 1991).

Anna P. Sofaer and Rolf M. Sinclair, 'Astronomical Markings at Three Sites on Fajada Butte', in J. B. Carlson and W. J. Judge, eds., *Astronomy and Ceremony in the Prehistoric Southwest*, (Albuquerque: University of New Mexico, 1983), pp. 43–70.

Edward W. Soja, *Postmodern Geographies: The Reassertion of Space in Critical Social Theory*, (London: Verso, 1989).

Edward Soja, *Thirdspace: Journeys to Los Angeles and Other Real-and-Imagined Places*, (Cambridge, Mass: Blackwell, 1996).

K. R. Sreenivasan, *The Turbulent Boundary Layer*, (Mason Lab, Yale University, 1989).

Susan Leigh Star, *Regions of Mind: Brain Research and the Quest for Scientific Certainty*, (Stanford: Stanford University Press, 1989).

Susan Leigh Star, 'Simplification in Science Work: An Example from Neuroscience Research', *Social Studies of Science*, Vol. 13, (1983), pp. 205–28.

Susan Leigh Star, 'The Structure of Ill-Structured Solutions: Boundary Objects and Heterogeneous Distributed Problem Solving', in L. Gasser and N. Huhns, eds., *Distributed Artificial Intelligence*, (New York: Morgan Kauffman Publications, 1989), pp. 37–54.

Susan Leigh Star, 'The Sociology of the Invisible: The Primacy of Work in the Writings of Anselm Strauss', in D. Maines, ed., *Social Organisation and Social Processes: Essays in Honour of Anselm Strauss*, (New York: Aldine de Gruyter, 1990).

Susan Leigh Star and James Griesmer, 'Institutional Ecology, "Translations" and Boundary Objects: Amateurs and Professionals in Berkeley's Museum of Vertebrate Zoology, 1907–39', *Social Studies of Science*, Vol. 19, (1989), pp. 387–420.

Werner Stark, *The Sociology of Knowledge*, (London: Routledge and Kegan Paul, 1958).

Nancy Stepan, 'The Interplay Between Socio-economic Factors and Medical Science: Yellow Fever Research, Cuba, and the United States', *Social Studies of Science*, Vol. 8, (1978), pp. 397–423.

Terry Stokes and David Turnbull, 'Manipulable Systems and Laboratory Strategies in a Biomedical Research Institute', in H. L. Grand, ed., *Experimental Inquiries: Historical, Philosophical and Social Studies in Science*, (Dordrecht: Kluwer Academic Publishers, 1990), pp. 167–192.

Brian V. Street, *Literacy in Theory and Practice*, (Cambridge: Cambridge University Press, 1984).

Lucy Suchman, *Plans and Situated Actions: The Problem of Human-Machine Communication*, (Cambridge: Cambridge University Press, 1987).

Lucy Sullivan, 'Language Map Gives Few Wrong Directions', *The Australian*, (Melbourne: 1994), p. 29.

Peter Sutton, *Dreamings: The Art of Aboriginal Australia*, (Ringwood: Viking, 1988).

Peter Sutton, ed., *Country: Aboriginal Boundaries and Land Ownership in Australia. Aboriginal History Monograph 3*, (Canberra: Aboriginal History Inc., 1995).

Stanley Jeyaraja Tambiah, *Magic, Science, Religion, and the Scope of Rationality*, (Cambridge University Press: Cambridge, 1990).

Luke Taylor, 'Seeing the "Inside": Kunwinjku Paintings and the Symbol of the Divided Body', in H. Morphy, ed., *Animals into Art*, (London: Unwin Hyman, 1989), pp. 371–389.

T. Theocharis and M. Psimopoulos, 'Where Science Has Gone Wrong', *Nature*, Vol. 329, 15th Oct, (1987), pp. 595–98.

Stephen D. Thomas, *The Last Navigator*, (New York: Ballantine Books, 1988).

Clare Thompson, 'Malaria Pill Stands Accused', *New Scientist*, Vol. 150, April 27, (1996), pp. 14–15.

Nigel Thrift, 'Flies and Germs: A Geography of Knowledge', in D. Gregory and J. Urry, eds., *Social Relations and Spatial Structures*, (London: Macmillan, 1985), pp. 366–403.

David Turnbull, 'Relativism, Reflexivity and the Sociology of Scientific Knowledge', *Metascience: Annual Review of the Australasian Association for the History, Philosophy and Social Studies of Science*, Vol. 1/2, (1984), pp. 47–61.

David Turnbull, 'The Push For a Malaria Vaccine', *Social Studies of Science*, Vol. 19, (1989), pp. 283–300.

David Turnbull, *Mapping the World in the Mind: An Investigation of the Unwritten Knowledge of the Micronesian Navigators*, (Geelong: Deakin University Press, 1991).

David Turnbull, *Technoscience Worlds*, (Geelong: Deakin University Press, 1991).

David Turnbull, 'The Ad Hoc Collective Work of Building Gothic Cathedrals with Templates, String, and Geometry', *Science Technology and Human Values*, Vol. 18, (1993), pp. 315–40.

David Turnbull, 'Local Knowledge and Comparative Scientific Traditions', *Knowledge and Policy*, Vol. 6, 3/4, (1993), pp. 29–54.

David Turnbull, *Maps Are Territories: Science Is an Atlas*, (Chicago: Chicago University Press, 1993).

David Turnbull, 'Comparing Knowledge Systems: Pacific Navigation and Western Science', in J. Morrison, P. Geraghty and L. Crowl, eds., *Science of the Pacific Island Peoples: Vol.1, Ocean and Coastal Studies*, (Suva: Institute of Pacific Studies, 1994), pp. 129–144.

David Turnbull, 'Rendering Turbulence Orderly', *Social Studies of Science*, Vol. 25, (1995), pp. 9–33.

David Turnbull, 'Cartography and Science in Early Modern Europe: Mapping the Construction of Knowledge Spaces', *Imago Mundi*, Vol. 48, (1996), pp. 5–24.

David Turnbull, 'Constructing Knowledge Spaces and Locating Sites of Resistance in the Early Modern Cartographic Transformation', in R. Paulston, ed., *Social Cartography: Mapping Ways of Seeing Social and Educational Change*, (New York: Garland Publishing Inc., 1996), pp. 53–79.

David Turnbull, 'Reframing Science and Other Local Knowledge Traditions', *Futures*, Vol. 29, 6, (1997), pp. 551–62.

David Turnbull, 'Mapping Encounters and (En)countering Maps: A Critical Examination of Cartographic Resistance', *Knowledge and Society*, Vol. 11, (1998), pp. 15–44.

David Turnbull, 'Cook and Tupaia, a Tale of Cartographic Méconnaissance?', in M. Lincoln, ed., *Science and Exploration: European Voyages to the Southern Oceans in the Eighteenth Century*, (London: Boydell and Brewer, 1998).

Sarah Tyacke, ed., *English Map-Making 1500–1650: Historical Essays*, (London: British Library, 1983).

J. Van der Muelen, 'Recent Literature on the Chronology of Chartres Cathedral', *Art Bulletin*, Vol. 4, (1967), pp. 152–72.

Giorgio Vasari, *The Lives of the Painters, Sculptors and Architects, Vol. 1*, (New York: Everyman's Library, 1550 reprinted 1963).

Garcilaso de la Vega, *The Incas: The Royal Commentaries of the Inca*, (New York: Avon Books, 1961).

R. Gwinn Vivian, 'Conservation and Diversion: Water-control Systems in the Anasazi Southwest', in T. E. Downing and M. Gibson, eds., *Irrigation's Impact on Society*, (Tucson: University of Arizona Press, 1974), pp. 95–112.

Helen Wallis, ed., *The Maps and Text of the Boke of Idrography Presented by Jean Rotz to Henry VIII, Now in the British Library*, (Oxford: Viscount Eccles for the Roxburghe Club, 1981).

Helen Wallis, *Did The Portuguese Discover Australia? The Map Evidence.* International Cartographic Association, (Perth, Australia: 1984).

Helen Wallis, 'Java La Grande: The Enigma of the Dieppe Maps', in G. Williams and A. Frost, eds., *Terra Australis to Australia*, (Melbourne: Oxford University Press, 1988), pp. 39–81.

Talbot H. Waterman, *Animal Navigation*, (New York: Scientific American Library, 1989).

David W. Waters, *The Art of Navigation in England in Elizabethan and Early Stuart Times*, (London: Hollis and Carter, 1958).

David W. Waters, 'Science and the Techniques of Navigation in the Renaissance', *Maritime Monographs and Reports*, Vol. 19, (1974).

Sian Watkins, 'Sky-high Jigsaw', *Age*, (Melbourne: 1990), p. 7.

Helen Watson, with the Yolgnu community at Yirrkala and David Wade Chambers, *Singing the Land, Signing the Land*, (Geelong: Deakin University Press, 1989).

Helen Watson-Verran, 'Working Where Knowledge Systems Overlap', *Knowledge and Policy*, Vol. 14, (1993).

Helen Watson-Verran and David Turnbull, 'Science and Other Indigenous Knowledge Systems', in S. Jasanoff, G. Markle, T. Pinch and J. Petersen, eds., *Handbook of Science and Technology Studies*, (Thousand Oaks: Sage Publications, 1995), pp. 115–139.

Max Weber, 'Law, Rationalism and Capitalism', in C. M. Campbell and P. Wiles, eds., *Law and Society*, (Oxford: Martin Robertson, 1979), pp. 51–89.

Stephen Webster, 'Dialogue and Fiction in Ethnography', *Dialectical Anthropology*, Vol. 7, (1982), pp. 91–114.

Steven Weinberg, *The Search for the Fundamental Laws of Nature*, (New York: Pantheon, 1992).

T. F. West and G. A. Campbell, *DDT: the Synthetic Insecticide*, (London: Chapman and Hall, 1946).

Lynn White Jnr, ed., *Medieval Religion and Technology: Collected Essays*, (Berkeley: University of California Press, 1978).

Lynn White Jnr, 'The Medieval Roots of Modern Technology and Science', in L. White Jnr, ed., *Medieval Religion and Technology: Collected Essays*, pp. 75–92.

Sven Widmalm, 'Accuracy, Rhetoric and Technology: The Paris-Greenwich Triangulation, 1784–88', in T. Frängsmyr, J. L. Heilbron and R. E. Rider, eds., *The Quantifying Spirit in the 18th Century*, (Berkeley: University of California Press, 1990), pp. 179–206.

Nancy M. Williams, *The Yolngu and their Land: A System of Land Tenure and the Fight for its Recognition*, (Canberra: Australian Institute of Aboriginal Studies, 1986).

R.R. Wilson, 'The Humanness of Physics', in D. M. Borchert and D. Stewart, eds., *Being Human in a Technological Age*, (Athens Ohio: 1979), pp. 25–36.

Keith Windschuttle, *The Killing of History: How a Discipline is Being Murdered by Literary Critics and Social Theorists*, (Sydney: Macleay Press, 1994).

Langdon Winner, *The Whale and the Reactor*, (Chicago: University of Chicago Press, 1986).

Ludwig Wittgenstein, *Philosophical Investigations*, (Oxford: Blackwell, 1958).

Denis Wood, 'How Maps Work', *Cartographica*, Vol. 29, 3&4, (1992), pp. 66–74.

Denis Wood, *The Power of Maps*, (New York: The Guilford Press, 1992).

Denis Wood, 'Maps and Mapmaking', *Cartographica*, Vol. 30, 1, (1993), pp. 1–9.

Denis Wood, 'Mapmaking', in H. Selin, ed., *Encyclopedia of the History of Science, Technology and Medicine in Non-Western Cultures*, (New York: Garland, 1995).

Steve Woolgar, 'Irony in the Social Study of Science', in K. D. Knorr and M. Mulkay, eds., *Science Observed: Perspectives on the Social Study of Science*, (London: Sage, 1983), pp. 239–266.

Steve Woolgar, ed., *Knowledge and Reflexivity: New Frontiers in the Sociology of Knowledge*, (London: Sage, 1988).

Steve Woolgar, *Science: The Very Idea*, (London: Tavistock, 1988).

Christopher Wren, *Life and Works of Sir Christopher Wren from the Parentalia or Memoirs by his Son Christopher*, (London: 1750 reprinted 1903).

Worsley, P. 1997, *Knowledges: Culture, Counterculture, Subculture*, New Press, New York.

Ronald Wright, *Cut Stones and Crossroads: Journey in Peru*, (New York: Penguin Books, 1984).

Brian Wynne, 'May the Sheep Safely Graze?', in S. Lash, B. Szerszynski and B. Wynne, eds., *Risk, Environment and Modernity: Towards a New Ecology*, (London: Sage, 1996), pp. 44–83.

Bob Young, 'Science *is* Social Relations', *Radical Science Journal*, Vol. 5, (1977), pp. 165–129.

Jane Young, 'The Nature of the Evidence: Archaeoastronomy in the Prehistoric Southwest', in J. B. Carlson and W. J. Judge, eds., *Astronomy and Ceremony in the Prehistoric Southwest*, (Albuquerque: University of New Mexico, 1983), pp. 169–190.

E. Yoxen, 'Life as a Productive Force: Capitalising the Science and Technology of Molecular Biology', in L. Levidow and B. Young, eds., *Science Technology and the Labour Process*, vol.1, (London: Free Association Books, 1981), pp. 66–122.

Michael Zeilik, 'Anticipation in Ceremony: The Readiness Is All', in J. B. Carlson and W. J. Judge, eds., *Astronomy and Ceremony in the Prehistoric Southwest*, (Albuquerque: University of New Mexico, 1983), pp. 25–42.

Michael Zeilik, 'A Reassessment of the Fajada Butte Solar Marker', *Archaeoastronomy, Supp n9, Journal for the History of Astronomy*, Vol. 16, (1985), pp. S69–S85.

John Ziman, *Public Knowledge: The Social Dimension of Science*, (Cambridge: Cambridge University Press, 1968).

R. Tom Zuidema, 'The Inca Calender', in A. Aveni, ed., *Native American Astronomy*, (Austin: University of Texas Press, 1977), pp. 219–259.

R. Tom Zuidema, 'Anthropology and Archaeoastronomy', in R. A. Williamson, ed., *Archaeoastronomy in the Americas*, (Los Altos: Ballena Press, 1981), pp. 29–32.

R. Tom Zuidema, 'Bureaucracy and Systematic Knowledge in Andean Civilization', in G. A. Collier, R. I. Rosaldo and J. D. Wirth, eds., *The Inca and Aztec States, 1400–1800 Anthropology and History*, (New York: Academic Press, 1982), pp. 419–458.

R. Tom Zuidema, 'The Sidereal Lunar Calender of the Incas', in A. Aveni, ed., *Archaeoastronomy in the New World*, (Cambridge: Cambridge University Press, 1982), pp. 59–107.

Ronald Edward Zupko, *Revolution in Measurement: Western European Weights and Measures Since the Age of Science*, (Philadelphia: American Philosophical Society, 1990).

Index